HBJ MATHEMATICS

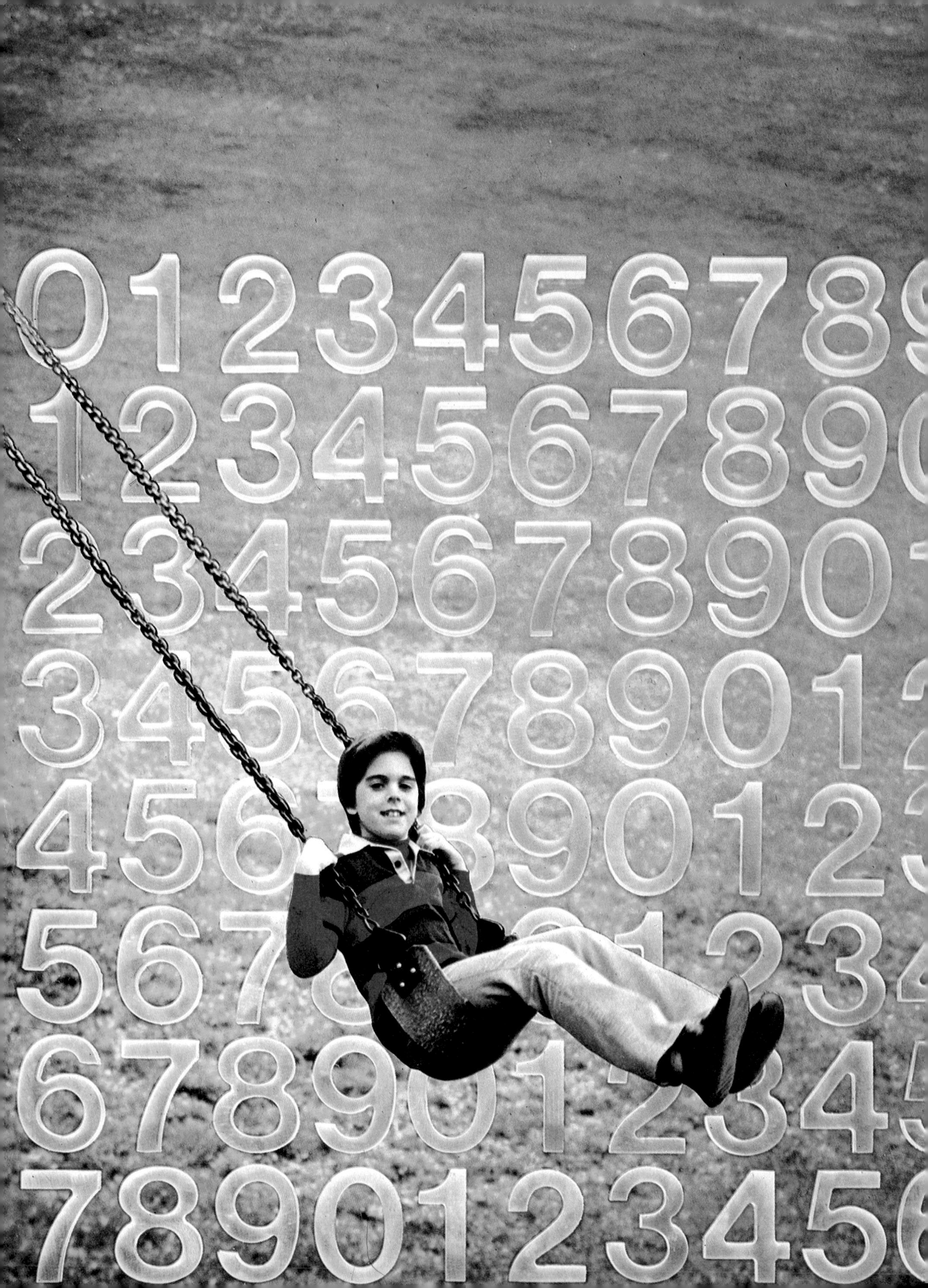

LOLA J. MAY
Mathematics Consultant
Winnetka Public Schools
Winnetka, Illinois

SHIRLEY M. FRYE
Mathematics Coordinator
Scottsdale Unified School District
Scottsdale, Arizona

DONNA CYRIER JACOBS
Director of Publications
Winnetka Public Schools
Winnetka, Illinois

HBJ MATHEMATICS

CONSULTING EDUCATORS

DELPHINA B. BRISCOE
Supervisor—Instructional Specialist
Pittsburgh Public Schools
Pittsburgh, Pennsylvania

SISTER MARY FREDERICK
Educational Consultant
Diocese of Syracuse
Syracuse, New York

DONALD A. KAMP
Mathematics Consultant
Spokane Public Schools
Spokane, Washington

MARJORIE H. COLEMAN
Amherst Elementary School
Amherst, Virginia

ANN HOLMAN
Lu Sutton School
Novato, California

KAREN LIEBERMAN
Harry L. Bain School
West New York, New Jersey

HBJ **HARCOURT BRACE JOVANOVICH**
New York   Chicago   San Francisco   Atlanta   Dallas   *and*   London

PHOTOGRAPH ACKNOWLEDGMENTS

KEY: T, Top; B, Bottom; L, Left; C, Center; R, Right.

HBJ PHOTOS: 283, 298CL.

HBJ PHOTOS by Josephine Coatsworth: 298C.

HBJ PHOTOS by Rick Der: 17, 34, 37, 56, 57, 58, 59, 60, 62, 65, 67, 68, 74, 79, 91, 93, 94, 95, 102, 103T, 107T, 112, 114, 127, 128, 129T, 130B, 131B, 138, 155, 172T, 183T, 184, 191, 192T, 201, 215T, 245, 260, 266L, 281, 289, 290, 291, 293, 295R, 298L, 298R, 300, 301, 320T.

HBJ PHOTOS by Elliott Varner Smith, courtesy of American Airlines: 2, 90, 122, 134, 164, 198, 222, 246, 280, 298CR.

RESEARCH CREDITS: © Black Star 1979, Edward Pieratt: 1. © Time/Life, Sports Illustrated, Neil Leifer: 29. Roy King: 30. Focus on Sports, Tom Kennedy: 45B. Focus on Sports, Mickey Palmer: 53. © Elliott Varner Smith: 54. Bruce Coleman Inc., © Clem Haagner: 89. Frank Wing: 121. © Peter Arnold Inc., Manfred Kage: 133. © ICON, Elizabeth Crews: 163. Woodfin Camp, © Chuck O'Rear: 177. Roy King: 197. © Woodfin Camp, John Marmaras: 221. Tom Burke: 279. Sports Illustrated, © Time Inc., Heinz Kluetmeir: 294R.

COVER CREDITS

HBJ Photo by Rick Der. Background © Roy King. Numbers by Walter Gasper.

ART ACKNOWLEDGMENTS

Robert Bausch: 292, 299.   Ellen Blonder: 136, 182B, 193C, 207, 272, 273.   Elizabeth Callen: 14–15, 32, 35, 36T, 40B, 47L, 92, 96R, 108–109, 116–117, 144R, 158T, 165, 166, 167, 172B, 173, 179L, 180B, 212, 223, 230, 231, 247, 259, 267, 282.   Walter Gasper, constructions: 34, 37, 61, 67, 68, 74, 107, 114, 155, 184, 191, 192T, 260T, 295.   Barbara Hack: 12T, 16, 32, 36B, 40T, 41R, 43, 47R, 75B, 126C, 129C, 129B, 144L, 148B, 158C, 179T, 179R, 180T, 180B, 181, 182T, 183B, 185, 186, 187, 188, 189, 190, 192B, 193T, 193B, 194, 195, 199, 200, 205, 206, 210, 211, 212, 213T, 214L, 218, 219, 230, 234B, 269, 271, 278, 281T, 283T, 285, 286T, 287, 288, 291T, 293T, 294L, 295L, 296L, 297T, 302B, 313, 314, 321, 323, 324, 327, 328, 329, 330.   Aleta Jenks: 3, 21, 22R, 33, 41L, 48, 55, 63, 77, 81, 84–85, 98, 99, 105, 106, 115, 154, 156, 157, 159, 204, 208, 209, 211TR, 214R, 226, 228, 229, 234T, 235, 236, 237, 251, 261, 264, 265B, 268, 286B, 296R.   Tony Naganuma: 9, 11, 19L, 20, 22L, 23, 31, 38, 45T, 60, 66, 78, 96L, 100, 104, 123, 124, 125, 130T, 131T, 135, 139, 141, 142, 146, 149, 213C, 224R, 225R, 227R, 250, 252, 253, 254, 256, 257, 258, 265T, 270, 284, 310T, and all Challenge, Review, and Calculate graphics, and Chapter Review, Chapter Test, and Brush-Up borders.   Sharron O'Neill: 25, 72–73.   Julie Peterson: 7, 13, 24, 39, 42, 46, 49, 64, 101, 113, 126, 148T, 150, 151, 215B, 239, 240, 241.   Barbara Reinertson: 6, 10, 69, 82, 83, 103B, 107B, 145, 147, 153, 216, 217, 238, 255, 266L, 275, 297B.   Judy Sakaguchi: 4, 5, 8, 12B, 71, 75T, 110, 111, 140, 143, 224L, 225L, 227L, 248, 249.   Marta Thoma: 18, 19R, 19B, 152, 202, 203, 232, 233, 263.

PRINTED IN THE UNITED STATES OF AMERICA

ISBN   0-15-352049-3

Contents

CHAPTER 1

Warm Up

Using Subtraction at Work

John Walker is a flight attendant on an airliner. During a 6-hour flight, a passenger asks him how long before they will arrive. Since they have been flying for 4 hours, he subtracts 6 − 4. He explains that they will arrive in 2 hours.

Addition Facts

addition fact

$$\begin{array}{r} 9 \\ +\ 4 \\ \hline 13 \end{array}$$

9   addend
+ 4   addend
13   sum

Find the sums.

1. $\begin{array}{r} 3 \\ +\ 9 \\ \hline 12 \end{array}$
2. $\begin{array}{r} 9 \\ +\ 9 \\ \hline 13 \end{array}$
3. $\begin{array}{r} 5 \\ +\ 4 \\ \hline \end{array}$
4. $\begin{array}{r} 5 \\ +\ 6 \\ \hline 1\!\!\!\!\;\!4 \end{array}$
5. $\begin{array}{r} 8 \\ +\ 3 \\ \hline \end{array}$
6. $\begin{array}{r} 3 \\ +\ 0 \\ \hline \end{array}$
7. $\begin{array}{r} 4 \\ +\ 9 \\ \hline \end{array}$

8. $\begin{array}{r} 7 \\ +\ 4 \\ \hline \end{array}$
9. $\begin{array}{r} 8 \\ +\ 4 \\ \hline \end{array}$
10. $\begin{array}{r} 9 \\ +\ 6 \\ \hline \end{array}$
11. $\begin{array}{r} 7 \\ +\ 8 \\ \hline \end{array}$
12. $\begin{array}{r} 6 \\ +\ 7 \\ \hline \end{array}$
13. $\begin{array}{r} 8 \\ +\ 6 \\ \hline \end{array}$
14. $\begin{array}{r} 5 \\ +\ 0 \\ \hline \end{array}$

15. $\begin{array}{r} 7 \\ +\ 5 \\ \hline \end{array}$
16. $\begin{array}{r} 8 \\ +\ 5 \\ \hline \end{array}$
17. $\begin{array}{r} 4 \\ +\ 7 \\ \hline \end{array}$
18. $\begin{array}{r} 6 \\ +\ 5 \\ \hline \end{array}$
19. $\begin{array}{r} 8 \\ +\ 9 \\ \hline \end{array}$
20. $\begin{array}{r} 2 \\ +\ 5 \\ \hline \end{array}$
21. $\begin{array}{r} 4 \\ +\ 6 \\ \hline \end{array}$

 Challenge

22. There are 9 birds in a tree.
7 more come. How many now?

More Addition Facts

Use Sam the snake to add.

Start near my head.
Move toward my tail.
You will be able to
add without fail.

$7 + 4 = 11$

Start on 7. Move 4.
Land on 11.

Add.

1. $6 + 7$ 13
2. $7 + 5$
3. $8 + 3$
4. $9 + 4$
5. $6 + 5$
6. $9 + 8$
7. $5 + 7$
8. $7 + 8$
9. $8 + 5$
10. $6 + 8$
11. $9 + 5$
12. $8 + 4$
13. $9 + 6$
14. $7 + 7$
15. $5 + 6$
16. $7 + 4$
17. $6 + 9$
18. $9 + 3$
19. $3 + 7$
20. $9 + 2$
21. $8 + 7$
22. $7 + 9$
23. $7 + 2$
24. $6 + 6$
25. $0 + 5$
26. $8 + 8$

Adding One-Digit Numbers

Add.

1. 6
   + 4
   ___
   10

2. 4
   + 4
   ___

3. 6
   + 6
   ___

4. 5
   + 3
   ___

5. 3
   + 7
   ___

6. 8
   + 2
   ___

7. 3
   + 4
   ___

8. 6
   + 5
   ___

9. 7
   + 4
   ___

10. 3
    + 8
    ___

11. 5
    + 7
    ___

12. 9
    + 3
    ___

13. 2
    + 9
    ___

14. 4
    + 5
    ___

15. 5
    + 4
    ___

16. 7
    + 0
    ___

17. 5
    + 8
    ___

18. 6
    + 8
    ___

19. 4 + 8   20. 9 + 4

21. 7 + 0   22. 2 + 2

23. 1 + 2   24. 3 + 3   25. 9 + 1   26. 8 + 2   27. 6 + 3

28. 7 + 7   29. 9 + 0   30. 3 + 1   31. 9 + 7   32. 5 + 5

33. 5 + 9   34. 8 + 9   35. 7 + 8   36. 9 + 9   37. 7 + 3

Subtraction Facts

subtraction fact

$$\begin{array}{r} 15 \\ -\ 7 \\ \hline 8 \end{array}$$ difference

Find the differences.

1. $\begin{array}{r} 13 \\ -\ 7 \\ \hline 6 \end{array}$	**2.** $\begin{array}{r} 17 \\ -\ 8 \\ \hline \end{array}$	**3.** $\begin{array}{r} 11 \\ -\ 8 \\ \hline \end{array}$	**4.** $\begin{array}{r} 12 \\ -\ 9 \\ \hline \end{array}$

1. $\begin{array}{r} 13 \\ -\ 7 \\ \hline 6 \end{array}$ **2.** $\begin{array}{r} 17 \\ -\ 8 \\ \hline \end{array}$ **3.** $\begin{array}{r} 11 \\ -\ 8 \\ \hline \end{array}$ **4.** $\begin{array}{r} 12 \\ -\ 9 \\ \hline \end{array}$ **5.** $\begin{array}{r} 13 \\ -\ 8 \\ \hline \end{array}$ **6.** $\begin{array}{r} 15 \\ -\ 6 \\ \hline \end{array}$

7. $\begin{array}{r} 14 \\ -\ 9 \\ \hline \end{array}$ **8.** $\begin{array}{r} 15 \\ -\ 9 \\ \hline \end{array}$ **9.** $\begin{array}{r} 16 \\ -\ 7 \\ \hline \end{array}$ **10.** $\begin{array}{r} 11 \\ -\ 9 \\ \hline \end{array}$ **11.** $\begin{array}{r} 12 \\ -\ 7 \\ \hline \end{array}$ **12.** $\begin{array}{r} 10 \\ -\ 4 \\ \hline \end{array}$

13. $\begin{array}{r} 13 \\ -\ 9 \\ \hline \end{array}$ **14.** $\begin{array}{r} 14 \\ -\ 8 \\ \hline \end{array}$ **15.** $\begin{array}{r} 15 \\ -\ 6 \\ \hline \end{array}$ **16.** $\begin{array}{r} 17 \\ -\ 9 \\ \hline \end{array}$ **17.** $\begin{array}{r} 18 \\ -\ 9 \\ \hline \end{array}$ **18.** $\begin{array}{r} 11 \\ -\ 8 \\ \hline \end{array}$

19. $12 - 6$ **20.** $13 - 5$ **21.** $9 - 4$ **22.** $9 - 0$ **23.** $16 - 5$

24. $11 - 6$ **25.** $16 - 9$ **26.** $17 - 8$ **27.** $12 - 5$ **28.** $18 - 7$

 Challenge

29. There were 9 bowls on a shelf. Jeffrey brought more. Then there were 18. How many did Jeffrey bring?

More Subtraction Facts

Move back to subtract.

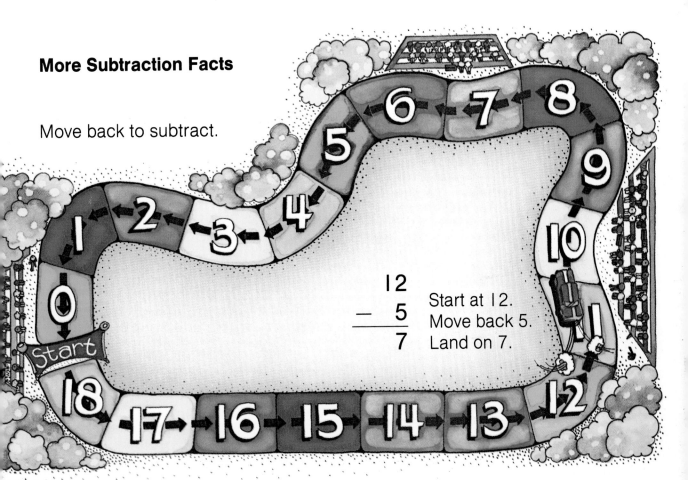

$$
\begin{array}{r}
12 \\
-\ 5 \\
\hline
7
\end{array}
$$

Start at 12.
Move back 5.
Land on 7.

Subtract. Use the subtraction track if you need help.

1. 13
   − 4
   9

2. 12
   − 5

3. 15
   − 6

4. 14
   − 5

5. 11
   − 4

6. 11
   − 8

7. 12
   − 3

8. 13
   − 5

9. 15
   − 7

10. 14
    − 8

11. 16
    − 7

12. 14
    − 9

13. 11
    − 3

14. 12
    − 4

15. 13
    − 6

16. 17
    − 8

17. 14
    − 6

18. 15
    − 8

19. 16
    − 9

20. 11
    − 2

21. 12
    − 7

22. 15
    − 9

23. 13
    − 8

24. 16
    − 5

Subtracting One-Digit Numbers

Subtract.

1. 9 − 3 6	2. 10 − 5	3. 11 − 7	4. 12 − 8	5. 17 − 9	6. 11 − 2
7. 11 − 9	8. 13 − 4	9. 8 − 5	10. 10 − 2	11. 13 − 6	12. 9 − 5
13. 11 − 3	14. 8 − 3	15. 12 − 9	16. 11 − 8	17. 10 − 6	18. 9 − 4
19. 8 − 5	20. 10 − 0	21. 11 − 6	22. 13 − 5	23. 12 − 8	24. 10 − 8
25. 9 − 6	26. 11 − 4	27. 7 − 7	28. 13 − 7	29. 10 − 7	30. 9 − 2

31. 12 − 6   32. 10 − 5

33. 18 − 9   34. 15 − 0

35. 14 − 7   36. 12 − 6

37. 10 − 7   38. 15 − 6

39. 17 − 8   40. 15 − 7

41. 16 − 7   42. 9 − 2

43. 6 − 3   44. 11 − 3

Picture Problems

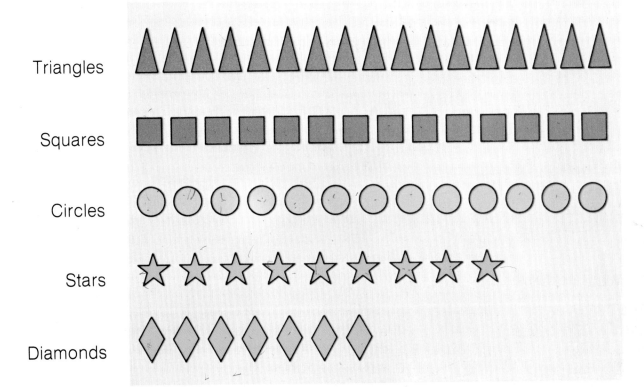

Triangles

Squares

Circles

Stars

Diamonds

Use the pictures to answer the questions.

1. How many more triangles than squares? 3

2. How many more squares than circles?

3. How many more stars than diamonds?

4. How many more squares than stars?

5. How many more triangles than circles?

6. How many more triangles than diamonds?

7. How many more squares than diamonds?

8. How many stars and diamonds together?

Finding Sums and Differences

$$\begin{array}{r} 4 \\ + 4 \\ \hline 8 \end{array}$$

$$\begin{array}{r} 4 \\ + 3 \\ \hline 7 \end{array}$$ I less than 4
I less than 8

$$\begin{array}{r} 4 \\ + 5 \\ \hline 9 \end{array}$$ I more than 4
I more than 8

Write the sums.

1a. $\begin{array}{r} 9 \\ + 2 \\ \hline 11 \end{array}$	1b. $\begin{array}{r} 9 \\ + 1 \\ \hline 10 \end{array}$	1c. $\begin{array}{r} 9 \\ + 3 \\ \hline 12 \end{array}$	2a. $\begin{array}{r} 5 \\ + 5 \\ \hline \end{array}$	2b. $\begin{array}{r} 5 \\ + 4 \\ \hline \end{array}$	2c. $\begin{array}{r} 5 \\ + 6 \\ \hline \end{array}$
3a. $\begin{array}{r} 8 \\ + 2 \\ \hline \end{array}$	3b. $\begin{array}{r} 8 \\ + 3 \\ \hline \end{array}$	3c. $\begin{array}{r} 8 \\ + 1 \\ \hline \end{array}$	4a. $\begin{array}{r} 6 \\ + 4 \\ \hline \end{array}$	4b. $\begin{array}{r} 6 \\ + 5 \\ \hline \end{array}$	4c. $\begin{array}{r} 6 \\ + 6 \\ \hline \end{array}$
5a. $\begin{array}{r} 7 \\ + 7 \\ \hline \end{array}$	5b. $\begin{array}{r} 7 \\ + 8 \\ \hline \end{array}$	5c. $\begin{array}{r} 7 \\ + 6 \\ \hline \end{array}$	6a. $\begin{array}{r} 9 \\ + 4 \\ \hline \end{array}$	6b. $\begin{array}{r} 9 \\ + 3 \\ \hline \end{array}$	6c. $\begin{array}{r} 9 \\ + 5 \\ \hline \end{array}$

Subtract.

7a. $\begin{array}{r} 8 \\ - 1 \\ \hline \end{array}$	7b. $\begin{array}{r} 8 \\ - 0 \\ \hline \end{array}$	7c. $\begin{array}{r} 8 \\ - 2 \\ \hline \end{array}$	8a. $\begin{array}{r} 9 \\ - 7 \\ \hline \end{array}$	8b. $\begin{array}{r} 9 \\ - 6 \\ \hline \end{array}$	8c. $\begin{array}{r} 9 \\ - 5 \\ \hline \end{array}$
9a. $\begin{array}{r} 13 \\ - 8 \\ \hline \end{array}$	9b. $\begin{array}{r} 13 \\ - 9 \\ \hline \end{array}$	9c. $\begin{array}{r} 13 \\ - 7 \\ \hline \end{array}$	10a. $\begin{array}{r} 15 \\ - 7 \\ \hline \end{array}$	10b. $\begin{array}{r} 15 \\ - 8 \\ \hline \end{array}$	10c. $\begin{array}{r} 15 \\ - 9 \\ \hline \end{array}$

Fact Families

Fact family for 6, 4, and 10.

$$6 + 4 = 10$$
$$4 + 6 = 10$$

$$10 - 4 = 6$$

$$10 - 6 = 4$$

Write the fact family for each group of numbers.

1. 7, 5, 12 $7 + 5 = 12, 5 + 7 = 12, 12 - 7 = 5, 12 - 5 = 7$

2. 9, 3, 12

3. 3, 8, 11

4. 8, 6, 14

5. 6, 10, 4

6. 7, 8, 15

7. 9, 5, 14

8. 6, 5, 11

9. 13, 5, 8

10. 7, 4, 11

11. 8, 9, 17

12. 4, 5, 9

13. 16, 7, 9

Review   (pp. 3–11)

1.	**2.**	**3.**	**4.**	**5.**	**6.**
4	3	11	18	9	15
+9	+7	− 3	− 7	+6	− 8

Addition and Subtraction Code

Crack the code to spell the names of three birds.

Code	o	y	s	k	t	g	r	a	i	e	c	h	l	u
	17	12	9	0	8	2	14	7	16	5	3	6	11	4

Add or subtract.

1. $\begin{array}{r} 10 \\ -\ 5 \\ \hline \end{array}$ 5, e

2. $\begin{array}{r} 10 \\ -\ 3 \\ \hline \end{array}$

3. $\begin{array}{r} 7 \\ -\ 5 \\ \hline \end{array}$

4. $\begin{array}{r} 5 \\ +\ 6 \\ \hline \end{array}$

5. $\begin{array}{r} 11 \\ -\ 6 \\ \hline \end{array}$

6. $\begin{array}{r} 8 \\ +\ 9 \\ \hline \end{array}$

7. $\begin{array}{r} 13 \\ -\ 4 \\ \hline \end{array}$

8. $\begin{array}{r} 15 \\ -\ 7 \\ \hline \end{array}$

9. $\begin{array}{r} 6 \\ +\ 8 \\ \hline \end{array}$

10. $\begin{array}{r} 7 \\ +\ 9 \\ \hline \end{array}$

11. $\begin{array}{r} 12 \\ -\ 9 \\ \hline \end{array}$

12. $\begin{array}{r} 3 \\ +\ 3 \\ \hline \end{array}$

13. $\begin{array}{r} 4 \\ +\ 4 \\ \hline \end{array}$

14. $\begin{array}{r} 12 \\ -\ 8 \\ \hline \end{array}$

15. $\begin{array}{r} 7 \\ +\ 7 \\ \hline \end{array}$

16. $\begin{array}{r} 9 \\ -\ 9 \\ \hline \end{array}$

17. $\begin{array}{r} 3 \\ +\ 2 \\ \hline \end{array}$

18. $\begin{array}{r} 8 \\ +\ 4 \\ \hline \end{array}$

19. The three big birds are an __ __ __ __ __,
                                        1. 2. 3. 4. 5.

   an __ __ __ __ __ __ __,
       6. 7. 8. 9. 10. 11. 12.

   and a __ __ __ __ __ __.
       13. 14. 15. 16. 17. 18.

Addition and Subtraction Facts to 18

Choose + or − to complete the problem.

1. $3 \oplus 8 = 11$ 2. $12 \ominus 5 = 7$

3. $4 \bigcirc 9 = 13$ 4. $14 \bigcirc 8 = 6$

5. $10 \bigcirc 9 = 1$ 6. $5 \bigcirc 9 = 14$

7. $6 \bigcirc 6 = 12$ 8. $9 \bigcirc 3 = 6$

Add or subtract.

9. $\begin{array}{r} 5 \\ + 8 \\ \hline \end{array}$	10. $\begin{array}{r} 12 \\ - 9 \\ \hline \end{array}$	11. $\begin{array}{r} 6 \\ + 9 \\ \hline \end{array}$	12. $\begin{array}{r} 11 \\ - 3 \\ \hline \end{array}$	13. $\begin{array}{r} 8 \\ + 8 \\ \hline \end{array}$	14. $\begin{array}{r} 7 \\ + 9 \\ \hline \end{array}$
15. $\begin{array}{r} 11 \\ - 7 \\ \hline \end{array}$	16. $\begin{array}{r} 7 \\ + 8 \\ \hline \end{array}$	17. $\begin{array}{r} 12 \\ - 4 \\ \hline \end{array}$	18. $\begin{array}{r} 9 \\ + 6 \\ \hline \end{array}$	19. $\begin{array}{r} 10 \\ - 6 \\ \hline \end{array}$	20. $\begin{array}{r} 11 \\ + 5 \\ \hline \end{array}$
21. $\begin{array}{r} 8 \\ + 6 \\ \hline \end{array}$	22. $\begin{array}{r} 15 \\ - 9 \\ \hline \end{array}$	23. $\begin{array}{r} 9 \\ + 8 \\ \hline \end{array}$	24. $\begin{array}{r} 13 \\ - 7 \\ \hline \end{array}$	25. $\begin{array}{r} 7 \\ + 4 \\ \hline \end{array}$	26. $\begin{array}{r} 12 \\ - 7 \\ \hline \end{array}$

 Calculate

Add and subtract.

27. $8 + 3 - 5 + 9 - 8 = \boxed{?}$

28. $16 - 8 + 4 - 5 + 6 - 7 = \boxed{?}$

29. $7 + 5 - 3 + 6 - 8 + 7 = \boxed{?}$

Beach Problems

Write an addition or subtraction fact for each problem.

1. There are 3 people playing ball. 8 more people come. How many people now? $3 + 8 = 11$

2. There are 16 swimmers. 7 swimmers leave. How many swimmers now?

3. There are 13 sand castles on the beach. 9 are washed away by the tide. How many are left?

4. Mike found 5 white shells and 8 brown shells. How many shells did he find in all?

5. There are 6 seagulls on the shore. More seagulls fly down. Now there are 12. How many seagulls came?

6. The lifeguard works 8 hours on Monday and 7 hours on Tuesday. How many hours does she work in all?

7. 8 people are flying kites. 5 more fly kites. How many people fly kites?

8. 4 crabs creep on the beach. 7 more crabs come out of the sea. How many crabs now?

9. 12 friends have a picnic. Some people go home. There are 7 people left. How many people went home?

10. There are 15 striped beach umbrellas and 6 plain beach umbrellas. How many more striped umbrellas?

11. There are 9 sailboats. There are 4 motorboats. How many boats in all?

12. Jim finds 7 clams. Maria finds 6 clams. How many clams have they found?

Puzzles

The rule is add 6.

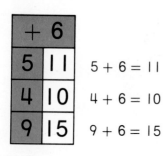

+ 6	
5	11
4	10
9	15

5 + 6 = 11

4 + 6 = 10

9 + 6 = 15

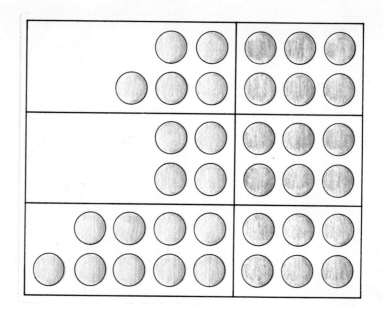

Add or subtract. Write the missing numbers.

1.
+ 7	
6	13
8	
7	

2.
− 5	
13	
14	
12	

3.
− 7	
15	
14	
12	

4.
+ 6	
6	
8	
7	

5.
+ 8	
7	
9	
6	

6.
− 3	
11	
9	
10	

7.
− 9	
18	
14	
16	

8.
+ 9	
5	
6	
7	

9.
+ 4	
8	
7	
9	

10.
− 8	
17	
14	
15	

11.
− 6	
12	
14	
13	

12.
+ 5	
8	
7	
6	

Three Addends

To add three numbers,
add any two numbers
at a time.

$$\begin{array}{r} 3 \\ 4 \\ + 5 \\ \hline 12 \end{array} \quad \begin{array}{r} 7 \\ + 5 \\ \hline 12 \end{array}$$

$$\begin{array}{r} 3 \\ 4 \\ + 5 \\ \hline 12 \end{array} \quad \begin{array}{r} 3 \\ + 9 \\ \hline 12 \end{array}$$

Add.

1. $\begin{array}{r} 8 \\ 2 \\ + 7 \\ \hline 17 \end{array}$
2. $\begin{array}{r} 6 \\ 3 \\ + 1 \\ \hline \end{array}$
3. $\begin{array}{r} 4 \\ 9 \\ + 2 \\ \hline \end{array}$
4. $\begin{array}{r} 5 \\ 4 \\ + 8 \\ \hline \end{array}$
5. $\begin{array}{r} 8 \\ 3 \\ + 6 \\ \hline \end{array}$
6. $\begin{array}{r} 4 \\ 7 \\ + 6 \\ \hline \end{array}$
7. $\begin{array}{r} 9 \\ 1 \\ + 8 \\ \hline \end{array}$

8. $\begin{array}{r} 5 \\ 3 \\ + 7 \\ \hline \end{array}$
9. $\begin{array}{r} 8 \\ 2 \\ + 4 \\ \hline \end{array}$
10. $\begin{array}{r} 6 \\ 3 \\ + 7 \\ \hline \end{array}$
11. $\begin{array}{r} 8 \\ 1 \\ + 6 \\ \hline \end{array}$
12. $\begin{array}{r} 3 \\ 7 \\ + 2 \\ \hline \end{array}$
13. $\begin{array}{r} 9 \\ 1 \\ + 4 \\ \hline \end{array}$
14. $\begin{array}{r} 5 \\ 8 \\ + 1 \\ \hline \end{array}$

15. $\begin{array}{r} 2 \\ 3 \\ + 6 \\ \hline \end{array}$
16. $\begin{array}{r} 3 \\ 4 \\ + 5 \\ \hline \end{array}$
17. $\begin{array}{r} 6 \\ 2 \\ + 7 \\ \hline \end{array}$
18. $\begin{array}{r} 5 \\ 2 \\ + 6 \\ \hline \end{array}$
19. $\begin{array}{r} 4 \\ 3 \\ + 6 \\ \hline \end{array}$
20. $\begin{array}{r} 5 \\ 2 \\ + 8 \\ \hline \end{array}$
21. $\begin{array}{r} 6 \\ 3 \\ + 8 \\ \hline \end{array}$

22. $3 + 1 + 9$
23. $6 + 2 + 4$
24. $7 + 4 + 8$
25. $5 + 9 + 2$

26. $6 + 3 + 2$
27. $5 + 5 + 3$
28. $7 + 6 + 4$
29. $4 + 7 + 7$

Two-Step Problems

( ) mean **Do me first.**

Step 1

$$(4 + 5) - 3 = \boxed{?}$$
$$9$$

Step 2

$$(4 + 5) - 3 = \boxed{?}$$
$$9 - 3 = 6$$

Solve each problem.

1. $(4 + 6) - 7$ 3

2. $(14 - 10) - 1$

3. $5 + (12 - 3)$

4. $7 + (6 - 2)$

5. $(8 + 5) - 3$

6. $8 + (4 - 4)$

7. $(3 + 6) - 8$

8. $8 + (10 - 5)$

9. $7 + (4 - 3)$

10. $3 + (12 - 8)$

11. $6 + (16 - 8)$

12. $8 + (12 - 6)$

13. $(6 - 2) + 5$

14. $(6 + 4) + 5$

15. $(6 + 8) - 9$

16. $(18 - 8) + 4$

17. $(13 - 6) + 2$

18. $(12 - 5) + 3$

 Challenge

Write two facts to solve the problem.

19. Peggy brought 7 sandwiches for the picnic. Anthony brought 3. People at the picnic ate 9 sandwiches. How many sandwiches were left?

Adding Tens

$$3 \atop {+4} \over 7$$

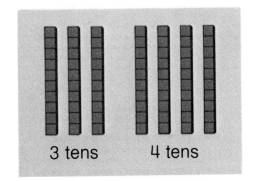

3 ones   4 ones

$$30 \atop {+40} \over 70$$

3 tens   4 tens

Add.

1. 50
   + 20
   70

2. 20
   + 40

3. 70
   + 10

4. 30
   + 40

5. 20
   + 20

6. 60
   + 20

7. 20
   + 30

8. 80
   + 20

9. 60
   + 30

10. 50
    + 40

11. 70
    + 20

12. 30
    + 50

13. 20
    + 60

14. 10
    + 40

15. 40
    + 40

16. 10
    + 20

17. 90
    + 10

18. 70
    + 30

19. Bob read 30 pages in his book. The next day he read 20 more. How many pages did he read in all?

Adding Two-Digit Numbers

Step 1
Add ones.

$$\begin{array}{r} 31 \\ +\ 27 \\ \hline 8 \end{array}$$

Step 2
Add tens.

$$\begin{array}{r} 31 \\ +\ 27 \\ \hline 58 \end{array}$$

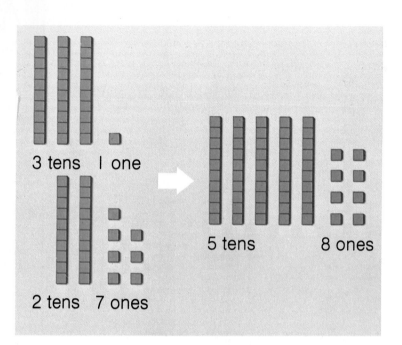

3 tens   1 one

2 tens   7 ones

5 tens   8 ones

Add.

1. $\begin{array}{r} 52 \\ +\ 27 \\ \hline 79 \end{array}$

2. $\begin{array}{r} 43 \\ +\ 25 \\ \hline \end{array}$

3. $\begin{array}{r} 6 \\ +\ 30 \\ \hline \end{array}$

4. $\begin{array}{r} 51 \\ +\ 32 \\ \hline \end{array}$

5. $\begin{array}{r} 73 \\ +\ 4 \\ \hline \end{array}$

6. $\begin{array}{r} 12 \\ +\ 36 \\ \hline \end{array}$

7. $\begin{array}{r} 46 \\ +\ 12 \\ \hline \end{array}$

8. $\begin{array}{r} 73 \\ +\ 25 \\ \hline \end{array}$

9. $\begin{array}{r} 24 \\ +\ 33 \\ \hline \end{array}$

10. $\begin{array}{r} 41 \\ +\ 18 \\ \hline \end{array}$

11. $\begin{array}{r} 20 \\ +\ 70 \\ \hline \end{array}$

12. $\begin{array}{r} 34 \\ +\ 61 \\ \hline \end{array}$

13. $\begin{array}{r} 43 \\ +\ 6 \\ \hline \end{array}$

14. $\begin{array}{r} 50 \\ +\ 19 \\ \hline \end{array}$

15. $\begin{array}{r} 34 \\ +\ 4 \\ \hline \end{array}$

16. $\begin{array}{r} 62 \\ +\ 5 \\ \hline \end{array}$

17. $\begin{array}{r} 71 \\ +\ 18 \\ \hline \end{array}$

18. $\begin{array}{r} 16 \\ +\ 53 \\ \hline \end{array}$

19. $\begin{array}{r} 23 \\ +\ 61 \\ \hline \end{array}$

20. $\begin{array}{r} 80 \\ +\ 9 \\ \hline \end{array}$

21. $\begin{array}{r} 39 \\ +\ 50 \\ \hline \end{array}$

22. $\begin{array}{r} 60 \\ +\ 34 \\ \hline \end{array}$

23. $\begin{array}{r} 48 \\ +\ 20 \\ \hline \end{array}$

24. $\begin{array}{r} 74 \\ +\ 15 \\ \hline \end{array}$

25. $\begin{array}{r} 13 \\ +\ 54 \\ \hline \end{array}$

26. $\begin{array}{r} 20 \\ +\ 49 \\ \hline \end{array}$

27. $\begin{array}{r} 10 \\ +\ 87 \\ \hline \end{array}$

28. $\begin{array}{r} 12 \\ +\ 45 \\ \hline \end{array}$

29. $\begin{array}{r} 17 \\ +\ 32 \\ \hline \end{array}$

30. $\begin{array}{r} 27 \\ +\ 62 \\ \hline \end{array}$

Three Addends

Add three addends the same way you add two addends.

```
  45
  10
+ 23
----
  78
```

Add.

1.	2.	3.	4.	5.	6.
19	14	55	24	12	17
40	34	3	24	53	22
+ 20	+ 31	+ 31	+ 21	+ 14	+ 40
79					

7.	8.	9.	10.	11.	12.
17	22	10	14	57	23
30	24	34	13	22	15
+ 30	+ 21	+ 25	+ 72	+ 20	+ 61

13.	14.	15.	16.	17.	18.
20	21	23	31	41	32
20	31	34	12	28	14
+ 20	+ 42	+ 31	+ 26	+ 10	+ 53

 Review (pp. 3–21)

Add or subtract.

1.	2.	3.	4.	5.	6.
7	13	9	16	3	23
+ 6	− 8	+ 7	− 9	5	+ 46
				+ 7	

Subtracting Tens

$$\begin{array}{r} 60 \\ -\ 20 \\ \hline 40 \end{array}$$

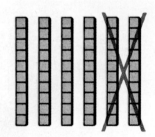

Subtract.

1. $\begin{array}{r} 80 \\ -\ 70 \\ \hline 10 \end{array}$

2. $\begin{array}{r} 60 \\ -\ 40 \\ \hline \end{array}$

3. $\begin{array}{r} 70 \\ -\ 50 \\ \hline \end{array}$

4. $\begin{array}{r} 40 \\ -\ 20 \\ \hline \end{array}$

5. $\begin{array}{r} 90 \\ -\ 30 \\ \hline \end{array}$

6. $\begin{array}{r} 50 \\ -\ 10 \\ \hline \end{array}$

7. $\begin{array}{r} 60 \\ -\ 20 \\ \hline \end{array}$

8. $\begin{array}{r} 70 \\ -\ 30 \\ \hline \end{array}$

9. $\begin{array}{r} 50 \\ -\ 50 \\ \hline \end{array}$

10. $\begin{array}{r} 80 \\ -\ 30 \\ \hline \end{array}$

11. $\begin{array}{r} 90 \\ -\ 60 \\ \hline \end{array}$

12. $\begin{array}{r} 40 \\ -\ 40 \\ \hline \end{array}$

13. $\begin{array}{r} 80 \\ -\ 60 \\ \hline \end{array}$

14. $\begin{array}{r} 70 \\ -\ 20 \\ \hline \end{array}$

15. $\begin{array}{r} 60 \\ -\ 30 \\ \hline \end{array}$

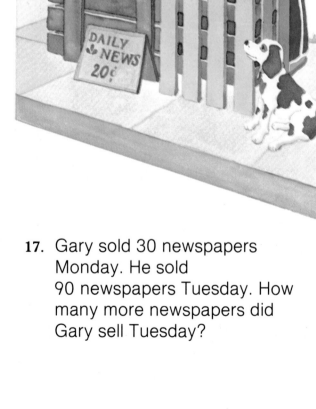

16. Tina sold 40 newspapers in one week. She sold 60 newspapers the next week. How many more newspapers did Tina sell the second week?

17. Gary sold 30 newspapers Monday. He sold 90 newspapers Tuesday. How many more newspapers did Gary sell Tuesday?

Subtracting Two-Digit Numbers

Step 1
Subtract ones.

```
  47
- 35
-----
   2
```

Step 2
Subtract tens.

```
  47
- 35
-----
  12
```

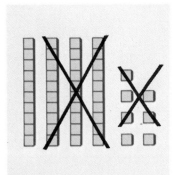

Subtract.

1. 78 − 33 45	2. 87 − 56	3. 27 − 13	4. 74 − 54	5. 48 − 6	6. 39 − 18
7. 55 − 35	8. 39 − 4	9. 35 − 22	10. 77 − 45	11. 33 − 12	12. 46 − 21
13. 39 − 19	14. 59 − 9	15. 47 − 27	16. 86 − 23	17. 36 − 6	18. 74 − 33
19. 87 − 81	20. 64 − 61	21. 78 − 40	22. 87 − 2	23. 59 − 3	24. 68 − 43

 Challenge

25. 29 − 14   26. 76 − 44   27. 87 − 52   28. 46 − 25

29. 64 − 34   30. 93 − 22   31. 57 − 24   32. 48 − 16

Adding and Subtracting Two-Digit Numbers

Add or subtract.

1. 67
  − 32
  35
	2. 71
	  + 23
		3. 59
		  − 7
			4. 86
			  + 12
				5. 98
				  − 42
					6. 37
					  − 24

7. 65
  − 20
	8. 49
	  − 2
		9. 74
		  + 23
			10. 56
			  − 23
				11. 60
				  + 20
					12. 94
					  − 72

13. 33
  + 20
	14. 84
	  − 40
		15. 68
		  − 33
			16. 46
			  + 32
				17. 80
				  − 30
					18. 27
					  + 42

19. 21
  + 68
	20. 78
	  − 42
		21. 53
		  + 34
			22. 99
			  − 4
				23. 74
				  − 34
					24. 16
					  + 43

25. 78
  − 25
	26. 80
	  + 11
		27. 87
		  − 47			

28. 24
  + 52
	29. 38
	  − 38
		30. 26
		  − 16			

 Calculate

Find the missing number in each problem.

31. $99 - \boxed{?} = 88$

32. $99 - \boxed{?} = 77$

33. $99 - \boxed{?} = 66$

Pond Problems

Add or subtract to solve these problems.

1. There are 27 frogs and 68 tadpoles in the pond. How many more tadpoles than frogs? 68 − 27 = 41

2. 38 ducks and 15 swans swim in the pond. How many more ducks than swans?

3. The goldfish catch 24 waterbugs. The minnows catch 63 waterbugs. How many waterbugs are caught?

4. 22 small dragonflies and 45 large dragonflies fly over the pond. How many dragonflies in all?

5. 29 turtles live in the pond. 17 are box turtles. The rest are snapping turtles. How many snapping turtles live in the pond?

6. There are 31 white waterlilies, 5 pink waterlilies, and 13 yellow waterlilies growing in the pond. How many waterlilies in all?

Chapter Review

Add.   (ex. 1–14: p. 3)

1.	2.	3.	4.	5.	6.	7.
5	6	8	6	5	7	8
+4	+5	+4	+7	+8	+9	+7

8.	9.	10.	11.	12.	13.	14.
8	9	5	9	9	7	6
+6	+3	+7	+6	+9	+4	+4

Subtract.   (ex. 15–26: p. 6)

15.	16.	17.	18.	19.	20.
10	12	15	13	16	11
− 5	− 4	− 7	− 4	− 9	− 5

21.	22.	23.	24.	25.	26.
14	16	18	11	17	15
− 6	− 8	− 9	− 4	− 8	− 9

Add or subtract.   (ex. 27–30: p. 17),   (ex. 31–33: p. 19),   (ex. 34–36: p. 22),

(ex. 37–39, 43–45: p. 20),   (ex. 40–42, 46–47: p. 23)

27. $4 + 6 + 2$ **28.** $7 + 5 + 3$ **29.** $5 + 2 + 8$ **30.** $3 + 4 + 6$

31.	32.	33.	34.	35.	36.
40	10	20	90	70	80
+ 20	+ 70	+ 50	− 30	− 50	− 40

37.	38.	39.	40.	41.	42.
34	75	53	42	33	67
+ 23	+ 3	+ 34	− 21	− 20	− 43

43. $52 + 7$ **44.** $71 + 23$ **45.** $40 + 19$ **46.** $83 - 23$ **47.** $98 - 42$

Chapter Test

Add.

1. 5 + 7	**2.** 3 + 9	**3.** 8 + 2	**4.** 7 + 4	**5.** 9 + 8	**6.** 7 + 6	**7.** 4 + 9
8. 8 + 5	**9.** 6 + 9	**10.** 7 + 7	**11.** 7 + 9	**12.** 5 + 6	**13.** 8 + 8	**14.** 6 + 8

Subtract.

15. 16 − 7	**16.** 13 − 4	**17.** 10 − 5	**18.** 11 − 2	**19.** 18 − 9	**20.** 15 − 5
21. 17 − 8	**22.** 14 − 6	**23.** 15 − 7	**24.** 12 − 9	**25.** 11 − 7	**26.** 13 − 8

Add or subtract.

27. $6 + 2 + 4$ **28.** $5 + 5 + 6$ **29.** $8 + 3 + 4$ **30.** $6 + 3 + 7$

31. 30 + 40	**32.** 60 − 20	**33.** 35 + 21	**34.** 84 − 23	**35.** 46 + 12	**36.** 65 − 41

Brush Up

Add or subtract.

1. $7 + 9$ 2. $12 - 4$ 3. $9 + 5$ 4. $9 - 6$

5. $17 - 9$ 6. $13 - 6$ 7. $8 + 5$ 8. $7 - 2$

9. $8 + 6$ 10. $15 - 6$ 11. $9 + 6$ 12. $5 + 4$

13. $13 - 7$ 14. $13 - 4$ 15. $6 + 7$ 16. $8 - 2$

17. $12 - 8$ 18. $11 - 7$ 19. $9 + 2$ 20. $10 - 3$

21. $15 - 8$ 22. $14 - 5$ 23. $9 + 7$ 24. $9 + 9$

25. $11 - 9$ 26. $12 - 3$ 27. $8 + 3$ 28. $8 - 3$

Find the sums and differences.

29. $\begin{array}{r} 8 \\ +9 \\ \hline \end{array}$
30. $\begin{array}{r} 17 \\ -\ 8 \\ \hline \end{array}$
31. $\begin{array}{r} 9 \\ +8 \\ \hline \end{array}$
32. $\begin{array}{r} 0 \\ +9 \\ \hline \end{array}$
33. $\begin{array}{r} 16 \\ -\ 9 \\ \hline \end{array}$
34. $\begin{array}{r} 15 \\ -\ 7 \\ \hline \end{array}$

35. $\begin{array}{r} 7 \\ +5 \\ \hline \end{array}$
36. $\begin{array}{r} 6 \\ +2 \\ \hline \end{array}$
37. $\begin{array}{r} 5 \\ +6 \\ \hline \end{array}$
38. $\begin{array}{r} 13 \\ -\ 8 \\ \hline \end{array}$
39. $\begin{array}{r} 8 \\ +6 \\ \hline \end{array}$
40. $\begin{array}{r} 9 \\ -4 \\ \hline \end{array}$

41. $\begin{array}{r} 14 \\ -\ 8 \\ \hline \end{array}$
42. $\begin{array}{r} 11 \\ -\ 5 \\ \hline \end{array}$
43. $\begin{array}{r} 9 \\ +3 \\ \hline \end{array}$
44. $\begin{array}{r} 8 \\ -2 \\ \hline \end{array}$
45. $\begin{array}{r} 8 \\ +7 \\ \hline \end{array}$
46. $\begin{array}{r} 16 \\ -\ 7 \\ \hline \end{array}$

47. $\begin{array}{r} 6 \\ +5 \\ \hline \end{array}$
48. $\begin{array}{r} 4 \\ +3 \\ \hline \end{array}$
49. $\begin{array}{r} 12 \\ -\ 5 \\ \hline \end{array}$
50. $\begin{array}{r} 14 \\ -\ 6 \\ \hline \end{array}$
51. $\begin{array}{r} 7 \\ +8 \\ \hline \end{array}$
52. $\begin{array}{r} 9 \\ -3 \\ \hline \end{array}$

CHAPTER 2

Numbers

Using Numbers at Work

Barbara Clinton owns a dairy farm. In one herd she has 135 cows. In another herd she has 153 cows. She knows that the herd with 153 cows has the greatest number of cows.

Tens and Ones

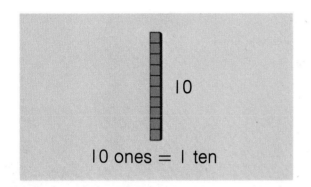

10 ones = 1 ten

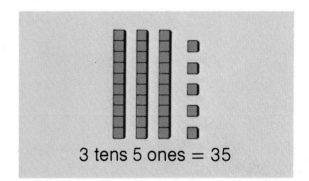

3 tens 5 ones = 35

How many tens and ones?

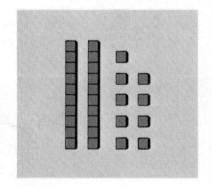

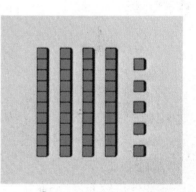

1. ☐ tens ☐ ones   2, 9

2. ☐ tens ☐ ones

3. ☐ tens ☐ ones

Write the numbers.

4. 8 tens 7 ones

5. 3 tens 9 ones

6. 5 tens 0 ones

7. 9 tens 9 ones

8. 7 tens 4 ones

9. 6 tens 2 ones

Copy and complete.

10. 48 = ☐ tens ☐ ones

11. 67 = ☐ tens ☐ ones

12. 97 = ☐ tens ☐ ones

13. 55 = ☐ tens ☐ ones

Names for Tens

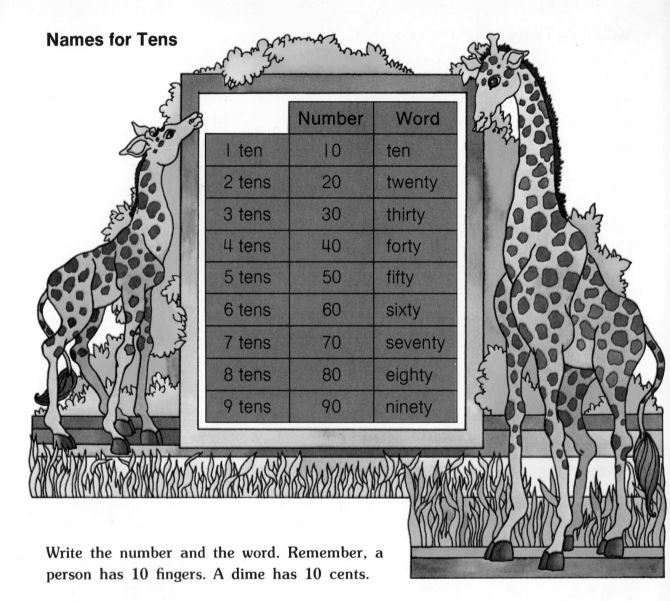

	Number	Word
1 ten	10	ten
2 tens	20	twenty
3 tens	30	thirty
4 tens	40	forty
5 tens	50	fifty
6 tens	60	sixty
7 tens	70	seventy
8 tens	80	eighty
9 tens	90	ninety

Write the number and the word. Remember, a person has 10 fingers. A dime has 10 cents.

1. How many fingers on 4 people?   40, forty

2. How many cents in 4 dimes?

3. How many cents in 7 dimes?

4. How many fingers on 5 people?

5. How many cents in 8 dimes?

6. How many cents in 9 dimes?

7. How many fingers on 6 people?

8. How many fingers on 8 people?

9. How many cents in 6 dimes?

Ordering Two-Digit Numbers

Which is greater, 72 or 58?
If tens are not the same,
compare tens.

72   58

7 tens is greater than 5 tens,
so 72 is greater than 58.

Which is greater, 46 or 42?
If tens are the same,
compare ones.

46   42

6 ones is greater than 2 ones,
so 46 is greater than 42.

Write the number that is greater.

1. 64 or 57   64
2. 83 or 91
3. 38 or 34
4. 27 or 72

5. 29 or 30
6. 13 or 31
7. 72 or 78
8. 98 or 99

9. 8 or 11
10. 18 or 11
11. 26 or 62
12. 84 or 94

13. 45 or 35
14. 33 or 44
15. 51 or 49
16. 50 or 49

17. 13 or 9
18. 46 or 34
19. 81 or 18
20. 16 or 36

 Challenge

21. Joellen and her dog went past 35 birds and 30 squirrels. Did they pass more birds or squirrels?

Using Symbols to Order Numbers

$>$ means **is greater than.**
28 is greater than 17.
$28 > 17$

$<$ means **is less than.**
17 is less than 28.
$17 < 28$

Replace the words with a symbol.

1. 5 is greater than 1 $5 > 1$

2. 2 is less than 9

3. 43 is greater than 23

4. 8 is greater than 3

5. 24 is less than 39

6. 35 is less than 39

7. 9 is less than 15

8. 32 is greater than 26

9. 49 is less than 50

 Challenge

Write true or false for each of these number sentences.

10. $4 + 3 > 10$

11. $4 + 3 = 10$

12. $4 + 3 < 10$

13. $10 - 3 > 5$

14. $10 - 3 = 5$

15. $10 - 3 < 5$

Writing Two-Digit Numbers

11 eleven
12 twelve
13 thirteen
14 fourteen
15 fifteen
16 sixteen
17 seventeen
18 eighteen
19 nineteen

21 twenty-one
32 thirty-two
43 forty-three
54 fifty-four
65 sixty-five
76 seventy-six
87 eighty-seven
98 ninety-eight

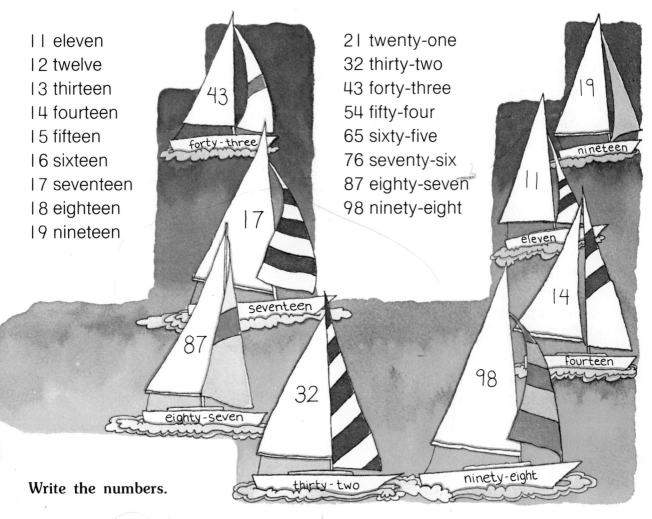

Write the numbers.

1. thirty-nine 39

2. fifteen

3. forty-eight

4. eleven

5. twenty-one

6. seventy

Write the words for these numbers.

7. 17   8. 34   9. 82   10. 60   11. 18   12. 29

13. 57   14. 13   15. 76   16. 15   17. 48   18. 91

Rounding to the Nearest Ten

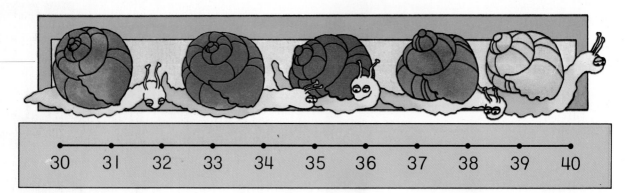

31 to 34 are nearer to 30. They **round** to 30.

35 is in the middle. It **rounds** to 40.

36 to 39 are nearer to 40. They **round** to 40.

Think about the nearest ten. Write the answers.

1a. 24 is between ⬚ and ⬚. 20, 30
 b. 24 rounds to ⬚. 20

2a. 43 is between ⬚ and ⬚.
 b. 43 rounds to ⬚.

3a. 65 is between ⬚ and ⬚.
 b. 65 rounds to ⬚.

4a. 59 is between ⬚ and ⬚.
 b. 59 rounds to ⬚.

5. Write the numbers between 30 and 40 that round to 30.

6. Write the numbers between 80 and 90 that round to 90.

Round to the nearest ten.

7. 19 **8.** 27 **9.** 21 **10.** 64 **11.** 98 **12.** 77

13. 12 **14.** 88 **15.** 67 **16.** 85 **17.** 93 **18.** 54

19. 74 **20.** 11 **21.** 55 **22.** 18 **23.** 15 **24.** 36

Rounding to the Nearest Ten Cents

Sometimes you want to know
about how much the total cost will be
before you get to the check-out counter.

Round each price to the
nearest ten cents. Then add.

19¢   rounds to **20¢**

39¢   rounds to **40¢**

WHEAT CEREAL 34¢   rounds to **30¢**

$$\begin{array}{r} 20\text{¢} \\ 40\text{¢} \\ +\ 30\text{¢} \\ \hline 90\text{¢} \end{array}$$

**Round to the nearest ten cents.
Add to find about how much
the total cost will be.**

1. orange 17¢   20¢
    milk 37¢   40¢
    soup 33¢   + 30¢
                 90¢

2. peas 23¢
    carrots 36¢
    onions 15¢

3. bananas 16¢
    juice 12¢
    potatoes 25¢

4. corn 21¢
    salt 9¢
    grapes 25¢

5. bread 47¢
    crackers 10¢
    peppers 19¢

6. tomatoes 33¢
    apples 16¢
    mustard 17¢

7. soap 17¢
    cream 42¢
    beans 38¢

 Review (pp. 31–37)

Choose the greater number. Round that number to
the nearest ten.

1. 36 or 63   2. 85 or 77   3. 98 or 89   4. 76 or 57   5. 45 or 30

Hundreds, Tens, and Ones

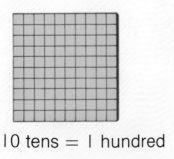

10 tens = 1 hundred

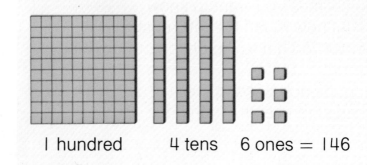

1 hundred   4 tens   6 ones = 146

Write the numbers.

1. 5 hundreds 9 tens 3 ones   593

2. 8 hundreds 3 tens 9 ones

3. 9 hundreds 0 tens 6 ones

4. 3 hundreds 7 tens 0 ones

5. 2 hundreds 3 tens 8 ones

6. 4 hundreds 2 tens 0 ones

Copy and complete.

7. 793 = ⬚ hundreds ⬚ tens ⬚ ones

8. 860 = ⬚ hundreds ⬚ tens ⬚ ones

9. 384 = ⬚ hundreds ⬚ tens ⬚ ones

10. 999 = ⬚ hundreds ⬚ tens ⬚ ones

11. 653 = ⬚ hundreds ⬚ tens ⬚ ones

12. 495 = ⬚ hundreds ⬚ tens ⬚ ones

Calculate

13. How many tens are there in 40?

14. How many tens are there in 140?

Place Value and Sums

Number: 879
This number is the sum of the total values of its digits.

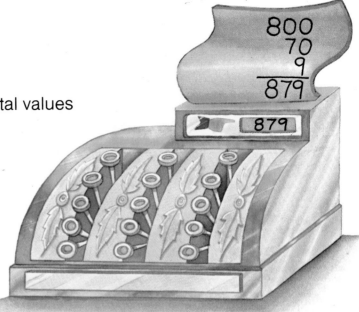

8 has a total value of   800
7 has a total value of   70
9 has a total value of $+$ 9
               879

Write the sums.

1.	2.	3.	4.	5.
600	500	900	300	800
80	90	80	70	80
+ 4	+ 4	+ 6	+ 7	+ 3
684				

Write a sum that shows the total value of each digit.

6. 536   500
            30
       $+$ 6
          536

7. 492   8. 619   9. 857

10. 280   11. 705   12. 333   13. 975   14. 509

 Calculate

15. Which is greater: 3 tens and 9 ones, or 4 tens and 2 ones?

Using Place Value

Number: 879

Hundreds	Tens	Ones
8	7	9

8 is the **digit** in the hundreds place. It has a **total value** of 800.

7 is the digit in the tens place. It has a total value of 70.

9 is the digit in the ones place. It has a total value of 9.

Answer these questions.

1. In 836, what is the total value of the digit in the tens place? 30

2. In 368, what is the total value of the digit in the ones place?

3. Use the number 638.
   a. What is the total value of the digit 8?
   b. What is the total value of the digit 6?
   c. What is the total value of the digit 3?

4. Use the number 863.
   a. What is the total value of the digit 8?
   b. What is the total value of the digit 6?
   c. What is the total value of the digit 3?

5. Use the number 386.
   a. What is the total value of the digit 8?
   b. What is the total value of the digit 6?
   c. What is the total value of the digit 3?

6. Use the number 683.
   a. What is the total value of the digit 6?
   b. What is the total value of the digit 3?
   c. What is the total value of the digit 8?

Names for Hundreds

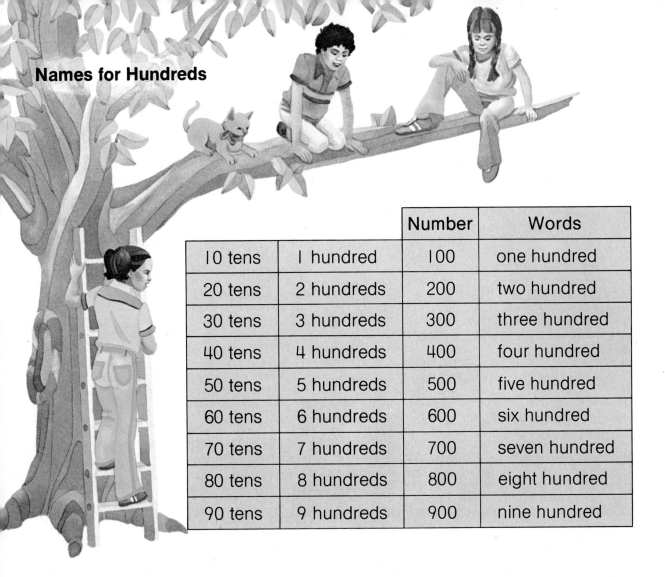

		Number	Words
10 tens	1 hundred	100	one hundred
20 tens	2 hundreds	200	two hundred
30 tens	3 hundreds	300	three hundred
40 tens	4 hundreds	400	four hundred
50 tens	5 hundreds	500	five hundred
60 tens	6 hundreds	600	six hundred
70 tens	7 hundreds	700	seven hundred
80 tens	8 hundreds	800	eight hundred
90 tens	9 hundreds	900	nine hundred

Write the number and the words. Remember, a person
has 10 fingers. A dollar has 100 cents.

1. How many fingers on 10 people?   100, one hundred

2. How many cents in 7 dollars?   3. How many cents in 5 dollars?

4. How many fingers on 80 people?   5. How many cents in 3 dollars?

6. How many fingers on 50 people?   7. How many cents in 4 dollars?

8. How many cents in 2 dollars?   9. How many fingers on 60 people?

Ordinal Numbers

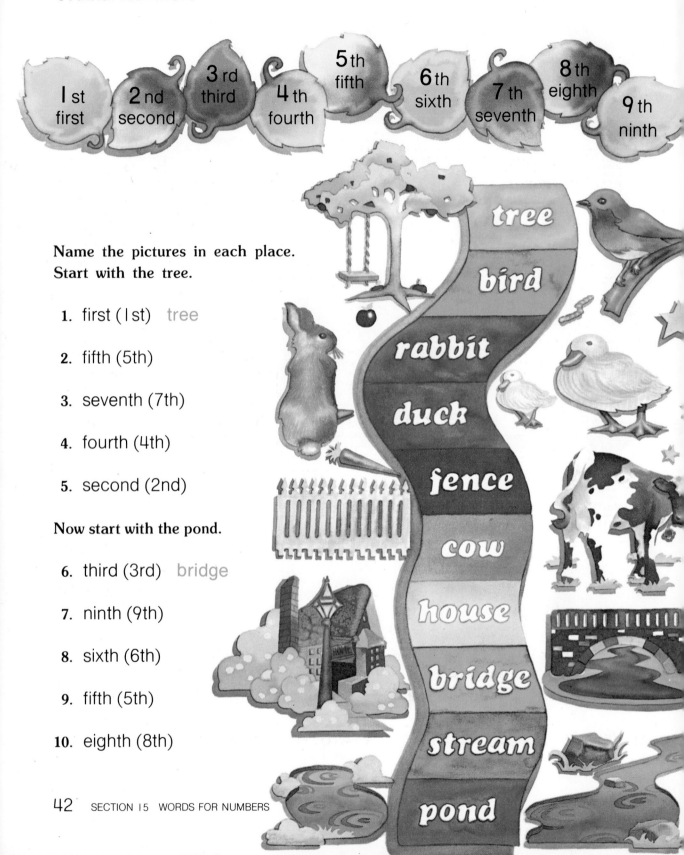

1st first **2nd** second **3rd** third **4th** fourth **5th** fifth **6th** sixth **7th** seventh **8th** eighth **9th** ninth

Name the pictures in each place.
Start with the tree.

1. first (1st) tree

2. fifth (5th)

3. seventh (7th)

4. fourth (4th)

5. second (2nd)

Now start with the pond.

6. third (3rd) bridge

7. ninth (9th)

8. sixth (6th)

9. fifth (5th)

10. eighth (8th)

tree
bird
rabbit
duck
fence
cow
house
bridge
stream
pond

Tens and Hundreds

Move right to count by tens.
Move down to count by hundreds.

Tens

0	10	20	30	40	50	60	70	80	90
100	110	120	130	140	150	160	170	180	190
200	210	220	230	240	250	260	270	280	290
300	310	320	330	340	350	360	370	380	390
400	410	420	430	440	450	460	470	480	490
500	510	520	530	540	550	560	570	580	590
600	610	620	630	640	650	660	670	680	690
700	710	720	730	740	750	760	770	780	790
800	810	820	830	840	850	860	870	880	890
900	910	920	930	940	950	960	970	980	990

(Hundreds — row labels down the left side)

Which number is 10 greater than each of these?

1. 40 50
2. 170
3. 750
4. 980
5. 190

6. 30
7. 580
8. 300
9. 450
10. 410

Which number is 100 greater than each of these?

11. 200
12. 530
13. 370
14. 890
15. 300

16. 90
17. 660
18. 410
19. 720
20. 110

Ordering Three-Digit Numbers

Which is greater, 634 or 712?
If hundreds are not the same,
compare hundreds.

634   712

6 hundreds is less than 7
hundreds, so 634 is less than 712.

634 < 712

Which is greater, 471 or 439?
If hundreds are the same,
compare tens.

471   439

7 tens is greater than 3 tens,
so 471 is greater than 439.

471 > 439

Order these numbers. Use > for is greater than and
< for is less than. Remember, if hundreds and tens
are the same, compare ones.

1. 600 ⬭> 400   2. 673 ◯ 698   3. 831 ◯ 837   4. 926 ◯ 949

5. 618 ◯ 809   6. 753 ◯ 735   7. 333 ◯ 337   8. 928 ◯ 908

9. 298 ◯ 299   10. 683 ◯ 638   11. 427 ◯ 724   12. 640 ◯ 670

13. 750 ◯ 705   14. 996 ◯ 991   15. 803 ◯ 809   16. 834 ◯ 843

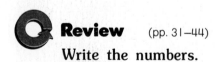 **Review**   (pp. 31–44)

Write the numbers.

1. 6 hundreds 8 tens 3 ones

2. 5 hundreds 0 tens 6 ones

3. 9 hundreds 4 tens 2 ones

4. 1 hundred 2 tens 3 ones

Thousands

10 hundreds = 1 thousand
1 thousand = 1 thousand 0 hundreds 0 tens 0 ones

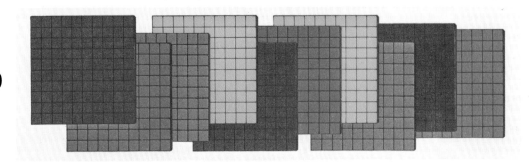

1000

Copy and complete.

1. 4674 = ▨ thousands ▨ hundreds ▨ tens ▨ ones   4, 6, 7, 4

2. 3041 = ▨ thousands ▨ hundreds ▨ tens ▨ ones

3. 2247 = ▨ thousands ▨ hundreds ▨ tens ▨ ones

Write the numbers.

4. 3 thousands 4 hundreds 6 tens 1 one

5. 1 thousand 0 hundreds 7 tens 3 ones

6. 2 thousands 7 hundreds 5 tens 0 ones

 Challenge

7. Write the words for 8796.

Place Value for Thousands

Number: 4873

This number is the sum of the total values
of its digits.

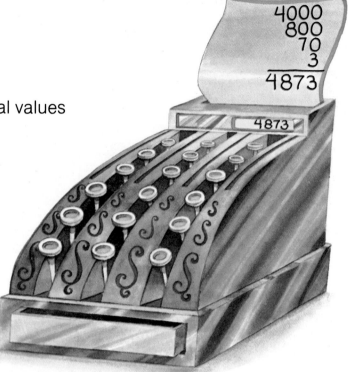

4 has a total value of   4000

8 has a total value of   800

7 has a total value of   70

3 has a total value of $+$ 3

                     4873

Answer these questions.

1. Use the number 5482.
   a. What is the total value
   of the digit 4?   400
   b. What is the total value
   of the digit 8?
   c. What is the total value
   of the digit 5?

2. Use the number 6981.
   a. What is the total value
   of the digit 6?
   b. What is the total value
   of the digit 1?
   c. What is the total value
   of the digit 8?

Write a sum that shows the total value of each digit.

3. 7482	4. 2994	5. 5039	6. 8340	7. 7425
8. 4006	9. 6175	10. 8384	11. 2301	12. 5312
13. 7840	14. 3647	15. 1179	16. 1329	17. 3761

Names for Thousands

10 hundreds	1 thousand	Number	Words
10 hundreds	1 thousand	1000	one thousand
20 hundreds	2 thousand	2000	two thousand
30 hundreds	3 thousand	3000	three thousand
40 hundreds	4 thousand	4000	four thousand
50 hundreds	5 thousand	5000	five thousand
60 hundreds	6 thousand	6000	six thousand
70 hundreds	7 thousand	7000	seven thousand
80 hundreds	8 thousand	8000	eight thousand
90 hundreds	9 thousand	9000	nine thousand

Write the number and the words.

1. A dollar is 100 pennies. How many pennies in 10 dollars?   1000, one thousand

2a. There are 100 centimeters in 1 meter. How many centimeters in 10 meters?

2b. How many centimeters in 40 meters?

3a. A century is 100 years. How many years in 10 centuries?

3b. How many years in 20 centuries?

4a. A kilometer is 1000 meters. How many meters in 6 kilometers?

4b. How many meters in 5 kilometers?

Number Patterns

Add 10   Add 10   Add 10

The rule is add 10.
The next number is 150.

110   120   130   140   ▢

Find the rule and the next number.

1. 300, 400, 500, 600, ▢
   a. The rule is ___.   Add 100
   b. The next number is ___.   700

2. 50, 60, 70, 80, ▢
   a. The rule is ___.
   b. The next number is ___.

3. 15, 20, 25, 30, ▢
   a. The rule is ___.
   b. The next number is ___.

4. 289, 389, 489, 589, ▢
   a. The rule is ___.
   b. The next number is ___.

5. 28, 27, 26, 25, ▢
   a. The rule is ___.
   b. The next number is ___.

6. 225, 235, 245, 255, ▢
   a. The rule is ___.
   b. The next number is ___.

 **Challenge**
Find the answer.

7. One month Ann and Maria made $25 mowing lawns. Then they earned $5 each week for 3 weeks. How much did they earn together?

SWITCH DIGITS

A game for two players.

Get ready:
Both players need ten digit slips. Each player writes one of the digits from 0 to 9 on a small slip of paper. Use each digit only once.

To play:
Use all twenty digit slips. Put them face down. Each player takes two digit slips and makes a two-digit number with them. (For example, the digits 2 and 3 make 23 or 32.) Each player writes the number on a sheet of paper. The player with the number that is less gets all four digit slips. Keep going until all the digit slips are used. The player with more digit slips wins.

Chapter Review

Copy and complete. (ex. 1–4: p. 31)

1. 38 = ? tens ? ones

2. 65 = ? tens ? ones

3. 72 = ? tens ? ones

4. 89 = ? tens ? ones

Write the number that is greater. (ex. 5–6: p. 33), (ex. 7–8: p. 44)

5. 26 or 62

6. 51 or 49

7. 640 or 670

8. 753 or 735

Round each number to the nearest ten. (ex. 9–14: p. 36)

9. 18

10. 72

11. 35

12. 64

13. 55

14. 86

Answer the questions. (ex. 15–16: p. 40)

15. Use the number 238.
    a. What is the total value of the digit 2?
    b. What is the total value of the digit 3?
    c. What is the total value of the digit 8?

16. Use the number 587.
    a. What is the total value of the digit 5?
    b. What is the total value of the digit 8?
    c. What is the total value of the digit 7?

Copy and complete. (ex. 17–18: p. 45)

17. 2351 = ? thousands ? hundreds ? tens ? ones

18. 7405 = ? thousands ? hundreds ? tens ? ones

Chapter Test

Copy and complete.

1. $46 = $ ▢ tens ▢ ones

2. $70 = $ ▢ tens ▢ ones

3. $85 = $ ▢ tens ▢ ones

4. $59 = $ ▢ tens ▢ ones

Write the number that is greater.

5. 44 or 34

6. 10 or 13

7. 816 or 618

8. 352 or 353

Round each number to the nearest ten.

9. 37

10. 25

11. 59

12. 81

13. 13

14. 78

Answer the questions.

15. Use the number 587.
   a. What is the total value of the digit 5?
   b. What is the total value of the digit 8?
   c. What is the total value of the digit 7?

16. Use the number 460.
   a. What is the total value of the digit 4?
   b. What is the total value of the digit 6?
   c. What is the total value of the digit 0?

Copy and complete.

17. $4069 = $ ▢ thousands ▢ hundreds ▢ tens ▢ ones

18. $8231 = $ ▢ thousands ▢ hundreds ▢ tens ▢ ones

Brush Up

Add.

1. $9 + 4$ 2. $6 + 4$ 3. $7 + 8$ 4. $4 + 3$ 5. $6 + 8$

6. $7 + 4$ 7. $6 + 5$ 8. $8 + 2$ 9. $9 + 3$ 10. $4 + 4$

11. $8 + 6$ 12. $6 + 2$ 13. $7 + 5$ 14. $0 + 8$ 15. $3 + 8$

16. $9 + 8$ 17. $8 + 3$ 18. $9 + 1$ 19. $9 + 7$ 20. $4 + 6$

21. $6 + 7$ 22. $5 + 4$ 23. $8 + 5$ 24. $5 + 6$ 25. $5 + 8$

26. $4 + 8$ 27. $9 + 9$ 28. $7 + 6$ 29. $6 + 3$ 30. $0 + 6$

31. $5 + 9$ 32. $7 + 8$ 33. $9 + 2$ 34. $8 + 8$ 35. $9 + 2$

36. $1 + 7$ 37. $6 + 4$ 38. $6 + 9$ 39. $4 + 7$ 40. $2 + 8$

41. $9 + 5$ 42. $7 + 7$ 43. $4 + 0$ 44. $8 + 9$ 45. $4 + 1$

46. $5 + 5$ 47. $7 + 3$ 48. $6 + 6$ 49. $8 + 6$ 50. $3 + 1$

Copy and complete.

51. $17 = $ ⬚ tens ⬚ ones   52. $85 = $ ⬚ tens ⬚ ones

53. $357 = $ ⬚ hundreds ⬚ tens ⬚ ones   54. $139 = $ ⬚ hundreds ⬚ tens ⬚ ones

55. $8676 = $ ⬚ thousands ⬚ hundreds ⬚ tens ⬚ ones

56. $5026 = $ ⬚ thousands ⬚ hundreds ⬚ tens ⬚ ones

Using Addition at Work

Philip Austin is a poultry farmer. In May he used 23 bags of feed. In June he used 41 bags. In July he used 32 bags. To find the total number of bags, he adds 23 + 41 + 32. He used 96 bags of feed during the three months.

Adding One-Digit and Two-Digit Numbers

Find the sums.

1. 9 +4 = 13
2. 8 +3
3. 7 +9
4. 9 +8
5. 8 +8
6. 9 +9
7. 7 +5

8. 20 +78
9. 11 +76
10. 32 +15
11. 45 +44
12. 12 +26
13. 43 +16

14. 58 +11
15. 13 +55
16. 63 +16
17. 42 +6
18. 15 +81
19. 31 +67

20. 23 +72
21. 8 +51
22. 64 +15

23. 42 +22
24. 71 +4
25. 18 +21

26. Toshio drew 15 pictures. Then he drew 23 more. How many pictures in all?

27. Bert made 27 posters. Sally made 42 posters. How many did they make in all?

28. The third grade made 44 maps. The fourth grade made 35 maps. How many maps in all?

Adding Three-Digit Numbers

Step 1
Add ones.

$$
\begin{array}{r}
123 \\
+\ 214 \\
\hline
7
\end{array}
$$

Step 2
Add tens.

$$
\begin{array}{r}
123 \\
+\ 214 \\
\hline
37
\end{array}
$$

Step 3
Add hundreds.

$$
\begin{array}{r}
123 \\
+\ 214 \\
\hline
337
\end{array}
$$

Add.

1.
$$
\begin{array}{r}
132 \\
+\ 346 \\
\hline
478
\end{array}
$$

2.
$$
\begin{array}{r}
311 \\
+\ 446 \\
\hline
\end{array}
$$

3.
$$
\begin{array}{r}
265 \\
+\ 413 \\
\hline
\end{array}
$$

4.
$$
\begin{array}{r}
140 \\
+\ 255 \\
\hline
\end{array}
$$

5.
$$
\begin{array}{r}
406 \\
+\ 153 \\
\hline
\end{array}
$$

6.
$$
\begin{array}{r}
123 \\
+\ 345 \\
\hline
\end{array}
$$

7.
$$
\begin{array}{r}
583 \\
+\ 214 \\
\hline
\end{array}
$$

8.
$$
\begin{array}{r}
248 \\
+\ 31 \\
\hline
\end{array}
$$

9.
$$
\begin{array}{r}
752 \\
+\ 224 \\
\hline
\end{array}
$$

10.
$$
\begin{array}{r}
382 \\
+\ 4 \\
\hline
\end{array}
$$

11.
$$
\begin{array}{r}
523 \\
+\ 202 \\
\hline
\end{array}
$$

12.
$$
\begin{array}{r}
321 \\
+\ 200 \\
\hline
\end{array}
$$

13.
$$
\begin{array}{r}
42 \\
+\ 135 \\
\hline
\end{array}
$$

14.
$$
\begin{array}{r}
140 \\
+\ 315 \\
\hline
\end{array}
$$

15.
$$
\begin{array}{r}
17 \\
+\ 532 \\
\hline
\end{array}
$$

16.
$$
\begin{array}{r}
362 \\
+\ 123 \\
\hline
\end{array}
$$

17.
$$
\begin{array}{r}
81 \\
+\ 314 \\
\hline
\end{array}
$$

18.
$$
\begin{array}{r}
653 \\
+\ 124 \\
\hline
\end{array}
$$

19.
$$
\begin{array}{r}
412 \\
+\ 345 \\
\hline
\end{array}
$$

20.
$$
\begin{array}{r}
605 \\
+\ 293 \\
\hline
\end{array}
$$

21. Miguel saves 247 stamps in one month. The next month he saves 341 stamps. How many stamps does Miguel save in all?

Adding Four-Digit Numbers

Now you can do this!
Change from long to tall.
Keep digits in their places.

3402 + 465

$$
\begin{array}{r}
3402 \\
+\ \ 465 \\
\hline
3867
\end{array}
$$

Write the tall form. Find each sum.

1. 1145 + 1253
$$
\begin{array}{r}
1145 \\
+\ 1253 \\
\hline
2398
\end{array}
$$

2. 7342 + 1436

3. 2136 + 1000

4. 4033 + 224

5. 5172 + 24

6. 316 + 52

7. 472 + 25

8. 6320 + 200

9. 421 + 30

10. 4311 + 121

11. 1500 + 402

12. 5004 + 60

13. 950 + 30

14. 7420 + 159

15. 222 + 34

 Calculate

16. There are 3600 seconds in 1 hour.
How many seconds in 2 hours?

Trading Pennies for Dimes

You can trade 14 pennies for 1 dime and 4 pennies.

Make these trades. Trade 10 pennies for 1 dime.

1. Trade 17 pennies for
   ☐ dimes ☐ pennies. 1, 7

2. Trade 19 pennies for
   ☐ dimes ☐ pennies.

3. Trade 23 pennies for
   ☐ dimes ☐ pennies.

4. Trade 35 pennies for
   ☐ dimes ☐ pennies.

5. Trade 26 pennies for
   ☐ dimes ☐ pennies.

6. Trade 58 pennies for
   ☐ dimes ☐ pennies.

7. Trade 44 pennies for
   ☐ dimes ☐ pennies.

8. Trade 62 pennies for
   ☐ dimes ☐ pennies.

9. Trade 73 pennies for
   ☐ dimes ☐ pennies.

10. Trade 30 pennies for
    ☐ dimes ☐ pennies.

More Trading

Sometimes you trade to add.

2 dimes   3 pennies
+   8 pennies
——————————————
2 dimes   11 pennies

Trade for 3 dimes 1 penny.

Add. Trade to get the most dimes.

1.   7 pennies
   + 8 pennies
     ☐ pennies   15
Trade for ☐ dimes ☐ pennies.   1, 5

2.   6 pennies
   + 9 pennies
     ☐ pennies
Trade for ☐ dimes ☐ pennies.

3.   5 pennies
   + 7 pennies
     ☐ pennies
Trade for ☐ dimes ☐ pennies.

4.   4 pennies
   + 8 pennies
     ☐ pennies
Trade for ☐ dimes ☐ pennies.

5.   2 dimes 4 pennies
   +   7 pennies
     ☐ dimes ☐ pennies
Trade for ☐ dimes ☐ pennies.

6.   3 dimes 8 pennies
   +   7 pennies
     ☐ dimes ☐ pennies
Trade for ☐ dimes ☐ pennies.

7.   6 dimes 4 pennies
   +   9 pennies
     ☐ dimes ☐ pennies
Trade for ☐ dimes ☐ pennies.

8.   4 dimes 7 pennies
   +   8 pennies
     ☐ dimes ☐ pennies
Trade for ☐ dimes ☐ pennies.

Trading Ones for Tens

You can trade 10 pennies for 1 dime.
Now trade 10 ones for 1 ten.

10 ones = 1 ten

Step 1	Step 2
Add ones.	Add tens.
Trade.	

$$\begin{array}{r} \overset{1}{28} \\ +\ 16 \\ \hline 4 \end{array} \qquad \begin{array}{r} \overset{1}{28} \\ +\ 16 \\ \hline 44 \end{array}$$

Add and trade.

1. $\begin{array}{r} 24 \\ +\ 58 \\ \hline 82 \end{array}$
  2. $\begin{array}{r} 36 \\ +\ 16 \\ \hline \end{array}$
  3. $\begin{array}{r} 57 \\ +\ 46 \\ \hline \end{array}$

4. $\begin{array}{r} 43 \\ +\ 27 \\ \hline \end{array}$
  5. $\begin{array}{r} 55 \\ +\ 36 \\ \hline \end{array}$
  6. $\begin{array}{r} 47 \\ +\ 19 \\ \hline \end{array}$
  7. $\begin{array}{r} 65 \\ +\ 18 \\ \hline \end{array}$
  8. $\begin{array}{r} 53 \\ +\ 28 \\ \hline \end{array}$
  9. $\begin{array}{r} 67 \\ +\ 14 \\ \hline \end{array}$

10. $\begin{array}{r} 23 \\ +\ 8 \\ \hline \end{array}$
  11. $\begin{array}{r} 32 \\ +\ 18 \\ \hline \end{array}$
  12. $\begin{array}{r} 58 \\ +\ 26 \\ \hline \end{array}$
  13. $\begin{array}{r} 46 \\ +\ 5 \\ \hline \end{array}$
  14. $\begin{array}{r} 89 \\ +\ 12 \\ \hline \end{array}$
  15. $\begin{array}{r} 33 \\ +\ 56 \\ \hline \end{array}$

16. $\begin{array}{r} 67 \\ +\ 18 \\ \hline \end{array}$
  17. $\begin{array}{r} 34 \\ +\ 29 \\ \hline \end{array}$
  18. $\begin{array}{r} 62 \\ +\ 19 \\ \hline \end{array}$
  19. $\begin{array}{r} 44 \\ +\ 46 \\ \hline \end{array}$
  20. $\begin{array}{r} 65 \\ +\ 39 \\ \hline \end{array}$
  21. $\begin{array}{r} 49 \\ +\ 25 \\ \hline \end{array}$

22. $\begin{array}{r} 26 \\ +\ 64 \\ \hline \end{array}$
  23. $\begin{array}{r} 57 \\ +\ 9 \\ \hline \end{array}$
  24. $\begin{array}{r} 47 \\ +\ 33 \\ \hline \end{array}$
  25. $\begin{array}{r} 77 \\ +\ 25 \\ \hline \end{array}$
  26. $\begin{array}{r} 19 \\ +\ 32 \\ \hline \end{array}$
  27. $\begin{array}{r} 45 \\ +\ 35 \\ \hline \end{array}$

Trading Ones for Tens Again

Step 1
Add ones.
Trade 10 ones
for 1 ten.

Step 2
Add tens.

$$
\begin{array}{r}
\overset{1}{3}5 \\
+\ 47 \\
\hline
2
\end{array}
$$

$$
\begin{array}{r}
\overset{1}{3}5 \\
+\ 47 \\
\hline
82
\end{array}
$$

Add and trade.

1. 67
   + 29
   ___
   96

2. 37
   + 55

3. 56
   + 39

4. 46
   + 38

5. 56
   + 29

6. 19
   + 39

7. 48
   + 39

8. 24
   + 36

9. 47
   + 25

10. 72
    + 19

11. 28
    + 37

12. 46
    + 37

13. 48
    + 36

14. 28
    + 65

15. 43
    + 37

16. 57
    + 37

17. 45
    + 8

18. 29
    + 39

19. 56
    + 28

20. 19
    + 36

21. 44
    + 48

22. 36
    + 17

23. 19
    + 12

24. 17
    + 3

 Challenge

25. Don has 2 dimes and 8 pennies. Rosa had 3 dimes
    and 6 pennies. How much do they have together?

Adding More Than Two Numbers

Look for facts for 10.
Do them first.

Step 1
Add ones.
Trade ones.

Step 2
Add tens.

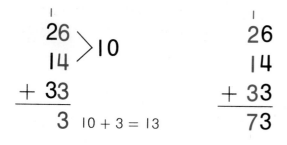

$$
\begin{array}{r}
\overset{1}{2}6 \\
14 \\
+\ 33 \\
\hline
3
\end{array}
\quad 10 + 3 = 13
$$

$$
\begin{array}{r}
\overset{1}{2}6 \\
14 \\
+\ 33 \\
\hline
73
\end{array}
$$

Add. First find the facts for 10.

1.
```
  36
  24
+ 37
----
  97
```
2.
```
  48
   3
+ 12
```
3.
```
  53
   7
+ 21
```
4.
```
  37
  21
+  9
```
5.
```
  27
   6
+ 34
```
6.
```
  42
  16
+  8
```

7.
```
  38
  11
+ 49
```
8.
```
  45
  28
+ 15
```
9.
```
  17
   6
+ 34
```
10.
```
  16
  47
+ 23
```
11.
```
  15
  35
+ 26
```
12.
```
  33
  48
+ 12
```

Add.

13.
```
  15
   8
   5
+ 20
```
14.
```
  23
  12
   8
+  4
```
15.
```
  47
  26
   2
+  4
```
16.
```
  39
   1
  22
+  4
```
17.
```
  20
   7
  44
+ 13
```

Weather Problems

Solve the problems.

1. There were 202 sunny days and 87 cloudy days. How many days were cloudy or sunny?   289

2. It rained on 76 days. It snowed on 15 days. How many days is that?

3. One rainy day, Joan's Rain Shop sold 35 umbrellas. Another rainy day Joan sold 45 umbrellas. How many is that?

4. One winter Lopez's Coat Store sold 56 warm coats. Next winter 73 coats were sold. How many is that?

5. The swimming pool was open 17 days in May and 29 days in June. How many days in all?

6. The ski slope was open 12 days in December, 26 days in January, and 24 days in February. How many days is that?

TARGET PUZZLE

Look at the score sheet below. Tell where each person's arrows landed. Remember, arrows could go to the same number.

		score	number of arrows	
1.	BOB	15	2	7 and 8
2.	PAT	21	3	
3.	RICK	23	2	
4.	SALLY	18	3	
5.	LIZ	17	3	
6.	PETE	22	3	
7.	ELAINE	23	3	
8.	TERESA	25	3	

Trading Dimes for Dollars

You can trade 12 dimes for 1 dollar and 2 dimes.

Add. Trade to get the most dollars.

1.   6 dimes
    + 9 dimes

       ⬚ dimes   15
  Trade for ⬚ dollars ⬚ dimes.   1,5

2.   5 dimes
    + 7 dimes

       ⬚ dimes
  Trade for ⬚ dollars ⬚ dimes.

3.   2 dollars 5 dimes
    +   5 dimes

       ⬚ dollars ⬚ dimes
  Trade for ⬚ dollars ⬚ dimes.

4.   3 dollars 8 dimes
    + 1 dollar   4 dimes

       ⬚ dollars ⬚ dimes
  Trade for ⬚ dollars ⬚ dimes.

5.   5 dollars 2 dimes
    + 2 dollars 8 dimes

       ⬚ dollars ⬚ dimes
  Trade for ⬚ dollars ⬚ dimes.

6.   4 dollars 3 dimes
    + 1 dollar   9 dimes

       ⬚ dollars ⬚ dimes
  Trade for ⬚ dollars ⬚ dimes.

Trading Tens for Hundreds

Trade 10 tens for 1 hundred.

Step 1
Add ones.

Step 2
Add tens.
Trade tens.

Step 3
Add hundreds.

```
    164          1              1
  + 153        164            164
  ─────      + 153          + 153
      7      ─────          ─────
               17            317
```

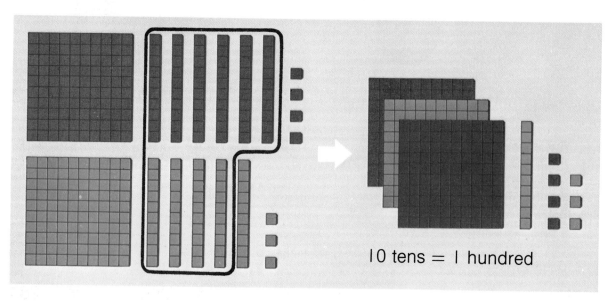

10 tens = 1 hundred

Add.

1. 152 + 353 **505**	2. 472 + 384	3. 681 + 234	4. 574 + 162	5. 426 + 293
6. 190 + 643	7. 584 + 172	8. 469 + 360	9. 785 + 193	10. 484 + 253

Practice Trading Tens

Step 1
Add ones.

Step 2
Add tens.
Trade tens.

Step 3
Add hundreds.

```
  276        ¹            ¹
            276          276
+ 183      + 183        + 183
─────      ─────        ─────
    9         59          459
```

Add.

1. 392
+ 546
─────
938

2. 588
+ 290

3. 383
+ 124

4. 172
+ 694

5. 273
+ 665

6. 91
+ 845

7. 483
+ 374

8. 468
+ 361

9. 364
+ 574

10. 452
+ 465

11. 431
+ 196

12. 255
+ 194

13. 598
+ 171

14. 147
+ 182

15. 382
+ 464

16. 223
+ 396

17. 151
+ 181

18. 334
+ 185

19. 390
+ 420

20. 283
+ 44

 Review   (pp. 55–67)

1. 3172
+ 424

2. 55
+ 36

3. 42
+ 18

4. 481
+ 344

5. 655
+ 91

Trading Twice

Step 1
Add ones.
Trade ones.

¹
378
+ 269
‾‾‾‾‾‾
7

Step 2
Add tens.
Trade tens.

¹ ¹
378
+ 269
‾‾‾‾‾‾
47

Step 3
Add hundreds.

¹ ¹
378
+ 269
‾‾‾‾‾‾
647

Find the sums.

1. 176 + 286 ‾‾‾‾‾ 462	2. 166 + 288	3. 658 + 194	4. 435 + 285	5. 345 + 76
6. 658 + 93	7. 608 + 298	8. 85 + 195	9. 216 + 188	10. 286 + 146
11. 856 + 866	12. 549 + 283	13. 345 + 165	14. 378 + 139	15. 446 + 284
16. 285 + 349	17. 265 + 489	18. 176 + 199	19. 237 + 86	20. 568 + 374
21. 647 + 186	22. 159 + 352	23. 465 + 266	24. 896 + 138	25. 179 + 265

More Trading

Write the tall form. Find each sum.

1. 174 + 456

$$\begin{array}{r} 174 \\ + 456 \\ \hline 630 \end{array}$$

2. 369 + 68

3. 459 + 183

4. 436 + 174

5. 631 + 179

6. 834 + 87

7. 139 + 83

8. 254 + 396

9. 878 + 56

Add.

10.
$$\begin{array}{r} 278 \\ + 196 \\ \hline \end{array}$$

11.
$$\begin{array}{r} 738 \\ + 195 \\ \hline \end{array}$$

12.
$$\begin{array}{r} 448 \\ + 164 \\ \hline \end{array}$$

13.
$$\begin{array}{r} 634 \\ + 78 \\ \hline \end{array}$$

14.
$$\begin{array}{r} 366 \\ + 244 \\ \hline \end{array}$$

15.
$$\begin{array}{r} 265 \\ + 396 \\ \hline \end{array}$$

16.
$$\begin{array}{r} 153 \\ + 378 \\ \hline \end{array}$$

17.
$$\begin{array}{r} 331 \\ + 179 \\ \hline \end{array}$$

18.
$$\begin{array}{r} 486 \\ + 278 \\ \hline \end{array}$$

19.
$$\begin{array}{r} 355 \\ + 198 \\ \hline \end{array}$$

20.
$$\begin{array}{r} 156 \\ + 776 \\ \hline \end{array}$$

21.
$$\begin{array}{r} 252 \\ + 268 \\ \hline \end{array}$$

22.
$$\begin{array}{r} 265 \\ + 535 \\ \hline \end{array}$$

23.
$$\begin{array}{r} 279 \\ + 686 \\ \hline \end{array}$$

24.
$$\begin{array}{r} 378 \\ + 262 \\ \hline \end{array}$$

25. The school store sold 267 notebooks in September and 135 notebooks in October. How many notebooks in all?

26. The school store sold 398 black pencils and 146 red pencils. How many pencils in all?

Practicing Addition

Remember these?

No trading.	Trading ones.	Trading tens.	Trading twice.
63 + 16 — 79	¹ 35 + 47 — 82	¹ 276 + 183 — 459	¹ ¹ 378 + 269 — 647

Find the sums.

1.   46
  + 8
  —
  54

2.   18
  + 24

3.   35
  + 37

4.   294
  + 161

5.   272
  + 23

6.   176
  + 230

7.   389
  + 37

8.   511
  + 386

9.   68
  + 437

10.   256
  + 446

11.   163
  + 278

12.   341
  + 114

13.   135
  + 124

14.   47
  + 583

15.   194
  + 382

 Challenge

Fill in the missing numbers.

16.   26
  + 3☐
  —
  65

17.   4☐
  + 48
  —
  97

18.   64
  + 29
  —
  ☐3

19.   123
  + ☐82
  —
  5☐5

20.   721
  + 1☐9
  —
  91☐

FISHING GAME

A game for 2 or 3 players.

Get ready:
The players copy the fish bowls. Each player needs eight number slips with these numbers written on them.

142	135	270	351
462	473	294	381

To play:
Each player takes two number slips, writes down the numbers, and finds the sum. Then the player puts a slip on a fish with that number. The winner is the first player to put slips on all the fish in one of the fish bowls.

Museum Problems

Solve these problems.

1. 345 people visit the Natural History Museum on Thursday and 192 visit on Friday. How many visitors in all? 537

2. The museum has 161 films about animals and 79 films about fish. How many films is that?

3. The museum has pictures of 379 plants from North America and 427 plants from South America. How many pictures in all?

4. One of the turtles at the museum weighed 97 kilograms. Another weighed 68 kilograms. How much did they weigh together?

5. There are 14 rocks in one case and 16 rocks in another. How many rocks in all?

6. The museum shows 174 large birds and 296 small birds. How many birds are shown?

7. The museum has 43 books about elephants and 57 books about lions and tigers. How many books is that?

8. 3422 people visit the museum in May and 4374 people visit the museum in June. How many people visit the museum in all?

 Challenge

9. There are 143 displays on the first floor, 75 displays on the second floor, and 102 displays on the third floor. How many displays in all?

10. An old bone was 1245 years old when it was found. It was found 86 years ago. How old is it now?

More Than Two Addends

Now try these.

```
  1 2
  146
   89
+ 225
-----
  460
```

Find the sums.

1.
```
  373
  213
+ 124
-----
  710
```

2.
```
  423
   82
+ 146
-----
```

3.
```
  631
   14
+ 245
-----
```

4.
```
  428
   34
+  38
-----
```

5.
```
   58
   62
+ 121
-----
```

6.
```
   32
  122
  343
+   8
-----
```

7.
```
  623
  102
   74
+  26
-----
```

8.
```
  424
   53
  102
+  44
-----
```

9.
```
  225
    5
   40
+  30
-----
```

10.
```
   12
   45
  124
+  61
-----
```

Write the tall form. Be sure the digits are
in their places. Add.

11. 42 + 8 + 350 + 20

12. 610 + 34 + 180 + 6

13. 205 + 100 + 35 + 84

14. 6 + 256 + 305 + 250

Addition Code

Crack the code to answer
the riddle.

If an elephant sat on a fence,
what time would it be?

Code	192	274	139	325	267	84	350	129	246	96	458
	e	o	g	a	n	w	m	i	t	c	f

Add.

1. 117
  + 129
  ___
  246, t

2. 110
  + 19

3. 225
  + 125

4. 146
  + 46

5. 219
  + 27

6. 156
  + 118

7.   14
  + 125

8. 174
  + 18

9. 133
  + 113

10. 217
  + 108

11. 238
  + 29

12.   65
  + 127

13. 63
  + 21

14. 329
  + 129

15. 172
  + 20

16.   48
  + 219

17. 84
  + 12

18. 154
  + 38

19. The answer is __ __ __ __   __ __   __ __ __
              1. 2. 3. 4.   5. 6.   7. 8. 9.

__   __ __ __ __   __ __ __ __ __
10.   11. 12. 13.   14. 15. 16. 17. 18.

Adding Thousands

10 hundreds = 1 thousand

Step 1
Add ones.
Trade.

```
    1
  5157
+ 2967
─────
     4
```

Step 2
Add tens.
Trade.

```
   1 1
  5157
+ 2967
─────
    24
```

Step 3
Add hundreds.
Trade.

```
  1 1 1
  5157
+ 2967
─────
   124
```

Step 4
Add thousands.

```
  1 1 1
  5157
+ 2967
─────
  8124
```

Find the sums.

1. 1452 + 2648 4100	2. 714 + 1796	3. 2488 + 1568	4. 1493 + 287	5. 3474 + 2856
6. 2724 + 587	7. 1894 + 238	8. 3627 + 1489	9. 784 + 1428	10. 4935 + 188
11. 2667 + 384	12. 1998 + 82	13. 5497 + 685	14. 2598 + 3412	15. 4261 + 3739

Now add these.

16. 8424 + 688

17. 1355 + 757

18. 6652 + 1759

19. 1497 + 3846

20. 2593 + 848

21. 6048 + 2986

22. 2689 + 1643

23. 1472 + 3639

24. 7528 + 1583

Same Ones Digit

Find the sums. The ones digits in each row are always the same.

1. 8 + 4 12	2. 58 + 4	3. 838 + 54	4. 8428 + 234
5. 6 + 6	6. 36 + 6	7. 526 + 6	8. 6476 + 1446
9. 7 + 3	10. 37 + 13	11. 237 + 483	12. 5827 + 1383
13. 5 + 2	14. 35 + 12	15. 165 + 422	16. 2295 + 4132
17. 5 + 9	18. 25 + 19	19. 355 + 99	20. 2335 + 269
21. 6 + 8	22. 36 + 8	23. 316 + 28	24. 4356 + 1458

 Calculate
Add.

25. 816 + 4893 + 2165 + 8792

26. 3483 + 8617 + 659 + 2376

27. 908 + 1462 + 375 + 5667

Practicing Addition

Watch out for trading.

```
   231        1 1         1 1 1
 + 453       336        3465
 ─────      +  79      +  555
   684      ─────      ──────
             415         4020
```

Find the sums.

1. 46 + 9 ── 55	2. 14 + 28	3. 37 + 35	4. 262 + 73	5. 461 + 284
6. 176 + 230	7. 299 + 37	8. 163 + 278	9. 256 + 394	10. 424 + 235

Now add these.

11. $436 + 58$ 12. $237 + 98$ 13. $483 + 67$

14. $565 + 387$ 15. $362 + 548$ 16. $1466 + 319$

17. $2478 + 52$ 18. $2664 + 1438$ 19. $973 + 428$

⚙ Review   (pp. 55–78)

1. 47 + 85	2. 482 + 193	3. 476 + 194	4. 195 + 357	5. 5492 + 868

More Than Two Addends

```
  I
  2713
   601
+ 3485
  6799
```

Find the sums.

```
1.   2841      2.     24      3.   1244      4.   3092      5.    764
      609          4601            672          2471          1950
  + 1382        + 3578        + 7156        + 4242        + 5236
     4832
```

```
6.    349      7.   1290      8.    537      9.   3041     10.     94
     1008            437           1148           409          1038
  +  827        +   814        + 7254        + 1264        + 7211
```

```
11.  6428     12.   2044     13.     29     14.    182     15.   3419
       99           1328          1046          2309           284
  +   536        + 4760        +  532        + 4615        +  576
```

16. 276 people visit the park on Saturday. 345 people visit on Sunday. 161 people visit on Monday. How many people visit the park in all?

17. 129 people buy ham sandwiches for lunch. 274 people buy chicken sandwiches. 89 people buy tuna sandwiches. How many sandwiches in all?

Grocery Problems

This grocery store keeps a chart of what is sold each day. This is part of the chart.

	Monday	Tuesday	Wednesday
Loaves of bread	268	253	271
Cartons of eggs	125	115	110
Cartons of milk	300	276	252
Cans of soup	76	49	60

Use the chart to answer these questions.

1. How many loaves of bread were sold on Monday and Tuesday? 521

2. How many cartons of eggs were sold Tuesday and Wednesday?

3. How many cartons of milk were sold Monday and Tuesday?

4. How many cans of soup were sold Tuesday and Wednesday?

5. How many cartons of eggs were sold on all these days?

6. How many loaves of bread were sold on all these days?

7. Henry's Grocery Store sells 345 oranges one week and 466 the next week. How many oranges are sold?

8. The store sells 54 cans of orange juice and 67 cans of apple juice. How many cans of juice are sold?

9. The store sells 106 packages of swiss cheese and 79 packages of cream cheese. How many are sold in all?

10. The store sells 324 bars of soap one month and 292 bars of soap the next month. How many are sold in all?

⭐ **Challenge**

11. The grocery store sells 136 packages of beef. The store sells 30 more packages of chicken than packages of beef. How many packages of chicken were sold?

Adding Cents

For prices less than $1.00
you can write:

$$
\begin{array}{r}
55¢ \\
+\ 23¢ \\
\hline
78¢
\end{array}
\qquad \text{or} \qquad
\begin{array}{r}
\$0.55 \\
+\ 0.23 \\
\hline
\$0.78
\end{array}
$$

Write the sums two ways.

1. $\begin{array}{r} 46¢ \\ +\ 39¢ \\ \hline \end{array}$ 85¢, $0.85

2. $\begin{array}{r} 23¢ \\ +\ 24¢ \\ \hline \end{array}$

3. $\begin{array}{r} 52¢ \\ +\ 18¢ \\ \hline \end{array}$

4. $\begin{array}{r} 29¢ \\ +\ 13¢ \\ \hline \end{array}$

5. $\begin{array}{r} 34¢ \\ +\ 57¢ \\ \hline \end{array}$

6. $\begin{array}{r} 56¢ \\ +\ 13¢ \\ \hline \end{array}$

7. $\begin{array}{r} 18¢ \\ +\ 24¢ \\ \hline \end{array}$

8. $\begin{array}{r} 46¢ \\ +\ 16¢ \\ \hline \end{array}$

9. $\begin{array}{r} 29¢ \\ +\ 43¢ \\ \hline \end{array}$

10. $\begin{array}{r} 79¢ \\ +\ 11¢ \\ \hline \end{array}$

11. $\begin{array}{r} 55¢ \\ +\ 34¢ \\ \hline \end{array}$

12. $\begin{array}{r} 38¢ \\ +\ 27¢ \\ \hline \end{array}$

13. $\begin{array}{r} 5¢ \\ +\ 36¢ \\ \hline \end{array}$

14. $\begin{array}{r} 42¢ \\ +\ 38¢ \\ \hline \end{array}$

15. $\begin{array}{r} 69¢ \\ +\ 19¢ \\ \hline \end{array}$

16. $\begin{array}{r} 18¢ \\ +\ 59¢ \\ \hline \end{array}$

17. $\begin{array}{r} 51¢ \\ +\ 28¢ \\ \hline \end{array}$

18. $\begin{array}{r} 37¢ \\ +\ 44¢ \\ \hline \end{array}$

19. $\begin{array}{r} 73¢ \\ +\ 17¢ \\ \hline \end{array}$

20. $\begin{array}{r} 46¢ \\ +\ 51¢ \\ \hline \end{array}$

Adding Dollars and Cents

When one addend is $1.00
or more, use . and $ in the sum.

$4.00
+ 2.23
$6.23

Add.

1. $1.34
+ 2.29
$3.63

2. $4.08
+ 2.65

3. $3.18
+ 0.59

4. $1.98
+ 3.73

5. $6.75
+ 1.89

6. $6.79
+ 8.54

7. $1.86
+ 0.33

8. $3.73
+ 3.97

9. $4.44
+ 2.34

10. $8.79
+ 2.05

11. $4.38
+ 1.27

12. $6.54
+ 1.23

 Challenge

Use addition to solve these problems.

13. Flowers cost $0.25 each.
Mi-Yung has $1.00. Can she
buy 6 flowers?

14. Pots cost 52¢. Jack has
$2.00. How many pots can he
buy?

Sports Problems

KATE'S SPORTS SHOP

$3.50 SLUGGER Batter-Up POWER

$4.10

8.60 MITT MITT

Use the pictures to answer these questions.

1. Which two items could you buy for about $31.00?
   skis and baseball bat

2. What is the total cost of the catcher's mitt and the baseball bat?

3. Which two items would cost about $15.00?

4. What is the total cost of the skis and the tennis racket?

5. What is the total cost of the football, the basketball, and the catcher's mitt?

6. What is the total cost of the baseball bat and the tennis racket?

7. What is the total cost of the football, the catcher's mitt, and the tennis racket?

8. What is the total cost of the tennis racket and two tennis balls?

9. Which two items could you buy for less than $8.00?

10. Which three items could you buy for about $20.00?

11. You have $2.00. How many tennis balls can you buy?

12. You have $9.00. How many basketballs can you buy?

Use addition to answer these.

13. Pete makes $20.15 in one day. Julia makes $22.35 in one day. How much do they make together?

14. Leon works in the store. He makes $16.47 one day and $13.57 the next day. How much does he make in all?

Chapter Review

Add. (ex. 1–3: p. 56), (ex. 4, 5: p. 57)

1. 275 + 412	**2.** 348 + 40	**3.** 573 + 4	**4.** 3005 + 40	**5.** 5245 + 2331

Add. (ex. 6–10: p. 60), (ex. 11–15: p. 66)

(ex. 16–20: p. 68)

6. 22 + 18	**7.** 47 + 24	**8.** 13 + 8	**9.** 16 + 36	**10.** 48 + 19
11. 381 + 134	**12.** 169 + 560	**13.** 272 + 141	**14.** 685 + 183	**15.** 276 + 451
16. 237 + 86	**17.** 342 + 179	**18.** 608 + 198	**19.** 245 + 77	**20.** 578 + 374

Add. (ex. 21–25: p. 76), (ex. 26–31: p. 79), (ex. 32–36: p. 83)

21. 8543 + 953	**22.** 2616 + 1834	**23.** 3665 + 2946	**24.** 2642 + 381	**25.** 3247 + 4352

26. 228 + 98 + 101   **27.** 729 + 64 + 2381   **28.** 5259 + 408 + 21

29. 29 + 3017 + 682   **30.** 5119 + 186 + 83   **31.** 735 + 6707 + 209

32. $4.39 + 6.52	**33.** $6.03 + 4.52	**34.** $3.27 + 1.86	**35.** $1.86 + 3.09	**36.** $5.62 + 4.08

Chapter Test

Add.

1. $\begin{array}{r} 140 \\ + 315 \\ \hline \end{array}$

2. $\begin{array}{r} 348 \\ + 40 \\ \hline \end{array}$

3. $\begin{array}{r} 573 \\ + 14 \\ \hline \end{array}$

4. $\begin{array}{r} 8415 \\ + 362 \\ \hline \end{array}$

5. $\begin{array}{r} 3005 \\ + 31 \\ \hline \end{array}$

Add.

6. $\begin{array}{r} 28 \\ + 62 \\ \hline \end{array}$

7. $\begin{array}{r} 67 \\ + 32 \\ \hline \end{array}$

8. $\begin{array}{r} 896 \\ + 42 \\ \hline \end{array}$

9. $\begin{array}{r} 585 \\ + 181 \\ \hline \end{array}$

10. $\begin{array}{r} 785 \\ + 167 \\ \hline \end{array}$

Add.

11. $\begin{array}{r} 4827 \\ + 2383 \\ \hline \end{array}$

12. $\begin{array}{r} 2356 \\ + 377 \\ \hline \end{array}$

13. $\begin{array}{r} 7050 \\ + 891 \\ \hline \end{array}$

14. $\begin{array}{r} \$5.89 \\ + 4.79 \\ \hline \end{array}$

15. $\begin{array}{r} \$3.97 \\ + 8.04 \\ \hline \end{array}$

16. $102 + 23 + 4248$

17. $45 + 12 + 6175$

18. $245 + 15 + 6314$

Brush Up

Subtract.

1. 12 − 6	2. 7 − 4	3. 15 − 6	4. 11 − 8	5. 9 − 5	6. 8 − 6	7. 9 − 4
8. 18 − 9	9. 12 − 4	10. 14 − 8	11. 6 − 5	12. 10 − 6	13. 13 − 7	14. 7 − 5
15. 16 − 8	16. 9 − 6	17. 18 − 9	18. 12 − 8	19. 14 − 7	20. 8 − 3	21. 11 − 2
22. 10 − 5	23. 11 − 6	24. 12 − 9	25. 9 − 8	26. 7 − 2	27. 15 − 7	28. 15 − 9
29. 8 − 2	30. 15 − 8	31. 13 − 8	32. 7 − 7	33. 9 − 7	34. 13 − 5	35. 11 − 6
36. 12 − 7	37. 9 − 3	38. 14 − 7	39. 16 − 9	40. 8 − 7	41. 17 − 8	42. 14 − 5

Copy and complete.

43. 29 = ▯ tens ▯ ones

44. 83 = ▯ tens ▯ ones

45. 50 = ▯ tens ▯ ones

46. 374 = ▯ hundreds ▯ tens ▯ ones

47. 98 = ▯ tens ▯ ones

48. 789 = ▯ hundreds ▯ tens ▯ ones

49. 62 = ▯ tens ▯ ones

50. 963 = ▯ hundreds ▯ tens ▯ ones

CHAPTER 4

Subtraction

Using Subtraction at Work

Lynn Woods is an inventory clerk in a warehouse. She counted 954 baseball gloves in stock at the beginning of the month and 276 at the end of the month. She subtracts 954 − 276 to find how many were shipped. 678 baseball gloves were shipped that month.

Subtracting Two-Digit Numbers

Remember this?
Subtract the ones.
Then subtract the tens.

tens ⌐ ⌐ ones
37
− 14
23 ← difference

Find the differences.

1. 49 − 35 = 14	2. 87 − 56	3. 65 − 24
4. 48 − 34	5. 76 − 41	6. 54 − 13
7. 87 − 50	8. 79 − 25	9. 57 − 32
10. 70 − 10	11. 76 − 3	12. 68 − 45
13. 84 − 60	14. 78 − 35	15. 67 − 23
16. 96 − 45	17. 69 − 32	18. 57 − 27
19. 99 − 64	20. 17 − 3	21. 78 − 15
22. 23 − 11	23. 79 − 23	24. 65 − 34
25. 59 − 46	26. 57 − 12	27. 76 − 64
28. 38 − 5	29. 99 − 56	30. 76 − 42

Circus Problems

Find the differences.

1. There are 26 clowns in the circus. 14 are men. How many clowns are women? 12

2. There are 17 acrobats. 7 do an act together. How many are not in the act?

3. There are 48 lions. 24 lions do tricks. How many lions do not do tricks?

4. There are 32 bales of hay. The elephants eat 11. How many bales are left?

5. The circus has 95 performers. 23 work with animals. How many do not work with animals?

6. The monkeys can do 15 tricks. The ponies can do 9. How many more tricks can the monkeys do?

⭐ Challenge

7. There are 79 bags of peanuts. The elephants eat 34 bags and the monkeys eat 15. How many bags are left?

Trading Dimes for Pennies

To find 32¢ − 8¢, you can trade 1 dime for 10 pennies.

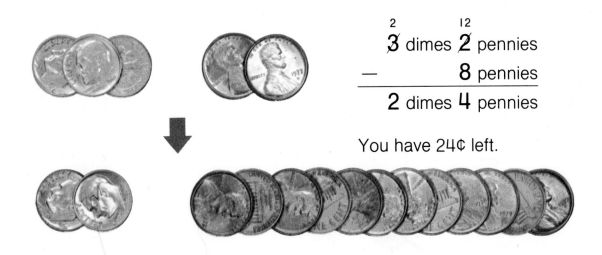

$$\begin{array}{r} \overset{2}{\cancel{3}} \text{ dimes } \overset{12}{\cancel{2}} \text{ pennies} \\ - \qquad\quad 8 \text{ pennies} \\ \hline 2 \text{ dimes } 4 \text{ pennies} \end{array}$$

You have 24¢ left.

Trade 1 dime for 10 pennies. Subtract.

1. 4 dimes 1 penny
    −   7 pennies
         3 dimes 4 pennies

2. 6 dimes 3 pennies
    −   5 pennies
         ☐ dimes ☐ pennies

3. 5 dimes 8 pennies
    −   9 pennies
         ☐ dimes ☐ pennies

4. 3 dimes 4 pennies
    −   6 pennies
         ☐ dimes ☐ pennies

5. 8 dimes 6 pennies
    −   8 pennies
         ☐ dimes ☐ pennies

6. 7 dimes 7 pennies
    −   8 pennies
         ☐ dimes ☐ pennies

Subtracting Ones

Are there enough
ones to subtract?

Look at
the ones.

Enough ones

$$89$$
$$-23$$
yes

Yes, you can
subtract 3 ones
from 9 ones.

Not enough ones

$$64$$
$$-29$$
no

No, you cannot
subtract 9 ones
from 4 ones.

**Are there enough ones to subtract? Write yes or no.
Do not subtract.**

1. 36	2. 48	3. 87	4. 46	5. 93	6. 76
− 28	− 29	− 61	− 24	− 28	− 43
no					

1. 36 − 28 no
2. 48 − 29
3. 87 − 61
4. 46 − 24
5. 93 − 28
6. 76 − 43

7. 45 − 20
8. 76 − 57
9. 63 − 18
10. 57 − 42
11. 81 − 25
12. 88 − 59

13. 90 − 74
14. 74 − 28
15. 96 − 36
16. 32 − 27
17. 85 − 33
18. 60 − 23

19. 71 − 23
20. 52 − 15
21. 57 − 48
22. 24 − 12
23. 78 − 53
24. 91 − 67

Trading Tens for Ones

Step 1
See if you need
more ones to subtract.

Step 2
Trade 1 ten
for 10 ones.

Step 3
Subtract ones.
Subtract tens.

$$\begin{array}{r} 90 \\ -\ 27 \\ \hline \end{array}$$ You cannot subtract 7 ones from 0 ones.

$$\begin{array}{r} {\scriptstyle 8\ 10} \\ 9\!\!\!/0 \\ -\ 27 \\ \hline \end{array}$$

$$\begin{array}{r} {\scriptstyle 8\ 10} \\ 9\!\!\!/0 \\ -\ 27 \\ \hline 63 \end{array}$$

Trade to subtract.

1.
$$\begin{array}{r} 70 \\ -\ 23 \\ \hline 47 \end{array}$$

2.
$$\begin{array}{r} 50 \\ -\ 49 \\ \hline \end{array}$$

3.
$$\begin{array}{r} 30 \\ -\ 18 \\ \hline \end{array}$$

4.
$$\begin{array}{r} 80 \\ -\ 56 \\ \hline \end{array}$$

5.
$$\begin{array}{r} 40 \\ -\ 21 \\ \hline \end{array}$$

6.
$$\begin{array}{r} 60 \\ -\ 49 \\ \hline \end{array}$$

7.
$$\begin{array}{r} 40 \\ -\ 15 \\ \hline \end{array}$$

8.
$$\begin{array}{r} 80 \\ -\ 54 \\ \hline \end{array}$$

9.
$$\begin{array}{r} 90 \\ -\ 22 \\ \hline \end{array}$$

10.
$$\begin{array}{r} 20 \\ -\ 7 \\ \hline \end{array}$$

11.
$$\begin{array}{r} 70 \\ -\ 66 \\ \hline \end{array}$$

12.
$$\begin{array}{r} 50 \\ -\ 25 \\ \hline \end{array}$$

13.
$$\begin{array}{r} 90 \\ -\ 64 \\ \hline \end{array}$$

14.
$$\begin{array}{r} 60 \\ -\ 23 \\ \hline \end{array}$$

15.
$$\begin{array}{r} 30 \\ -\ 17 \\ \hline \end{array}$$

16. Russell has 8 dimes. He buys some daisies for 37¢. What is his change?

17. Helen has 4 dimes. She pays 15¢ for a newspaper. What is her change?

More Trading

Step I
Trade I ten
for 10 ones.

$$\begin{array}{r} {}^{2}\cancel{3}{}^{14}\cancel{4} \\ -\ 15 \\ \hline \end{array}$$

Step 2
Subtract ones.
Subtract tens.

$$\begin{array}{r} {}^{2}\cancel{3}{}^{14}\cancel{4} \\ -\ 15 \\ \hline 19 \end{array}$$

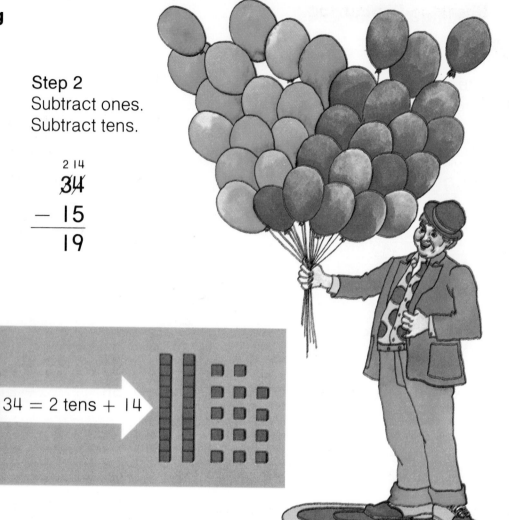

$34 = 2 \text{ tens} + 14$

Subtract.

1. 73 − 38 35	2. 86 − 49	3. 92 − 54	4. 51 − 27	5. 36 − 18	6. 64 − 15
7. 43 − 27	8. 24 − 9	9. 65 − 38	10. 83 − 34	11. 94 − 38	12. 43 − 29
13. 76 − 47	14. 26 − 19	15. 41 − 27	16. 63 − 37	17. 52 − 34	18. 77 − 68

Checking Subtraction

	Subtract	Check
	4 13	
	5̶3̶	27
	− 27	+ 26
	26	53

Check subtraction by adding.

Subtract. Add to check.

1. 65   28
   − 28 + 37
   37   65

2. 16
   − 7

3. 15
   − 8

4. 48
   − 15

5. 37
   − 22

6. 70
   − 34

7. 83
   − 57

8. 92
   − 38

9. 31
   − 16

10. 50
    − 23

11. 64
    − 48

12. 73
    − 29

13. 87
    − 39

14. 13
    − 7

15. 54
    − 6

16. 60
    − 38

17. 25
    − 8

 Calculate

Find the missing numbers.

18. ☐ − 18 = 27

19. 38 + ☐ = 72

20. ☐ − 47 = 35

Practicing Two-Digit Subtraction

Change from long to tall.

$$63 - 47$$

$$
\begin{array}{r}
5\ 13 \\
\cancel{63} \\
-\ 47 \\
\hline
16
\end{array}
$$

Write the tall form. Subtract.

1. 87 − 59
$$
\begin{array}{r}
87 \\
-\ 59 \\
\hline
28
\end{array}
$$

2. 94 − 67

3. 84 − 39

4. 78 − 59

5. 68 − 49

6. 23 − 16

7. 22 − 7

8. 46 − 19

9. 70 − 38

10. 80 − 41

11. 90 − 34

12. 50 − 16

13. 42 − 18

14. 61 − 23

15. 74 − 46

16. 85 − 39

17. 31 − 18

18. 60 − 25

19. 40 − 27

20. 91 − 56

21. Luisa put 2 rows of bricks on the wall. She used 83 bricks in all. One row has 37 bricks. How many bricks in the other row?

More Subtraction Practice

Subtract. Check the first row by adding.

1. $\begin{array}{r} 80 \\ -21 \\ \hline 59 \end{array}$ $\begin{array}{r} 21 \\ +59 \\ \hline 80 \end{array}$ 2. $\begin{array}{r} 90 \\ -56 \\ \hline \end{array}$ 3. $\begin{array}{r} 50 \\ -32 \\ \hline \end{array}$ 4. $\begin{array}{r} 30 \\ -17 \\ \hline \end{array}$ 5. $\begin{array}{r} 61 \\ -46 \\ \hline \end{array}$

6. $\begin{array}{r} 47 \\ -33 \\ \hline \end{array}$ 7. $\begin{array}{r} 90 \\ -74 \\ \hline \end{array}$ 8. $\begin{array}{r} 85 \\ -19 \\ \hline \end{array}$ 9. $\begin{array}{r} 63 \\ -18 \\ \hline \end{array}$ 10. $\begin{array}{r} 80 \\ -64 \\ \hline \end{array}$ 11. $\begin{array}{r} 37 \\ -9 \\ \hline \end{array}$

12. $\begin{array}{r} 73 \\ -18 \\ \hline \end{array}$ 13. $\begin{array}{r} 62 \\ -8 \\ \hline \end{array}$ 14. $\begin{array}{r} 71 \\ -7 \\ \hline \end{array}$ 15. $\begin{array}{r} 56 \\ -9 \\ \hline \end{array}$ 16. $\begin{array}{r} 72 \\ -27 \\ \hline \end{array}$ 17. $\begin{array}{r} 48 \\ -34 \\ \hline \end{array}$

18. $\begin{array}{r} 90 \\ -84 \\ \hline \end{array}$ 19. $\begin{array}{r} 93 \\ -56 \\ \hline \end{array}$ 20. $\begin{array}{r} 71 \\ -36 \\ \hline \end{array}$

21. $\begin{array}{r} 30 \\ -28 \\ \hline \end{array}$ 22. $\begin{array}{r} 26 \\ -15 \\ \hline \end{array}$ 23. $\begin{array}{r} 56 \\ -28 \\ \hline \end{array}$

24. Linda is 18 years old.
    Her grandmother is 63.
    How many years older is
    her grandmother?

 Review (pp. 91–99)

1. $\begin{array}{r} 49 \\ -35 \\ \hline \end{array}$ 2. $\begin{array}{r} 93 \\ -28 \\ \hline \end{array}$ 3. $\begin{array}{r} 71 \\ -35 \\ \hline \end{array}$ 4. $\begin{array}{r} 80 \\ -54 \\ \hline \end{array}$ 5. $\begin{array}{r} 53 \\ -47 \\ \hline \end{array}$ 6. $\begin{array}{r} 64 \\ -19 \\ \hline \end{array}$

Subtracting Three-Digit Numbers

Step 1
See if you need more ones to subtract.

253   Not enough ones
− 127

Step 2
Trade 1 ten for 10 ones.

⁴ ¹³
2̶5̶3̶
− 127

Step 3
Subtract ones.
Subtract tens.
Subtract hundreds.

⁴ ¹³
2̶5̶3̶
− 127
126

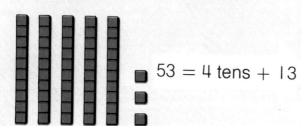

53 = 4 tens + 13

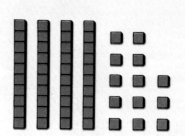

Subtract. Check the first row by adding.

1. 840   527
   − 527   + 313
    313   840

2. 957
   − 428

3. 890
   − 284

4. 761
   − 439

5. 672
   − 349

6. 698
   − 452

7. 978
   − 640

8. 532
   − 417

9. 653
   − 228

10. 381
    − 269

11. 464
    − 137

12. 280
    − 164

13. 563
    − 218

14. 785
    − 413

Three-Digit Subtraction

Subtract. Check the first row.

1. 630
    − 128
    502

2. 771
    − 236

3. 893
    − 456

4. 417
    − 103

5. 639
    − 214

6. 538
    − 112

7. 426
    − 105

8. 864
    − 521

9. 758
    − 232

10. 583
     − 219

11. 460
     − 237

12. 671
     − 249

13. 846
     − 231

14. 786
     − 236

15. 795
     − 432

16. 887
     − 143

17. 580
     − 224

18. 783
     − 346

19. 578
     − 346

20. 698
     − 350

21. 423
     − 208

22. 835
     − 526

23. 190
     − 145

 Challenge

24. A year has 365 days. It rained on 129 days one year. How many dry days that year?

25. One city has 296 days with sunshine. How many cloudy days in that city?

Trading Dollars for Dimes

To find $5.35 − $1.74, you have to trade
1 dollar for 10 dimes.

$$\begin{array}{llll} & \overset{4}{\cancel{5}} \text{ dollars} & \overset{13}{\cancel{3}} \text{ dimes} & 5 \text{ pennies} \\ - & 1 \text{ dollar} & 7 \text{ dimes} & 4 \text{ pennies} \\ \hline & 3 \text{ dollars} & 6 \text{ dimes} & 1 \text{ penny} \end{array}$$

You have $3.61 left.

Subtract.

1. 6 dollars 4 dimes 8 pennies
    − 2 dollars 7 dimes 4 pennies
    ⬚ dollars ⬚ dimes ⬚ pennies
    3 dollars 7 dimes 4 pennies

2. 5 dollars 2 dimes 7 pennies
    − 3 dollars 6 dimes 2 pennies
    ⬚ dollars ⬚ dimes ⬚ pennies

3. 4 dollars 2 dimes 5 pennies
    − 1 dollar 8 dimes 5 pennies
    ⬚ dollars ⬚ dimes ⬚ pennies

4. 2 dollars 3 dimes 9 pennies
    − 1 dollar 6 dimes 7 pennies
    ⬚ dollars ⬚ dimes ⬚ pennies

5. 7 dollars 1 dime 6 pennies
    − 5 dollars 3 dimes 5 pennies
    ⬚ dollars ⬚ dimes ⬚ pennies

6. 8 dollars 2 dimes 9 pennies
    − 4 dollars 6 dimes 4 pennies
    ⬚ dollars ⬚ dimes ⬚ pennies

7. 4 dollars 6 dimes 3 pennies
    − 2 dollars 7 dimes 1 penny
    ⬚ dollars ⬚ dimes ⬚ pennies

Subtracting Tens

First subtract ones. Then see if there are enough tens to subtract.

Look at the tens.

Enough tens

637
− 212
5 yes

Yes, you can subtract 1 ten from 3 tens.

Not enough tens

437
− 192
5 no

No, you cannot subtract 9 tens from 3 tens.

The ones are done for you. Are there enough tens to subtract? Write yes or no. Do not subtract.

1. 436
− 172
4 no

2. 684
− 261
3

3. 817
− 374
3

4. 905
− 382
3

5. 783
− 240
3

6. 578
− 234
4

7. 346
− 193
3

8. 259
− 174
5

9. 998
− 364
4

10. 389
− 164
5

11. 806
− 461
5

12. 346
− 124
2

13. 809
− 427
2

14. Betty is mailing a package. She has $2.94. The package costs $1.75 to mail. How much money will Betty have left?

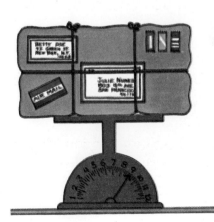

Trading Hundreds for Tens

I hundred = 10 tens

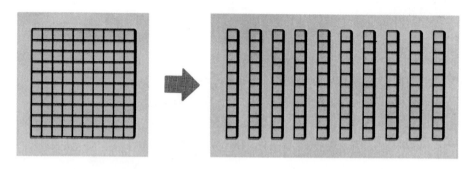

Step I	Step 2	
Subtract ones.	Subtract tens.	
Trade I hundred for I0 tens.	Subtract hundreds.	Check

$$\begin{array}{r} \overset{3\ 15}{\cancel{4}\cancel{5}7} \\ -\ 283 \\ \hline 4 \end{array}$$

$$\begin{array}{r} \overset{3\ 15}{\cancel{4}\cancel{5}7} \\ -\ 283 \\ \hline 174 \end{array}$$

$$\begin{array}{r} \overset{1}{283} \\ +\ 174 \\ \hline 457 \end{array}$$

Subtract. Write the check.

1. $\begin{array}{r} 628 \\ -\ 274 \\ \hline 354 \end{array}$ $\begin{array}{r} 274 \\ +\ 354 \\ \hline 628 \end{array}$

2. $\begin{array}{r} 735 \\ -\ 461 \\ \hline \end{array}$

3. $\begin{array}{r} 914 \\ -\ 480 \\ \hline \end{array}$

4. $\begin{array}{r} 847 \\ -\ 583 \\ \hline \end{array}$

5. $\begin{array}{r} 529 \\ -\ 175 \\ \hline \end{array}$

Subtract.

6. $\begin{array}{r} 537 \\ -\ 182 \\ \hline \end{array}$

7. $\begin{array}{r} 429 \\ -\ 163 \\ \hline \end{array}$

8. $\begin{array}{r} 762 \\ -\ 291 \\ \hline \end{array}$

9. $\begin{array}{r} 517 \\ -\ 263 \\ \hline \end{array}$

10. $\begin{array}{r} 889 \\ -\ 392 \\ \hline \end{array}$

11. $\begin{array}{r} 736 \\ -\ 354 \\ \hline \end{array}$

12. $\begin{array}{r} 637 \\ -\ 284 \\ \hline \end{array}$

13. $\begin{array}{r} 438 \\ -\ 273 \\ \hline \end{array}$

14. $\begin{array}{r} 445 \\ -\ 191 \\ \hline \end{array}$

15. $\begin{array}{r} 869 \\ -\ 394 \\ \hline \end{array}$

Practice Trading Hundreds for Tens

Subtract. Check the first row by adding.

1. 446
   − 192
   ___
   254

2. 324
   − 182

3. 567
   − 83

4. 183
   − 61

5. 551
   − 290

6. 445
   − 163

7. 328
   − 142

8. 483
   − 291

9. 625
   − 142

10. 858
    − 262

11. 568
    − 172

12. 628
    − 263

13. 328
    − 191

14. 625
    − 342

15. 436
    − 193

16. 459
    − 267

17. 946
    − 582

18. 815
    − 632

19. 715
    − 532

20. 213
    − 121

21. 666
    − 372

22. 389
    − 192

23. 416
    − 322

24. 537
    − 262

 Challenge

25. The cafeteria has 237 plates. They use 189 for lunch. How many left?

26. There are 210 slices of ham. 172 are used for sandwiches. How many slices left?

Trading Tens and Hundreds

Step 1
Trade 1 ten
for 10 ones.
Subtract ones.

$$\begin{array}{r} {}^{2\ 17} \\ 43\!\!\!/7 \\ -\ 158 \\ \hline 9 \end{array}$$

Step 2
Trade 1 hundred
for 10 tens.

$$\begin{array}{r} {}^{12} \\ {}^{3\ 2\ 17} \\ 43\!\!\!/7 \\ -\ 158 \\ \hline 9 \end{array}$$

Step 3
Subtract tens.
Subtract hundreds.

$$\begin{array}{r} {}^{12} \\ {}^{3\ 2\ 17} \\ 43\!\!\!/7 \\ -\ 158 \\ \hline 279 \end{array}$$

Subtract. Check the first row by adding.

1. $\begin{array}{r} 836 \\ -\ 578 \\ \hline 258 \end{array}$
2. $\begin{array}{r} 953 \\ -\ 454 \\ \hline \end{array}$
3. $\begin{array}{r} 718 \\ -\ 259 \\ \hline \end{array}$
4. $\begin{array}{r} 555 \\ -\ 276 \\ \hline \end{array}$
5. $\begin{array}{r} 844 \\ -\ 266 \\ \hline \end{array}$

6. $\begin{array}{r} 462 \\ -\ 198 \\ \hline \end{array}$
7. $\begin{array}{r} 321 \\ -\ 154 \\ \hline \end{array}$
8. $\begin{array}{r} 434 \\ -\ 267 \\ \hline \end{array}$
9. $\begin{array}{r} 411 \\ -\ 133 \\ \hline \end{array}$
10. $\begin{array}{r} 235 \\ -\ 47 \\ \hline \end{array}$

11. $\begin{array}{r} 334 \\ -\ 288 \\ \hline \end{array}$
12. $\begin{array}{r} 545 \\ -\ 286 \\ \hline \end{array}$
13. $\begin{array}{r} 213 \\ -\ 144 \\ \hline \end{array}$
14. $\begin{array}{r} 466 \\ -\ 188 \\ \hline \end{array}$
15. $\begin{array}{r} 354 \\ -\ 275 \\ \hline \end{array}$

16. $\begin{array}{r} 429 \\ -\ 235 \\ \hline \end{array}$
17. $\begin{array}{r} 824 \\ -\ 476 \\ \hline \end{array}$
18. $\begin{array}{r} 582 \\ -\ 297 \\ \hline \end{array}$
19. $\begin{array}{r} 634 \\ -\ 265 \\ \hline \end{array}$
20. $\begin{array}{r} 654 \\ -\ 275 \\ \hline \end{array}$

Practicing Subtraction

No trading.

```
  258
- 127
-----
  131
```

Trading
hundreds.

```
   3 15
  4̸5̸7
- 283
-----
  174
```

Trading tens
and hundreds.

```
     13
   6 3̸ 16
  7̸4̸6̸
- 589
-----
  157
```

Subtract. Check the first row by adding.

1. 521 − 298	2. 373 − 192	3. 985 − 742	4. 472 − 97	5. 259 − 146
223				

6. 434 − 139	7. 954 − 342	8. 652 − 268	9. 465 − 163	10. 728 − 345

11. 862 − 341	12. 624 − 576	13. 774 − 562	14. 486 − 294	15. 522 − 235

16. Cooper's Card Store had
347 birthday cards. They
sold 198 cards. How many cards
were left?

 Review (pp. 91–107)

1. 45 − 39	2. 462 − 348	3. 639 − 257	4. 854 − 275	5. 324 − 176

Starbound Problems

Add or subtract to solve these problems.

1. There are 426 people on the Starbound. 198 are children. How many are not children?
228

2. There are 156 rock samples from Venus and 568 rock samples from Mars. How many rock samples in all?

3. There are 417 space suits. 196 are new. How many are not new?

4. There are 228 adults on the Starbound. 188 are women. How many are men?

5. There are 85 engineers and 56 biologists on the Starbound. How many more engineers than biologists?

6. There are 148 children in the Starbound School. 129 are not third graders. How many are third graders?

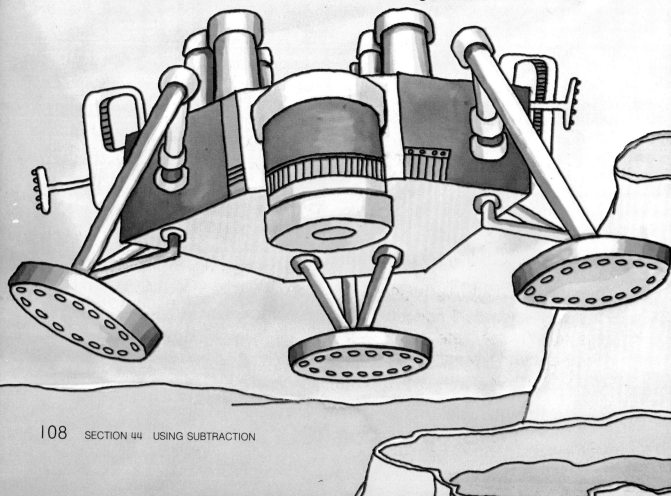

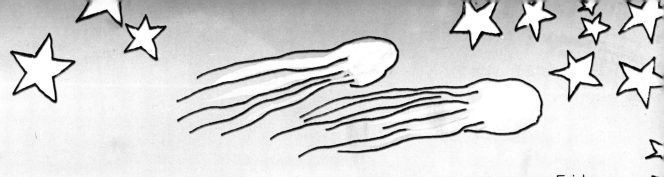

7. Ellen took 48 pictures on Sunday and 35 pictures on Monday. How many pictures did she take on those two days?

8. Matt saw 55 meteors on Friday and 23 meteors on Saturday. How many meteors did he see in all?

9. The Starbound cook made 26 pots of soup on Tuesday and 43 pots of soup on Wednesday. How many pots of soup were made on those two days?

10. The Starbound went to Venus in 15 days. Then it went to Mars in 46 days. How many days did the Starbound travel?

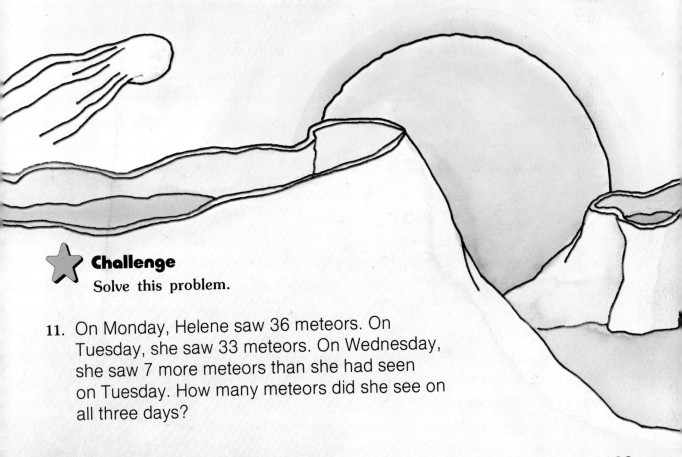

⭐ Challenge
Solve this problem.

11. On Monday, Helene saw 36 meteors. On Tuesday, she saw 33 meteors. On Wednesday, she saw 7 more meteors than she had seen on Tuesday. How many meteors did she see on all three days?

Subtracting with Zeros

Step 1
Look at the ones.
Look at the tens.

306
− 127

Not enough ones.
You cannot trade
0 tens for 10 ones.

Step 2
Trade 1 hundred
for 10 tens.

2 10
3̸0̸6
− 127

Step 3
Trade 1 ten for
10 ones. Subtract.

9
2 10 16
3̸0̸6̸
− 127
179

Subtract. Check the first row by adding.

1. 700
− 376
324

2. 300
− 157

3. 604
− 246

4. 500
− 317

5. 403
− 185

6. 900
− 563

7. 801
− 199

8. 200
− 47

9. 406
− 68

10. 200
− 186

11. 300
− 49

12. 502
− 133

13. 802
− 403

14. 607
− 329

15. 904
− 506

16. A pet store had 400 fish.
347 were goldfish. How many
were not goldfish?

Practice Subtracting with Zeros

Write the tall form. Then subtract.

1. $102 - 17$
$$\begin{array}{r} 102 \\ -\ \ 17 \\ \hline 85 \end{array}$$

2. $206 - 39$

3. $507 - 189$

4. $604 - 108$

5. $701 - 162$

6. $302 - 64$

7. $500 - 305$

8. $302 - 157$

9. $803 - 94$

10. $602 - 254$

11. $404 - 235$

Subtract.

12.
$$\begin{array}{r} 706 \\ -\ 548 \\ \hline \end{array}$$

13.
$$\begin{array}{r} 407 \\ -\ 129 \\ \hline \end{array}$$

14.
$$\begin{array}{r} 204 \\ -\ 159 \\ \hline \end{array}$$

15.
$$\begin{array}{r} 604 \\ -\ 368 \\ \hline \end{array}$$

16.
$$\begin{array}{r} 600 \\ -\ 549 \\ \hline \end{array}$$

17.
$$\begin{array}{r} 308 \\ -\ \ 99 \\ \hline \end{array}$$

18.
$$\begin{array}{r} 401 \\ -\ 335 \\ \hline \end{array}$$

19.
$$\begin{array}{r} 705 \\ -\ 488 \\ \hline \end{array}$$

20.
$$\begin{array}{r} 500 \\ -\ 376 \\ \hline \end{array}$$

21.
$$\begin{array}{r} 303 \\ -\ 214 \\ \hline \end{array}$$

22. A pet store had 121 birds. 63 were parrots. How many were not parrots?

23. A pet store had 301 canaries. 124 were sold in six months. How many were left?

 Calculate

24. Find the missing numbers. Do you see a pattern?
   a. $63 = 100 - \boxed{?}$
   b. $64 = 100 - \boxed{?}$
   c. $65 = 100 - \boxed{?}$

Practicing Subtraction

Do you remember these?

Trade 1 ten
for 10 ones.

Trade 1 ten
for 10 ones.
Trade 1 hundred
for 10 tens.

$$\begin{array}{r} \overset{5\ 14}{\cancel{64}} \\ -\ 29 \\ \hline 35 \end{array}$$

$$\begin{array}{r} \overset{10}{\underset{3\ \cancel{0}\ 12}{}} \\ \cancel{4}\cancel{1}2 \\ -\ 134 \\ \hline 278 \end{array}$$

Subtract. Check the first row.

1. 50 − 16 34	2. 85 − 39	3. 61 − 32	4. 43 − 37	5. 95 − 56	6. 38 − 19
7. 80 − 44	8. 75 − 19	9. 31 − 18	10. 22 − 7	11. 23 − 16	12. 61 − 24
13. 400 − 278	14. 653 − 167	15. 702 − 413	16. 500 − 109	17. 707 − 218	
18. 762 − 293	19. 441 − 195	20. 400 − 163	21. 732 − 364	22. 523 − 174	
23. 500 − 261	24. 316 − 127	25. 834 − 245	26. 702 − 134	27. 618 − 439	

Subtracting Thousands

Step 1
Trade 1 ten
for 10 ones.
Subtract ones.

$$
\begin{array}{r}
\overset{\scriptstyle 5\ 12}{436\!\!\!/2} \\
-\ 2178 \\
\hline
4
\end{array}
$$

Step 2
Trade 1 hundred
for 10 tens.
Subtract tens, hundreds,
and thousands.

$$
\begin{array}{r}
\overset{\scriptstyle 15}{\overset{\scriptstyle 2\ \not{3}\ 12}{436\!\!\!/2}} \\
-\ 2178 \\
\hline
2184
\end{array}
$$

Subtract.

1. $\begin{array}{r}4765\\-2388\\\hline 2377\end{array}$	2. $\begin{array}{r}7985\\-3527\\\hline\end{array}$	3. $\begin{array}{r}5963\\-2750\\\hline\end{array}$

4. $\begin{array}{r}4966\\-1482\\\hline\end{array}$ 5. $\begin{array}{r}3871\\-\ 265\\\hline\end{array}$

6. $\begin{array}{r}8303\\-3156\\\hline\end{array}$ 7. $\begin{array}{r}6450\\-3154\\\hline\end{array}$ 8. $\begin{array}{r}8442\\-\ 250\\\hline\end{array}$ 9. $\begin{array}{r}3700\\-1422\\\hline\end{array}$ 10. $\begin{array}{r}2319\\-1047\\\hline\end{array}$

11. $\begin{array}{r}4756\\-2480\\\hline\end{array}$ 12. $\begin{array}{r}9626\\-\ 348\\\hline\end{array}$ 13. $\begin{array}{r}3802\\-1434\\\hline\end{array}$ 14. $\begin{array}{r}5939\\-2747\\\hline\end{array}$ 15. $\begin{array}{r}6550\\-3355\\\hline\end{array}$

16. $\begin{array}{r}1842\\-\ 348\\\hline\end{array}$ 17. $\begin{array}{r}6640\\-2360\\\hline\end{array}$ 18. $\begin{array}{r}8484\\-\ 292\\\hline\end{array}$ 19. $\begin{array}{r}3805\\-1398\\\hline\end{array}$ 20. $\begin{array}{r}5177\\-4038\\\hline\end{array}$

Subtracting Money

Subtract money the same way you subtract numbers. Remember to use . and $ in your answer.

Subtract   Check

$$\begin{array}{r} \overset{\scriptstyle 12}{\cancel{5\ \overset{\scriptstyle 2}{\cancel{6}}}}{\scriptstyle 10} \\ \$6.3\cancel{0} \\ -\ 2.45 \\ \hline \$3.85 \end{array}$$

$$\begin{array}{r} {\scriptstyle 1\ \ 1} \\ \$2.45 \\ +\ 3.85 \\ \hline \$6.30 \end{array}$$

Subtract. Check the first row by adding.

1. $3.54
   − 1.95
   $1.59

2. $6.86
   − 3.94

3. $7.34
   − 1.23

4. $9.93
   − 7.84

5. $8.23
   − 2.46

6. $7.74
   − 2.78

7. $4.40
   − 1.25

8. $3.40
   − 0.50

9. $5.05
   − 0.85

10. $6.19
    − 3.34

11. $5.42
    − 1.73

12. $8.62
    − 1.05

13. $2.74
    − 1.62

14. $3.57
    − 2.86

15. $6.30
    − 0.54

16. $8.97
    − 4.84

17. $5.35
    − 1.84

18. $7.62
    − 5.49

19. $8.54
    − 6.07

20. $7.14
    − 2.25

21. Colin had $5.00. He bought a book for $2.59. How much money did he have left?

22. Sarah had $2.25. She bought lunch for $1.29. How much money did she have left?

Money Problems

Add or subtract.

1. $2.56
  + 4.46
  $7.02

2. $1.94
  − 1.82

3. $2.94
  − 1.61

4. $0.18
  + 0.24

5. $6.80
  − 1.24

6. $3.89
  − 0.97

7. $0.58
  + 1.69

8. $2.18
  − 1.17

9. $6.27
  − 1.08

10. $3.98
  + 3.25

11. $2.05
  + 1.00

12. $4.28
  + 0.34

13. $4.23
  − 1.89

14. $2.19
  + 3.78

15. $6.54
  − 1.63

Now do these.

16. 93¢ − 42¢

17. $1.78 + $0.64

18. $8.20 − $5.48

19. $0.29 + $4.93

20. $1.63 + $1.63

21. $3.45 − $2.80

22. $1.87 + $0.99

23. $2.16 − $0.67

24. $0.48 + $9.51

Add or subtract to solve these.

25. Bob had $2.47. He earned $1.35 washing dishes. How much did he have then?

26. Carol and Rich had $3.46. They spent $0.75 for apple cider. How much money did they have left?

Aquarium Problems

Add or subtract to solve these problems.

1. 3456 people visit the aquarium in May. 3745 people visit in June. How many visitors in all?
7201

2. A turtle can live 120 years. A goldfish can live 20 years. How much longer can a turtle live?

3. 128 fish live in one tank and 74 fish live in another tank. How many fish in both tanks?

4. There were 253 lake fish and 407 ocean fish. How many more ocean fish?

5. Last year the aquarium had 746 fish. Now they have 897 fish. How many more fish do they have now?

6. It costs $8.43 to feed an alligator each day. It costs $2.65 to feed an octopus. How much more to feed an alligator?

7. There are 365 days in a year. The aquarium is open 294 days. How many days is it closed?

8. A ticket costs $1.50 for an adult and $0.75 for a child. How much more for the adult?

9. There are 105 angel fish and 15 guppies in one tank. How many fish in the tank?

10. The gift shop has 316 post cards. They sell 98. How many are left?

 Challenge

11. A tank has starfish, seahorses, and crabs. There are 33 starfish and 16 seahorses. There are 13 more crabs than seahorses. How many animals in the tank in all?

Chapter Review

Subtract. (ex. 1–5: p. 95), (ex. 6–10: p. 96)

1. 60
   − 37

2. 70
   − 42

3. 60
   − 6

4. 80
   − 59

5. 50
   − 17

6. 81
   − 25

7. 66
   − 7

8. 93
   − 34

9. 42
   − 23

10. 35
    − 28

Subtract. (ex. 11–15: p. 100), (ex. 16–20: p. 104), (ex. 21–25: p. 106)

11. 784
    − 133

12. 381
    − 149

13. 456
    − 109

14. 380
    − 264

15. 632
    − 317

16. 338
    − 273

17. 229
    − 65

18. 445
    − 291

19. 637
    − 382

20. 546
    − 175

21. 654
    − 375

22. 721
    − 354

23. 635
    − 447

24. 877
    − 288

25. 713
    − 565

Subtract. (ex. 26–28: p. 110), (ex. 29–31: p. 113), (ex. 32–35: p. 114)

26. 400
    − 185

27. 604
    − 317

28. 800
    − 575

29. 3602
    − 1436

30. 1842
    − 348

31. 4711
    − 2455

32. $5.54
    − 3.63

33. $6.40
    − 1.50

34. $3.35
    − 1.30

35. $9.43
    − 2.81

Chapter Test

Subtract.

1. 50 − 27	2. 90 − 38	3. 30 − 9	4. 90 − 25	5. 60 − 58
6. 86 − 47	7. 43 − 29	8. 50 − 8	9. 65 − 38	10. 42 − 39

Subtract.

11. 831 − 216	12. 622 − 117	13. 532 − 417	14. 429 − 163	15. 536 − 254
16. 653 − 561	17. 429 − 75	18. 354 − 175	19. 313 − 44	20. 621 − 333

Subtract.

21. 400 − 263	22. 5119 − 3806	23. 4603 − 2881	24. $3.92 − 1.07	25. $7.74 − 5.78

Brush Up

Add.

1. 30 + 50	2. 46 + 12	3. 248 + 31	4. 752 + 224	5. 6172 + 324
6. 55 + 36	7. 43 + 27	8. 87 + 8	9. 72 + 19	10. 29 + 39
11. 426 + 293	12. 785 + 175	13. 355 + 87	14. 446 + 284	15. 608 + 298

Subtract.

16. 78 − 15	17. 57 − 12	18. 65 − 38	19. 54 − 6	20. 48 − 15
21. 40 − 15	22. 87 − 49	23. 62 − 41	24. 70 − 25	25. 91 − 56
26. 563 − 218	27. 280 − 164	28. 905 − 382	29. 318 − 247	30. 558 − 196

Order these numbers. Use > for is greater than
and < for is less than.

31. 305 ◯ 503   32. 200 ◯ 201   33. 444 ◯ 446   34. 397 ◯ 398

35. 600 ◯ 700   36. 406 ◯ 409   37. 351 ◯ 349   38. 867 ◯ 876

CHAPTER 5

Time and Money

Using Time at Work

Dick Lawson works in a clock shop. At 1:30 a customer brings a clock in to be fixed. It will take 3 hours to fix the clock. Dick has to find out what time to tell the customer to come back. He knows that in 3 hours the time will be 4:30. Dick tells the customer to come back at 4:30.

Hours, Half Hours, and Quarter Hours

The hour hand is past 2.
The minute hand points to 3.
The time is 2:15.

There are 60 minutes in 1 hour.

2:15
two-fifteen

Write the time shown on each clock.

1.

9:30

2.

3.

4.

5.

6.

 Calculate

7. It is now 2:15. One hour and 20 minutes from now, what time will it be?

Telling Time

The hour hand is past 4.
The minute hand is on 43.
The time is 4:43.

4:43

Write the time shown on each clock.

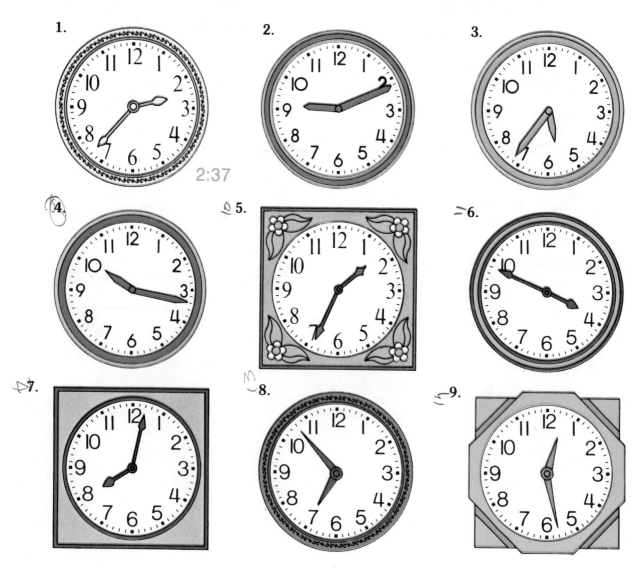

1.

2:37

2.

3.

4.

5.

6.

7.

8.

9.

Time Problems

At the Zoo	
Morning	**Afternoon**
8:00 Guided tour	12:00 Elephant walk
9:30 Pony ride	3:00 Bear feeding time
10:00 Tiger show	5:30 Closing time

1. It is 7:30 in the morning. How many hours until the pony ride starts?   2 hours

2. It is 1:00 in the afternoon. How many hours until bear feeding time?

3. How many hours and minutes are there between the start of the guided tour and the pony ride?

4. How many hours and minutes are there between closing time and bear feeding time?

5. How many minutes are there between the pony ride and the tiger show?

6. How many hours are there between the guided tour and the elephant walk?

 Review   (pp. 123–125)

Write the time shown on each clock.

1.

2.

3.

Reading a Calendar

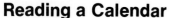

Use the calendar. Write the day for each date.

1. May 1   Monday   2. May 6   3. May 11   4. May 8

5. May 28   6. May 19   7. May 12   8. May 3

9. May 24   10. May 14   11. May 5   12. May 30

Write the date for each day.

13. the first Tuesday   May 2   14. the third Saturday

15. the second Friday   16. the fifth Wednesday

Money

 Penny
1¢
$0.01

 Nickel
5¢
$0.05

 Dime
10¢
$0.10

 Quarter
25¢
$0.25

 Half Dollar
50¢
$0.50

 Dollar
100¢
$1.00

Write the total amount in cents.

1.  20¢

2.

3.

4.

What is the total amount?

5. 5 nickels

6. 3 half dollars

7. 6 dimes

8. 20 pennies

9. 4 quarters

10. 8 nickels

Total Amounts of Coins

Write the total amounts.

1.

25¢ + 10¢ + 10¢ = 45¢

2.

3.

4.

5.

6.

7.

8.

★ Challenge

9. How many of these coins do you need to make 50¢?
   a. ☐ quarters
   b. ☐ dimes
   c. ☐ nickels
   d. I quarter ☐ dimes I nickel

Adding Dollars and Coins

Use the chart. Write the total amount.

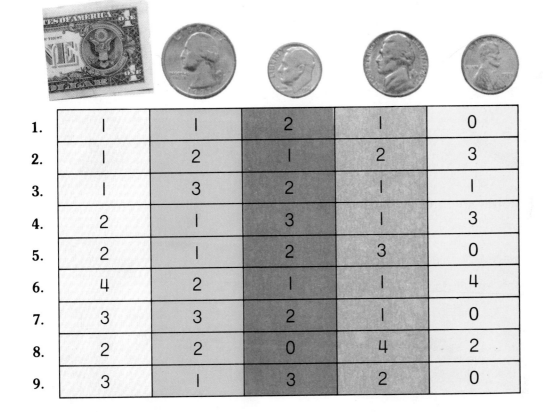

	Dollars	Quarters	Dimes	Nickels	Pennies	
1.	1	1	2	1	0	$1.50
2.	1	2	1	2	3	
3.	1	3	2	1	1	
4.	2	1	3	1	3	
5.	2	1	2	3	0	
6.	4	2	1	1	4	
7.	3	3	2	1	0	
8.	2	2	0	4	2	
9.	3	1	3	2	0	

 Challenge

Copy the chart. Show three ways to make the total amount.
Write one number in each box.

	Dollars	Quarters	Dimes	Nickels	Pennies
Total $2.75 10.	?	?	?	?	?
11.	?	?	?	?	?
12.	?	?	?	?	?

Chapter Review

Write the time shown on each clock. (ex. 1–3: p. 124)

1.

2.

3.

What is the total amount? (ex. 4–6: p. 127)

4. 6 nickels

5. 8 dimes

6. 7 pennies

Write the total amounts. (ex. 7–10: p. 128)

7.

8.

9.

10.

Chapter Test

Write the time shown on each clock.

1.

2.

3.

What is the total amount?

4. 6 dimes

5. 2 half dollars

6. 3 quarters

Write the total amounts.

7.

8.

9.

10.

Brush Up

Add or subtract.

1. 15
    − 8

2. 8
    + 9

3. 7
    + 6

4. 18
    − 9

5. 17
    − 8

6. 6
    + 8

7. 44
    + 35

8. 87
    + 8

9. 45
    − 23

10. 62
    + 29

11. 54
    − 6

12. 73
    − 19

13. 78
    − 25

14. 81
    − 56

15. 50
    − 35

16. 46
    + 84

17. 8
    + 98

18. 47
    − 38

19. 172
    + 241

20. 461
    + 206

21. 237
    + 86

22. 426
    − 205

23. 329
    − 85

24. 256
    + 394

25. 521
    + 786

26. 300
    − 175

27. 329
    − 291

28. 436
    + 384

29. 1335
    − 321

30. 4846
    + 783

31. 5602
    − 3436

32. 853
    + 1640

33. 2690
    − 847

Copy and complete.

34. 38 = ▢ tens ▢ ones

35. 469 = ▢ hundreds ▢ tens ▢ ones

36. 75 = ▢ tens ▢ ones

37. 105 = ▢ hundreds ▢ tens ▢ ones

38. 62 = ▢ tens ▢ ones

39. 300 = ▢ hundreds ▢ tens ▢ ones

40. 89 = ▢ tens ▢ ones

41. 261 = ▢ hundreds ▢ tens ▢ ones

CHAPTER 6

Multiplication

Using Multiplication at Work

Richard Alfaro is a commercial artist. His customers want to order 6 drawings. It takes him about 4 hours to do each drawing. He multiplies 4 × 6 to find how long 6 drawings will take. It will take him about 24 hours to do 6 drawings.

Adding to Multiply

Each shelf has an equal number of cans. How many cans in all?

3 fours = 12

$$\begin{array}{r} 4 \\ 4 \\ + \ 4 \\ \hline 12 \end{array}$$

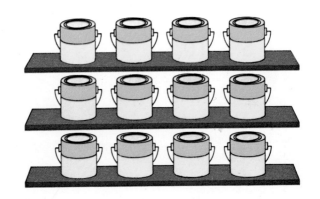

Solve these problems.

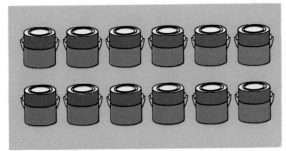

1a. How many cans in all? 12
 b. 2 sixes = ▢ 12

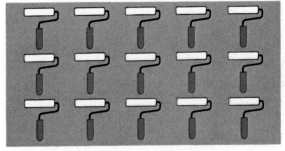

2a. How many rollers in all?
 b. 3 fives = ▢

3a. How many hats in all?
 b. 2 sevens = ▢

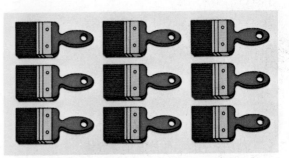

4a. How many brushes in all?
 b. 3 threes = ▢

Adding and Multiplying

There are 2 rows of bears with 5 bears in each row.
Find the total number of bears by adding or multiplying.

$$5 + 5 = 10 \qquad 2 \times 5 = 10$$

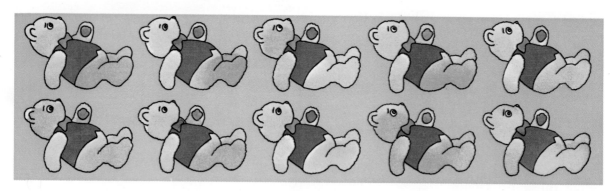

Write the answers.

1a. How many rows of 4?   3
 b. Write an addition fact.
 c. How many cars in all?
 d. ? × 4 = ?

2a. How many rows of 6?
 b. Write an addition fact.
 c. How many flowers in all?
 d. ? × 6 = ?

3a. How many rows of 8?
 b. Write an addition fact.
 c. How many leaves in all?
 d. ? × 8 = ?

Writing Multiplication Facts

You can write a multiplication fact for an addition problem with equal addends.

addition
problem

multiplication
fact

$$
\left.\begin{array}{r} 4 \\ 4 \\ + 4 \end{array}\right\} \begin{array}{l} \text{equal} \\ \text{addends} \end{array}
$$
$$
\begin{array}{r} 12 \end{array}
$$

$$
\begin{array}{r} 4 \quad \text{factor} \\ \times 3 \quad \text{factor} \\ \hline 12 \quad \text{product} \end{array}
$$
or
$3 \times 4 = 12$

factors   product

Find the sums. Write a multiplication fact for each problem.

1. $\begin{array}{r} 5 \\ 5 \\ 5 \\ + 5 \\ \hline 20 \end{array}$ $\begin{array}{r} 5 \\ \times 4 \\ \hline 20 \end{array}$

2. $\begin{array}{r} 1 \\ 1 \\ 1 \\ + 1 \\ \hline \end{array}$

3. $\begin{array}{r} 3 \\ 3 \\ + 3 \\ \hline \end{array}$

4. $\begin{array}{r} 4 \\ 4 \\ 4 \\ + 4 \\ \hline \end{array}$

5. $\begin{array}{r} 9 \\ 9 \\ + 9 \\ \hline \end{array}$

6. $\begin{array}{r} 8 \\ + 8 \\ \hline \end{array}$

7. $\begin{array}{r} 7 \\ 7 \\ + 7 \\ \hline \end{array}$

8. $\begin{array}{r} 10 \\ 10 \\ 10 \\ + 10 \\ \hline \end{array}$

9. $\begin{array}{r} 2 \\ 2 \\ 2 \\ 2 \\ + 2 \\ \hline \end{array}$

10. $\begin{array}{r} 8 \\ 8 \\ 8 \\ + 8 \\ \hline \end{array}$

11. $\begin{array}{r} 6 \\ 6 \\ 6 \\ + 6 \\ \hline \end{array}$

12. $\begin{array}{r} 5 \\ 5 \\ 5 \\ 5 \\ + 5 \\ \hline \end{array}$

13. $\begin{array}{r} 3 \\ 3 \\ 3 \\ 3 \\ + 3 \\ \hline \end{array}$

14. $3 + 3 + 3 + 3 + 3 + 3$

15. $1 + 1 + 1 + 1 + 1$

16. $9 + 9$

17. $4 + 4 + 4 + 4 + 4$

18. $7 + 7 + 7 + 7 + 7$

19. $2 + 2 + 2 + 2 + 2 + 2$

Deciding When to Multiply

Look for equal addends to
write a multiplication fact.

Addends are equal.
You can write a
multiplication fact.

$$\left.\begin{array}{r} 5 \\ 5 \\ + 5 \end{array}\right\} \begin{array}{l} \text{equal} \\ \text{addends} \end{array}$$
$$\overline{15}$$

$$\begin{array}{r} 5 \\ \times 3 \\ \hline 15 \end{array}$$

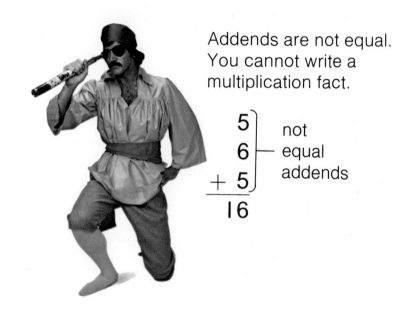

Addends are not equal.
You cannot write a
multiplication fact.

$$\left.\begin{array}{r} 5 \\ 6 \\ + 5 \end{array}\right\} \begin{array}{l} \text{not} \\ \text{equal} \\ \text{addends} \end{array}$$
$$\overline{16}$$

Find the sums. Write a multiplication fact if you can.

1.
$$\begin{array}{r} 7 \\ 7 \\ + 7 \\ \hline 21 \end{array}$$
$$\begin{array}{r} 7 \\ \times 3 \\ \hline 21 \end{array}$$

2.
$$\begin{array}{r} 3 \\ 2 \\ + 6 \end{array}$$

3.
$$\begin{array}{r} 5 \\ 5 \\ 5 \\ + 5 \end{array}$$

4.
$$\begin{array}{r} 3 \\ 3 \\ 3 \\ 3 \\ + 4 \end{array}$$

5.
$$\begin{array}{r} 8 \\ 7 \\ 2 \\ + 1 \end{array}$$

6.
$$\begin{array}{r} 6 \\ 4 \\ + 2 \end{array}$$

7.
$$\begin{array}{r} 10 \\ 10 \\ 10 \\ + 10 \end{array}$$

8.
$$\begin{array}{r} 4 \\ 7 \\ + 3 \end{array}$$

9.
$$\begin{array}{r} 2 \\ 2 \\ 2 \\ 2 \\ + 2 \end{array}$$

10.
$$\begin{array}{r} 11 \\ 17 \\ 11 \\ + 11 \end{array}$$

11.
$$\begin{array}{r} 5 \\ 4 \\ 5 \\ + 5 \end{array}$$

12.
$$\begin{array}{r} 4 \\ 4 \\ 4 \\ 4 \\ + 4 \end{array}$$

13.
$$\begin{array}{r} 8 \\ 6 \\ 2 \\ + 4 \end{array}$$

Multiplying by 2

—2—
2 in each row
× 2 rows
——
4

$2 \times 2 = 4$

—5——
5 in each row
× 2 rows
——
10

$2 \times 5 = 10$

Write a multiplication fact for each drawing.

1. —2—

$\begin{array}{r} 2 \\ \times\ 3 \\ \hline 6 \end{array}$

3

2. ———6———

2

3. ————8————

2

4. —2—

9

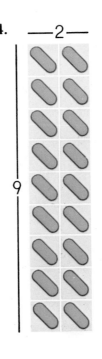

5. —2—

7

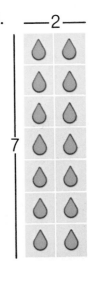

6. —2—

4

Practice Multiplying by 2

Count by 2.

1. 0, 2, 4, ▢, ▢, ▢, ▢, ▢, ▢, ▢, ▢

Find the products.

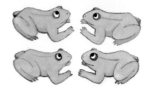

2. 8 ×2 16	3. 1 ×2	4. 3 ×2
5. 4 ×2	6. 5 ×2	7. 2 ×2

8. 7 ×2	9. 1 ×2	10. 9 ×2

11. 6 ×2	12. 7 ×2	13. 8 ×2

Write a multiplication fact for each product. Use **2** as one of the factors.

14. 10 5 × 2 = 10   15. 12   16. 8   17. 14   18. 16

19. 2   20. 18   21. 6   22. 16   23. 4   24. 10

 Challenge

25. 2 shoes in each box. How many shoes in 7 boxes?

26. 2 light bulbs in each box. How many light bulbs in 9 boxes?

Switching Factors

There are two ways to write a multiplication
fact about these drawings.
The factors are 2 and 4.
The product is 8.

$$2 \times 4 = 8 \qquad\qquad 4 \times 2 = 8$$

Write two multiplication facts for each drawing.

1.

$$2 \times 5 = 10 \qquad 5 \times 2 = 10$$

2.

3.
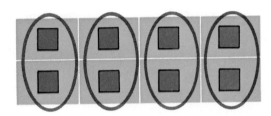

4.
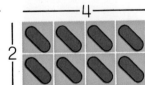

5.

6.
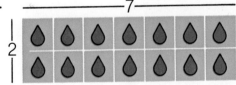

7.
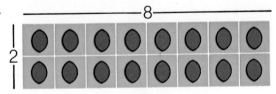

8.
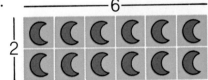

Multiplying by 3

You can write two multiplication facts about this drawing.

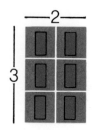

2 in each row
× 3 rows
6

3 rows
× 2 in each row
6

Write two multiplication facts for each drawing.

1.

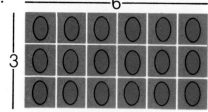

6
× 3
18

3
× 6
18

2.

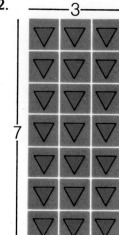

3.

4.

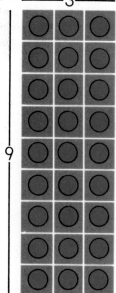

5.

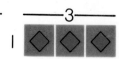

6.

7.

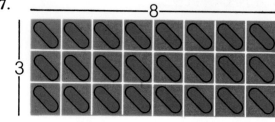

Practice Multiplying by 3

Count by 3.

1. 0, 3, 6, ?, ?, ?, ?, ?, ?, ?

Find the products.

2. 3
   × 7
   ——
   21

3. 2
   × 3

4. 9
   × 3

5. 3
   × 5

6. 1
   × 3

7. 3
   × 3

8. 3
   × 4

9. 3
   × 6

10. 4
    × 3

11. 8
    × 3

12. 7
    × 3

13. 3
    × 9

14. 3
    × 8

15. 6
    × 3

 Challenge

Find the missing factors.

16. 3 × ? = 24

17. ? × 3 = 15

18. ? × 3 = 12

19. 3 × ? = 18

20. 3 × ? = 6

21. ? × 3 = 21

22. ? × 3 = 3

23. 3 × ? = 27

Pattern Charts

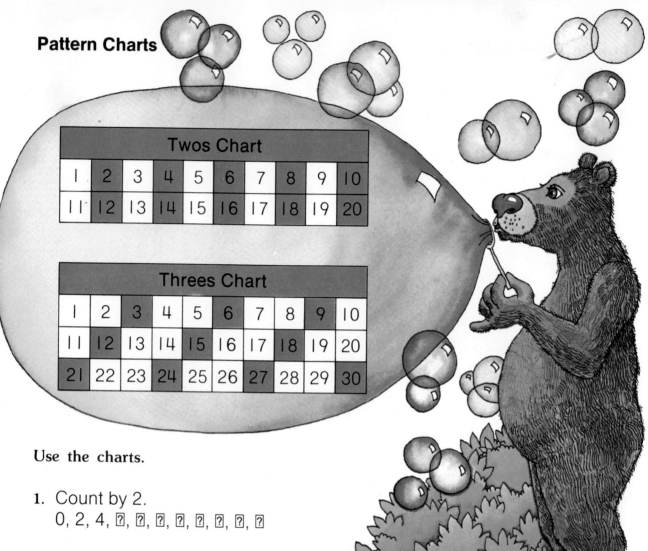

Twos Chart

1	2	3	4	5	6	7	8	9	10
11	12	13	14	15	16	17	18	19	20

Threes Chart

1	2	3	4	5	6	7	8	9	10
11	12	13	14	15	16	17	18	19	20
21	22	23	24	25	26	27	28	29	30

Use the charts.

1. Count by 2.
   0, 2, 4, ?, ?, ?, ?, ?, ?, ?, ?

2. Count by 3.
   0, 3, 6, ?, ?, ?, ?, ?, ?, ?, ?

Find the products. Use the charts if you need help.

3. 2 × 7 14	4. 2 × 8	5. 3 × 4	6. 2 × 5	7. 3 × 9	8. 3 × 7	9. 3 × 3
10. 2 × 9	11. 3 × 6	12. 2 × 4	13. 3 × 8	14. 2 × 1	15. 3 × 5	16. 2 × 6

Multiplication Problems

Write a multiplication fact for each problem.

1. How many wheels on
   5 tricycles?   5 × 3 = 15

2. How many eyes on 7 cats?

3. How many slices of bread for
   3 sandwiches?

4. How many tennis balls in
   3 cans?

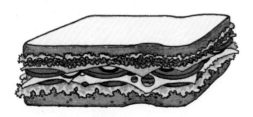

5. How many ears on 9 dogs?

6. How many wings on 7 birds?

Multiplying by 4

Write two multiplication facts for each drawing.

1.

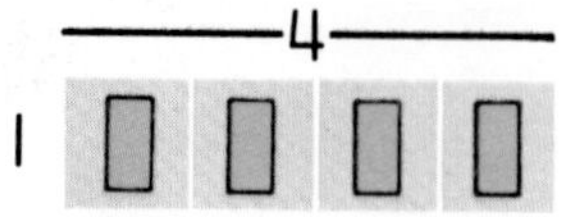

$$\begin{array}{r} 4 \\ \times\ 1 \\ \hline 4 \end{array} \qquad \begin{array}{r} 1 \\ \times\ 4 \\ \hline 4 \end{array}$$

2.

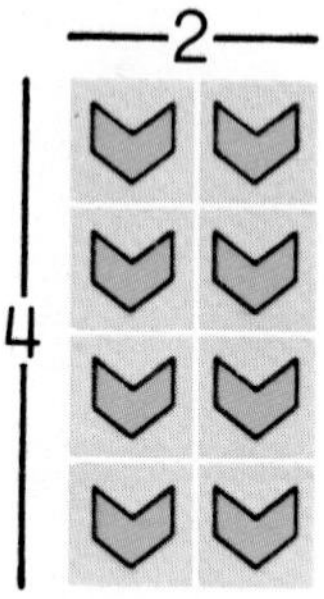

3.

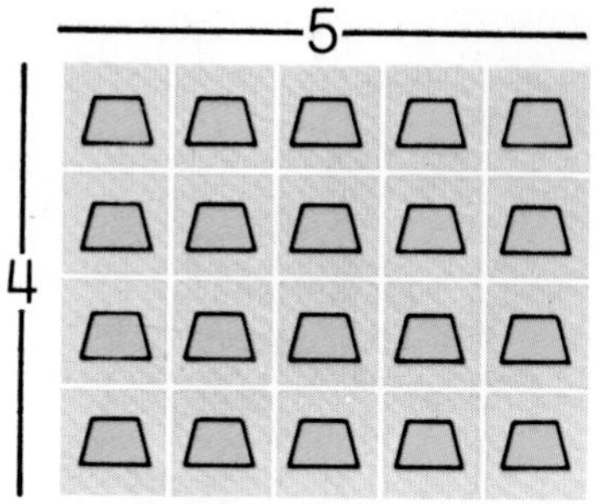

4.

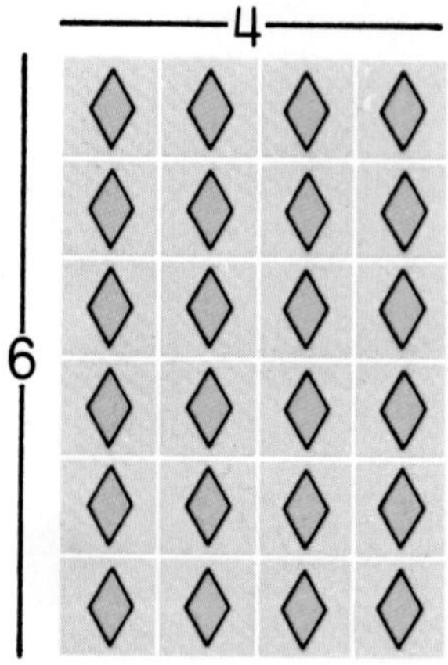

5.

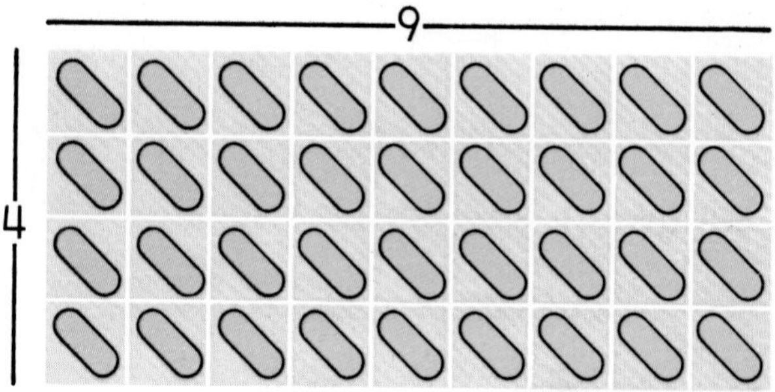

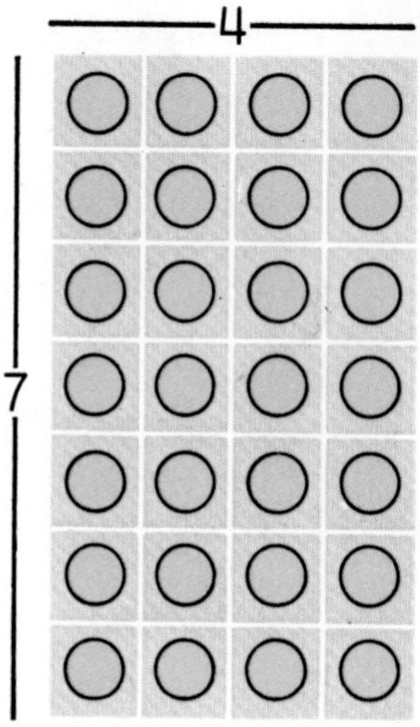

6.

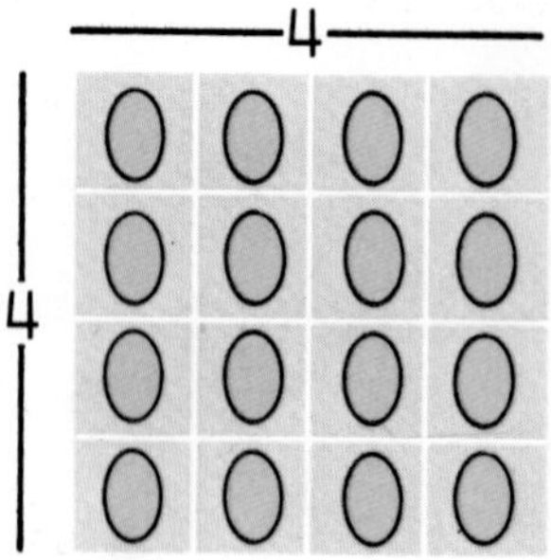

7.

8.

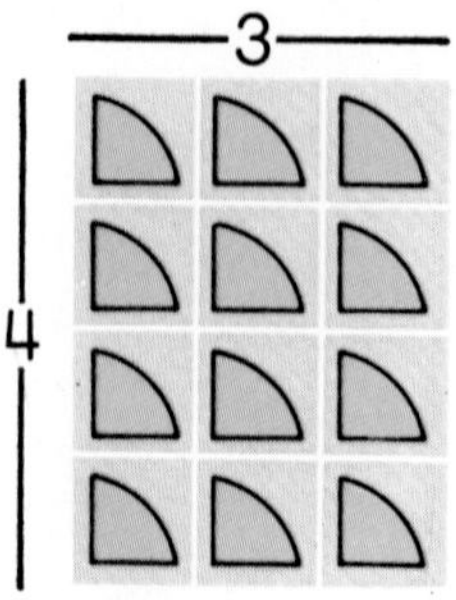

Practice Multiplying by 4

Count by 4.

1. 0, 4, ▢, ▢, ▢, ▢, ▢, ▢, ▢, ▢

Find the products.

2.	4 × 9 36	3.	4 × 4	4.	6 × 4	5.	2 × 4	6.	8 × 4	7.	5 × 4	8.	4 × 3

9.	4 × 5	10.	4 × 7	11.	1 × 4	12.	4 × 8	13.	4 × 6	14.	9 × 4	15.	7 × 4

Write a multiplication fact for each product. Use 4 as one of the factors.

16. 12   17. 16   18. 20   19. 8   20. 4   21. 28

22. 36   23. 20   24. 32   25. 16   26. 24   27. 8

 **Review**   (pp. 135–147)

1.	7 × 2	2.	9 × 3	3.	2 × 8	4.	3 × 6	5.	8 × 4	6.	4 × 5	7.	3 × 4

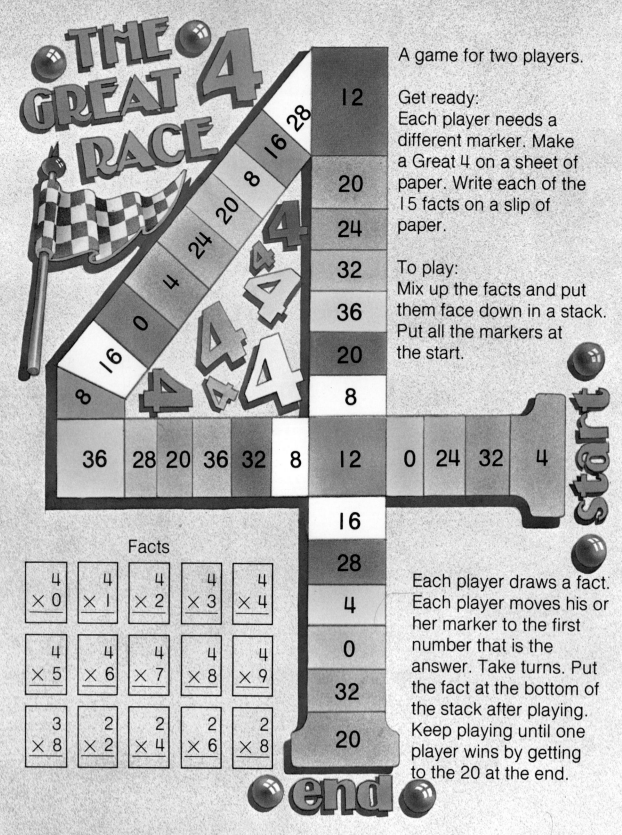

THE GREAT 4 RACE

			28
		8	16
	20		
4	24		
0			
16			
8			

12
20
24
32
36
20
8

| 36 | 28 | 20 | 36 | 32 | 8 | 12 | 0 | 24 | 32 | 4 |

start

16
28
4
0
32
20

end

A game for two players.

Get ready:
Each player needs a different marker. Make a Great 4 on a sheet of paper. Write each of the 15 facts on a slip of paper.

To play:
Mix up the facts and put them face down in a stack. Put all the markers at the start.

Each player draws a fact. Each player moves his or her marker to the first number that is the answer. Take turns. Put the fact at the bottom of the stack after playing. Keep playing until one player wins by getting to the 20 at the end.

Facts

$\begin{array}{r} 4 \\ \times\, 0 \\ \hline \end{array}$	$\begin{array}{r} 4 \\ \times\, 1 \\ \hline \end{array}$	$\begin{array}{r} 4 \\ \times\, 2 \\ \hline \end{array}$	$\begin{array}{r} 4 \\ \times\, 3 \\ \hline \end{array}$	$\begin{array}{r} 4 \\ \times\, 4 \\ \hline \end{array}$
$\begin{array}{r} 4 \\ \times\, 5 \\ \hline \end{array}$	$\begin{array}{r} 4 \\ \times\, 6 \\ \hline \end{array}$	$\begin{array}{r} 4 \\ \times\, 7 \\ \hline \end{array}$	$\begin{array}{r} 4 \\ \times\, 8 \\ \hline \end{array}$	$\begin{array}{r} 4 \\ \times\, 9 \\ \hline \end{array}$
$\begin{array}{r} 3 \\ \times\, 8 \\ \hline \end{array}$	$\begin{array}{r} 2 \\ \times\, 2 \\ \hline \end{array}$	$\begin{array}{r} 2 \\ \times\, 4 \\ \hline \end{array}$	$\begin{array}{r} 2 \\ \times\, 6 \\ \hline \end{array}$	$\begin{array}{r} 2 \\ \times\, 8 \\ \hline \end{array}$

Multiplying by 5

Write two multiplication facts for each drawing.

1.

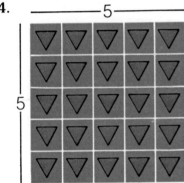

$$\begin{array}{cc} 5 & 1 \\ \times\,1 & \times\,5 \\ \hline 5 & 5 \end{array}$$

2.

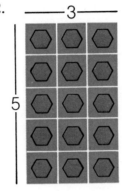

3.

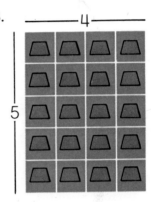

4.

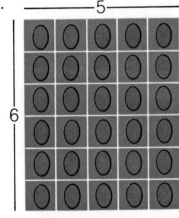

5.

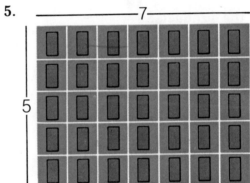

6.

7.

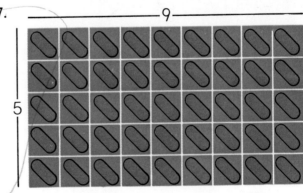

Practice Multiplying by 5

Count by 5.

1. 0, 5, ▢, ▢, ▢, ▢, ▢, ▢, ▢, ▢

Find the products.

2. 6
  × 5
  ——
  30

3. 5
  × 7
  ——

4. 3
  × 5
  ——

5. 5
  × 4
  ——

6. 5
  × 1
  ——

7. 8
  × 5
  ——

8. 5
  × 2
  ——

9. 5 × 6

10. 5 × 3

11. 5 × 5

12. 5 × 7

13. 9 × 5

14. 2 × 5

15. 6 × 5

16. 5 × 4

17. 5 × 9

18. 5 × 1

19. 3 × 5

20. 5 × 9

21. 1 × 5

22. 8 × 5

23. 4 × 5

 Calculate

Find the missing numbers.

24.

3	6	9	?	15	?	?	24	?
15	30	45	60	?	90	105	?	135

Picture Problems

Draw each picture. Write a multiplication fact.

1. Draw 3 large circles. Put
5 triangles in each circle.
How many triangles in all?

$$\begin{array}{r} 5 \\ \times\ 3 \\ \hline 15 \end{array}$$

2. Draw 2 large stars. Put
8 circles in each star.
How many circles in all?

3. Draw 7 large triangles. Put
4 moons in each triangle.
How many moons in all?

4. Draw 5 large squares. Put
9 stars in each square.
How many stars in all?

5. Draw 8 large diamonds. Put
3 circles in each diamond.
How many circles in all?

6. Draw 2 large moons. Put
7 squares in each moon.
How many squares in all?

Using Multiplication

Write a multiplication fact for each problem.

1. There are 3 tennis balls in each can. How many tennis balls in 4 cans? $4 \times 3 = 12$

2. There are 4 turtles on each rock. How many turtles on 6 rocks?

3. There are 7 books on a shelf. How many books on 2 shelves?

4. There are 5 pictures on each page. How many pictures on 5 pages?

5. There are 4 wheels on each car. How many wheels on 8 cars?

Multiply.

6. 2×7	7. 5×4	8. 3×7	9. 4×6	10. 7×3
11. 8×4	12. 3×9	13. 5×6	14. 2×8	15. 4×7
16. 9×4	17. 6×3	18. 5×8	19. 2×9	20. 4×4

Practicing Multiplication

Find the products.

1. $\begin{array}{r} 7 \\ \times\ 3 \\ \hline 21 \end{array}$ 2. $\begin{array}{r} 8 \\ \times\ 2 \\ \hline \end{array}$

3. $\begin{array}{r} 5 \\ \times\ 4 \\ \hline \end{array}$ 4. $\begin{array}{r} 2 \\ \times\ 6 \\ \hline \end{array}$

5. $\begin{array}{r} 6 \\ \times\ 3 \\ \hline \end{array}$ 6. $\begin{array}{r} 4 \\ \times\ 3 \\ \hline \end{array}$ 7. $\begin{array}{r} 5 \\ \times\ 3 \\ \hline \end{array}$

8. $\begin{array}{r} 5 \\ \times\ 9 \\ \hline \end{array}$ 9. $\begin{array}{r} 3 \\ \times\ 3 \\ \hline \end{array}$ 10. $\begin{array}{r} 9 \\ \times\ 2 \\ \hline \end{array}$

11. $\begin{array}{r} 4 \\ \times\ 7 \\ \hline \end{array}$ 12. $\begin{array}{r} 9 \\ \times\ 3 \\ \hline \end{array}$ 13. $\begin{array}{r} 1 \\ \times\ 4 \\ \hline \end{array}$ 14. $\begin{array}{r} 6 \\ \times\ 5 \\ \hline \end{array}$

15. $\begin{array}{r} 5 \\ \times\ 7 \\ \hline \end{array}$ 16. $\begin{array}{r} 4 \\ \times\ 9 \\ \hline \end{array}$ 17. $\begin{array}{r} 7 \\ \times\ 2 \\ \hline \end{array}$ 18. $\begin{array}{r} 8 \\ \times\ 3 \\ \hline \end{array}$

 Challenge

Multiply. ( ) mean **Do me first.**

19. $(3 \times 2) \times 5$ 20. $3 \times (2 \times 5)$

21. $4 \times (2 \times 1)$ 22. $(4 \times 2) \times 1$

23. $(4 \times 2) \times 6$ 24. $4 \times (2 \times 6)$

Fruit Problems

Solve each problem.

1. There are 3 bananas in each bunch. How many bananas in 8 bunches? 24

2. There are 6 grapes on each stem. How many grapes on 3 stems?

3. There are 4 melons in each box. How many melons in 9 boxes?

4. There are 8 oranges in each bag. How many oranges in 3 bags?

5. There are 5 apples in each basket. How many apples in 8 baskets?

6. There are 5 tomatoes in each basket. How many tomatoes in 9 baskets?

 **Review**   (pp. 137–154)

1.	2.	3.	4.	5.	6.	7.
8	6	7	8	5	9	5
×2	×3	×4	×5	×6	×5	×7

One and Zero as Factors

Any number times zero is zero.

product 0   factor 0

If 1 is a factor, the product is the same as the other factor.

$1 \times 3 = 3$ $1 \times 17 = 17$

If 0 is a factor, the product is 0.

$0 \times 3 = 0$ $0 \times 17 = 0$

Find the products.

1. 1×9 9
2. 6×0
3. 4×1
4. 1×6
5. 0×9

6. 0×15
7. 12×1
8. 10×0
9. 0×1
10. 3×1

11. 1
    $\times 2$
12. 0
    $\times 9$
13. 23
    $\times 1$
14. 11
    $\times 0$
15. 7
    $\times 1$
16. 14
    $\times 0$
17. 6
    $\times 1$

18. 0
    $\times 7$
19. 13
    $\times 1$
20. 2
    $\times 0$
21. 20
    $\times 1$
22. 0
    $\times 0$
23. 9
    $\times 1$
24. 8
    $\times 0$

25. 1
    $\times 5$
26. 5
    $\times 0$
27. 15
    $\times 1$
28. 10
    $\times 0$
29. 1
    $\times 1$
30. 20
    $\times 1$
31. 16
    $\times 0$

32. There are 4 envelopes. There is 1 letter in each envelope. How many letters in all?

33. There are 6 packages. There are 0 seeds in each package. How many seeds in all?

Ten as a Factor

You can write a multiplication
fact for sums of tens.

$10 + 10 + 10 + 10 = 40$

$4 \times 10 = 40$

4 tens $= 40$

Find the sums. Write a multiplication fact for each.

1. $10 + 10 + 10 + 10 + 10 + 10$ $60, 6 \times 10 = 60$

2. $10 + 10 + 10$

3. $10 + 10 + 10 + 10 + 10 + 10 + 10 + 10$

4. $10 + 10 + 10 + 10 + 10 + 10 + 10 + 10 + 10$

Find the products.

5. $\begin{array}{r}10\\ \times\ 6\\ \hline\end{array}$	**6.** $\begin{array}{r}10\\ \times\ 7\\ \hline\end{array}$	**7.** $\begin{array}{r}10\\ \times\ 3\\ \hline\end{array}$	**8.** $\begin{array}{r}10\\ \times\ 4\\ \hline\end{array}$	**9.** $\begin{array}{r}10\\ \times\ 9\\ \hline\end{array}$	**10.** $\begin{array}{r}10\\ \times\ 8\\ \hline\end{array}$
11. $\begin{array}{r}10\\ \times\ 8\\ \hline\end{array}$	**12.** $\begin{array}{r}10\\ \times\ 1\\ \hline\end{array}$	**13.** $\begin{array}{r}10\\ \times\ 5\\ \hline\end{array}$	**14.** $\begin{array}{r}10\\ \times\ 0\\ \hline\end{array}$	**15.** $\begin{array}{r}10\\ \times\ 2\\ \hline\end{array}$	**16.** $\begin{array}{r}10\\ \times\ 6\\ \hline\end{array}$

Practicing Multiplication

Find the products.

1. 2×5 10   2. 3×4 3. 2×8 4. 5×3 5. 4×5

6. 7×5 7. 10×6 8. 3×7 9. 10×7 10. 7×2

11. 7×4 12. 8×3 13. 5×8 14. 3×9 15. 6×4

16. $\begin{array}{r} 10 \\ \times\ 1 \\ \hline \end{array}$ 17. $\begin{array}{r} 4 \\ \times\ 8 \\ \hline \end{array}$ 18. $\begin{array}{r} 7 \\ \times\ 0 \\ \hline \end{array}$ 19. $\begin{array}{r} 2 \\ \times\ 9 \\ \hline \end{array}$ 20. $\begin{array}{r} 3 \\ \times\ 6 \\ \hline \end{array}$ 21. $\begin{array}{r} 5 \\ \times\ 5 \\ \hline \end{array}$ 22. $\begin{array}{r} 5 \\ \times\ 0 \\ \hline \end{array}$

23. $\begin{array}{r} 4 \\ \times\ 9 \\ \hline \end{array}$ 24. $\begin{array}{r} 1 \\ \times\ 9 \\ \hline \end{array}$ 25. $\begin{array}{r} 8 \\ \times\ 5 \\ \hline \end{array}$ 26. $\begin{array}{r} 3 \\ \times\ 0 \\ \hline \end{array}$ 27. $\begin{array}{r} 2 \\ \times\ 6 \\ \hline \end{array}$ 28. $\begin{array}{r} 9 \\ \times\ 5 \\ \hline \end{array}$ 29. $\begin{array}{r} 4 \\ \times\ 1 \\ \hline \end{array}$

30. $\begin{array}{r} 4 \\ \times\ 4 \\ \hline \end{array}$ 31. $\begin{array}{r} 5 \\ \times\ 6 \\ \hline \end{array}$ 32. $\begin{array}{r} 15 \\ \times\ 0 \\ \hline \end{array}$ 33. $\begin{array}{r} 8 \\ \times\ 4 \\ \hline \end{array}$ 34. $\begin{array}{r} 9 \\ \times\ 3 \\ \hline \end{array}$ 35. $\begin{array}{r} 19 \\ \times\ 1 \\ \hline \end{array}$ 36. $\begin{array}{r} 10 \\ \times\ 8 \\ \hline \end{array}$

37. $\begin{array}{r} 18 \\ \times\ 0 \\ \hline \end{array}$ 38. $\begin{array}{r} 9 \\ \times\ 1 \\ \hline \end{array}$

 Challenge

39. Larry buys 4 bags of rolls. Each bag has 5 rolls. How many rolls in all?

40. Sally buys 3 muffins. Each muffin has 6 raisins. How many raisins in all?

Using a Multiplication Table

Look for a product in the table. Then find
one factor at the top and one factor at the side.

×	0	1	2	3	4	5	6	7	8	9	10
0	0	0	0	0	0	0	0	0	0	0	0
1	0	1	2	3	4	5	6	7	8	9	10
2	0	2	4	6	8	10	12	14	16	18	20
3	0	3	6	9	12	15	18	21	24	27	30
4	0	4	8	12	16	20	24	28	32	36	40
5	0	5	10	15	20	25	30	35	40	45	50

Write as many facts as you can for each product.

1. 12 $4 \times 3 = 12, 2 \times 6 = 12$ 2. 10   3. 20   4. 15

5. 24   6. 28   7. 18   8. 36   9. 35   10. 16

11. 45   12. 4   13. 30   14. 10   15. 40   16. 27

 **Calculate**

17. $2 \times 5 + 25$ 18. $4 \times 8 + 48$ 19. $3 \times 6 + 36$

Exercise Problems

Write a multiplication fact to solve these problems.

1. Liana does 5 push-ups in one minute. How many push-ups can she do in 4 minutes?
$4 \times 5 = 20$

2. Tim runs around the field once in 2 minutes. How long does it take for him to run around the field 9 times?

3. Elena swims 3 times each week. How many times does she swim in 6 weeks?

4. Joan runs 10 minutes each day. How many minutes does she run in 7 days?

⭐ Challenge
Add and then multiply to solve these.

5. Mario jumps rope for 5 minutes and does sit-ups for 3 minutes each day. How many minutes of exercise in 4 days?

6. Linda runs 2 kilometers every morning and 6 kilometers every night. How many kilometers does she run in 3 days?

Chapter Review

Find the sums. Write a multiplication fact if you can.   (ex. 1–7: p. 138)

1. 4
    4
  + 4

2. 3
    3
  + 2

3. 6
    6
    6
  + 6

4. 7
  + 7

5. 5
    5
    6
  + 6

6. 0
    0
  + 0

7. 8
    8
    4
  + 4

Multiply.   (ex. 8–17: p. 139),   (ex. 18–26: p. 142),   (ex. 27–36: p. 146),
(ex. 37–46: p. 149),   (ex. 47–50: p. 155),   (ex. 51–55: p. 156)

8. 2
  × 5

9. 2
  × 1

10. 7
   × 2

11. 9
   × 2

12. 2
   × 2

13. 2
   × 8

14. 6
   × 2

15. 3
   × 2

16. 2
   × 8

17. 2
   × 4

18. 3
   × 3

19. 4
   × 3

20. 9
   × 3

21. 6
   × 3

22. 1
   × 3

23. 3
   × 8

24. 3
   × 5

25. 7
   × 3

26. 3
   × 9

27. 4
   × 1

28. 7
   × 4

29. 4
   × 4

30. 4
   × 2

31. 6
   × 4

32. 4
   × 7

33. 8
   × 4

34. 4
   × 5

35. 3
   × 4

36. 9×4 37. 5×4 38. 5×2 39. 1×5 40. 9×5

41. 6×5 42. 5×8 43. 3×5 44. 7×5 45. 5×5

46. 8×5 47. 5×0 48. 9×1 49. 0×4 50. 7×1

51. 0×10 52. 10×6 53. 8×10 54. 10×7 55. 3×10

Chapter Test

Find the sums. Write a multiplication fact if you can.

1. 8 +9	2. 2 2 +2	3. 4 8 8 +4	4. 9 9 +0	5. 7 7 7 +7	6. 1 1 1 +1	7. 5 5 6 +4

Multiply.

8. 5 ×7	9. 2 ×8	10. 6 ×2	11. 4 ×4	12. 2 ×1	13. 4 ×5	14. 9 ×5

15. 8 ×4	16. 7 ×3	17. 6 ×5	18. 7 ×2	19. 3 ×0	20. 2 ×9	21. 6 ×3

22. 4×3 23. 5×9 24. 1×2 25. 4×5 26. 8×5

27. 10×9 28. 8×4 29. 5×7 30. 3×10 31. 4×6

32. 1×7 33. 3×3 34. 9×4 35. 6×0 36. 7×3

Brush Up

Add or subtract.

1. 36	2. 424	3. 98	4. 57	5. 63
+ 13	+ 72	− 34	+ 28	− 7

6. 45	7. 439	8. 379	9. 564	10. 859
+ 19	− 78	− 189	+ 148	+ 181

11. 705	12. 300	13. 1845	14. 5462	15. 728
− 164	− 142	+ 3809	− 292	+ 1649

Answer the questions.

16. Use the number 218.
    a. What is the total value of the digit 2?
    b. What is the total value of the digit 1?

17. Use the number 4306.
    a. What is the total value of the digit 4?
    b. What is the total value of the digit 0?

Multiply.

18. 5	19. 4	20. 2	21. 0	22. 6	23. 3	24. 8
× 2	× 3	× 6	× 9	× 5	× 7	× 2

25. 9	26. 7	27. 8	28. 9	29. 2	30. 9	31. 5
× 2	× 5	× 3	× 4	× 7	× 3	× 1

32. 8×5 33. 2×8 34. 5×3 35. 4×8 36. 3×7

CHAPTER 7

Problem Solving

Using Problem Solving at Work

Ella Cross is a lawyer. She is working on writing a contract between two business partners. She must make sure that she knows what the important facts are. She must be sure that she has enough information.

Reading Problems

When you read a problem, look for the important information.

- What is the question?
- What are the important facts?

Read each problem. Then answer the questions about it.

1. One sail on a sailboat costs $87. The other sail costs $135. How much do both sails cost?
   a. What is the question?
      How much do both sails cost?
   b. What are the important facts?
      One sail costs $87, and the other costs $135.

2. A motorboat travels 8 hours in one day. How many hours does it travel in 7 days?
   a. What is the question?
   b. What are the important facts?

3. A large canoe holds 7 people. How many people do 6 canoes hold?
   a. What is the question?
   b. What are the important facts?

4. The boatyard paints 27 sailboats on Tuesday, 32 sailboats on Wednesday, and 29 sailboats on Thursday. How many sailboats are painted in all?
   a. What is the question?
   b. What are the important facts?

5. 183 motorboats are rented in two weeks. The first week 78 motorboats are rented. How many motorboats are rented the second week?
   a. What is the question?
   b. What are the important facts?

Choosing the Operation

To solve problems, think about whether to add, subtract, or multiply.

Choose the correct way to solve each problem. Then solve it.

1. Jack brings 218 cans to the recycling center. Sally brings 194 cans to the center. How many cans in all?

    218 − 194 or 218 + 194
    218 + 194 = 412

2. Bob and Jose collect 147 bundles of newspapers. Jose collects 88 bundles of newspapers. How many bundles does Bob collect?

    147 + 88 or 147 − 88

3. One month the recycling center sells cans and newspapers for $79.16. The next month the center earns $62.04. How much does the center earn?

    $79.16 − $62.04 or
    $79.16 + $62.04

4. The recycling center is open 4 days each week. How many days is the center open in 8 weeks?

    4 × 8 or 4 + 8

5. Laura has 7 bags of cans. Each bag hold 9 cans. How many cans in all?

    7 + 9 or 7 × 9

Choosing the Operation

In these problems triangles and squares take the place of numbers. You cannot solve the problems, but you can decide to add, subtract, or multiply.

Decide what to do. Write add, subtract, or multiply for each problem.

1. ■ ticket costs ▲ dollars. How much would 5 tickets cost?
   multiply

2. Larry is ■ years old. Tina is ▲ years old. How much older is Larry than Tina?

3. Rosa reads ■ stories about animals and ▲ stories about people. How many stories is that?

4. Carol buys ■ birthday cards and ▲ funny cards. How many cards does she buy?

5. You save ■ cents each week. You save for ▲ weeks. How much money will you have?

 Challenge

6. A pirate has ■ treasure chests. Each chest holds ■ bags of silver coins and ▲ bags of gold coins. How many bags in all the chests?

Choosing the Operation

Decide what to do. Write **add**, **subtract**, or **multiply** for each problem.

1. Porter's Pet Shop has ■ parakeets in each cage. There are ▲ cages. How many parakeets in all?   multiply

2. Goldfish cost ■ ¢ each. Susan buys ▲ goldfish. How much money does she pay?

3. The shop sells ■ dogs in the morning and ▲ dogs in the afternoon. How many dogs are sold in all?

4. The parrot is ■ years old. The parakeet is ▲ years old. How much older is the parrot?

5. William buys ■ snails. Anna buys ▲ snails. How many more snails does Anna buy?

6. The shop has ■ angelfish and ▲ guppies. How many fish is that?

7. The dogs eat ■ cans of food each day. How much food will they eat in ▲ days?

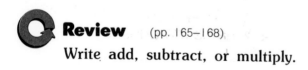

Review   (pp. 165–168)

Write add, subtract, or multiply.

1. Linda delivers ■ newspapers on Monday and ▲ newspapers on Tuesday. How many in all?

2. Newspapers cost ■ ¢ each. Fumio sells ▲ newspapers. How much does he make?

Too Much Information

Look for the important facts. Sometimes you might have too much information.

Read each problem. Then answer the questions about it.

1. You need 1 ball of string to tie 8 packages. String costs 30¢ a ball. How many packages can you tie with 3 balls?
   a. What is the question?
      How many packages can you tie with 3 balls?
   b. Will you add, subtract, or multiply?
   c. What numbers do you need?
   d. What number is not needed?
   e. Solve the problem.

2. Last year Sam was 7 years old. He was 121 centimeters tall. This year he is 188 centimeters tall. How much did he grow?
   a. What is the question?
   b. Will you add, subtract, or multiply?
   c. What numbers do you need?
   d. What number is not needed?
   e. Solve the problem.

3. There were 17 people on a bus. 3 got off at Main Street. 5 got off at Oak Street. How many people got off the bus?
   a. What is the question?
   b. Will you add, subtract, or multiply?
   c. What numbers do you need?
   d. What number is not needed?
   e. Solve the problem.

Estimating Answers

You can use rounding to estimate answers.

You spend
39¢ for a puzzle   39¢ rounds to 40¢.
49¢ for a ball   49¢ rounds to 50¢.

40¢ + 50¢ = 90¢   You spend about 90¢.

Round to the nearest ten. Then choose the best answer.

1. You have 90¢.
   You spend 36¢.
   Your change will be about
   40¢, 50¢, or 60¢?   50¢

2. You spend 14¢ for a pencil and
   35¢ for a pen.
   You spend about
   40¢, 50¢, or 60¢?

3. You pay 25¢ for an apple and
   16¢ for milk.
   You spend about
   30¢, 40¢, or 50¢?

4. You pay 23¢ for soup and
   81¢ for a hamburger.
   You spend about
   60¢, 90¢, or $1.00?

5. You spend 12¢ for an orange
   and 65¢ for a sandwich.
   You spend about
   30¢, 60¢, or 80¢?

6. You have 63¢.
   You spend 22¢.
   Your change will be about
   40¢, 50¢, or 60¢?

 Challenge

7. You pay 59¢ for a toy truck,
   38¢ for a boat, and 73¢ for
   a plane. You spend about
   $1.50, $1.60, or $1.70?

8. You pay 29¢ for thread and
   54¢ for pins. You have $1.20.
   Your change will be about
   40¢, 50¢, or 60¢?

Estimating Answers

Round to answer each question. Write **yes** or **no**.

1. You have $4.00. A clown's wig costs $1.69. Can you buy 2 wigs?   yes

2. The costume store's owners ordered 200 costumes. They received 83 clown suits and 98 space suits. Did they receive all the costumes?   *no*

3. You have $1.20. A paper hat costs 55¢. Can you buy 2 hats?   *yes*

4. A teacher needs 74 blonde wigs and 91 brown wigs for a school play. The store has 150 wigs. Does the store have enough wigs for the play?   *yes*

5. Each rabbit suit has 9 buttons. The costume maker has 80 buttons. Are there enough buttons for 8 rabbit suits?   *yes*

6. You have $6.00. A cat mask costs $2.79. A firefighter's hat costs $2.99. Can you buy both?   *yes*

 Calculate

7. A toy store sells 3 toys: a clown, a dog, and a car. There are 536 clowns, 297 dogs, and 1000 toys in all. How many cars?

Writing Problems

Writing problems will help you solve problems.

Some questions
1. How much do you get together?
2. How much less do you get than your sister?
3. How much more does your sister get?

You get 25¢ allowance.

Your sister gets 45¢ allowance.

Write a question about each. Answer the question.

1. Apples cost 8¢ each.
   You buy 4 apples.
   How much do you spend?   32¢

2. There are 17 red crayons and 23 blue crayons.

3. The birthday card costs 29¢.
   You have 50¢.

4. Today is May 10th.
   Tony's birthday is May 18th.

5. There are 18 elephants in the circus. There are 23 elephants in the zoo.

6. There are 6 monkey cages at the zoo. There are 6 monkeys in each cage.

 Challenge

7. Make up five problems. Find the answers.
   Exchange them with another student.

Problem-Solving Practice

Solve these problems.

1. Andrew and Toby hiked 5 hours
   one day, 7 hours the next day,
   and 9 hours the third day.
   How many hours did they hike?
   21 hours

2. Nora hiked 5 hours each day.
   How many hours did she hike
   in 3 days?

3. The Girl Scouts need 9 tents
   for camping. Each tent takes
   3 poles. How many poles in all?

4. The Boy Scouts made 37 tuna
   sandwiches, 24 cheese
   sandwiches, and 19 egg salad
   sandwiches. How many
   sandwiches in all?

5. The store had 428 canteens.
   65 canteens were sold. How
   many canteens were left?

6. Ellen and Terry plan to walk
   6 hours each day. How many
   hours will they walk in 8 days?

 Calculate

7. In 8 months, a sporting goods store sold 38, 42,
   51, 26, 59, 61, 47, and 32 backpacks. How many
   were sold in all?

Decide what to do. Write **add**, **subtract**, or **multiply** for each problem.   (ex. 1–4: p. 167)

1. Apples cost ■ ¢ each.
   Ginny buys ▲ apples.
   How much does she spend?

2. Eric buys ■ red pencils
   and ▲ blue pencils. How
   many pencils is that?

3. Pencils cost ■ ¢ each.
   Julio buys ▲ pencils.
   How much does he spend?

4. Brent weighs ■ kilograms.
   Mary weighs ▲ kilograms. How
   much more does Brent weigh?

Read each problem. Then answer the questions about it.   (ex. 5–6: p. 169)

5. You need I jar of paint to
   paint 3 pictures. Paint costs
   95¢ a jar. How many jars of
   paint do you need to paint
   9 pictures?
   a. What is the question?
   b. Will you add, subtract,
      or multiply?
   c. What numbers do you need?
   d. What number is not needed?
   e. Solve the problem.

6. There were 295 people on a
   train. I30 got off in Jefferson.
   50 got off in Pleasantville.
   How many people got off the
   train?
   a. What is the question?
   b. Will you add, subtract,
      or multiply?
   c. What numbers do you need?
   d. What number is not needed?
   e. Solve the problem.

Choose the best answer.   (ex. 7–8: p. 170)

7. You pay I5¢ for milk and
   63¢ for a sandwich. You
   spend about 70¢, 80¢, or 90¢?

8. You have 74¢. You spend 37¢.
   Your change will be about
   20¢, 30¢, or 40¢?

Chapter Test

Decide what to do. Write **add, subtract,** or **multiply** for each problem.

1. Vera has ■ books. Each book has ▲ stories. How many stories in all?

2. Paul has ▲ ¢. He spends ■ ¢. How much does he have left?

3. Grace spends ■ ¢ to buy one fish and ▲ ¢ to buy another fish. How much does she spend in all?

4. Barry learns ■ new songs one week and ▲ new songs the next week. How many songs is that?

Read each problem. Then answer the questions about it.

5. Karen's mother weighs 60 kilograms. Karen weighs 35 kilograms less than her mother. Karen's sister weighs 40 kilograms. How much does Karen weigh?
   a. What is the question?
   b. Will you add, subtract, or multiply?
   c. What numbers do you need?
   d. What number is not needed?
   e. Solve the problem.

6. There were 54 people on a bus. 13 got on the bus at Main Street. 9 got on the bus at Center Street. How many people got on the bus?
   a. What is the question?
   b. Will you add, subtract, or multiply?
   c. What numbers do you need?
   d. What number is not needed?
   e. Solve the problem.

Choose the best answer.

7. You spend 32¢ for a birthday card and 58¢ for a toy. You spend about 60¢, 70¢, or 90¢?

8. You have 89¢. You spend 65¢. Your change will be about 10¢, 20¢, or 30¢?

Brush Up

Add.

1. 18 + 21	2. 61 + 89	3. 431 + 343	4. 262 + 365	5. 893 + 465
6. 465 + 326	7. 5632 + 85	8. 91 + 36	9. 478 + 176	10. 653 + 79
11. 1653 + 2345	12. 89 + 42	13. 127 + 352	14. 691 + 9	15. 4065 + 3262

Subtract.

16. 68 − 46	17. 906 − 423	18. 91 − 6	19. 943 − 156	20. 2053 − 1142
21. 4865 − 1426	22. 705 − 312	23. 89 − 43	24. 600 − 211	25. 1859 − 763

Multiply.

26. 8 × 9	27. 6 × 4	28. 0 × 1	29. 2 × 9	30. 7 × 8	31. 9 × 9	32. 10 × 3
33. 6 × 0	34. 4 × 9	35. 7 × 3	36. 7 × 1	37. 7 × 7	38. 9 × 7	39. 6 × 2

40. 4×4 41. 2×2 42. 0×9 43. 6×5 44. 3×8

CHAPTER 8

Geometry

Using Geometry at Work

Lucy Chin is a surveyor. She wants to find the
distance around a square piece of land. One side
measures 60 meters. She knows that all 4 sides of a
square are equal, so she multiplies 60×4.
The distance around the land is 240 meters.

Squares and Rectangles

Squares and rectangles have four sides. The sides
of a square are the same length.

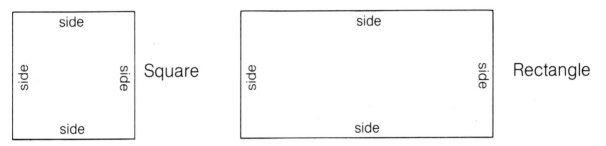

Square

Rectangle

Look at the shapes below.

1. Write the letters of the squares.
   b, h, f, d

2. Write the letters of the shapes
   that are neither squares nor
   rectangles.

3. Write the letters of the
   rectangles that are not squares.

Triangles and Circles

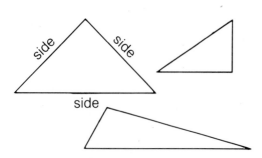

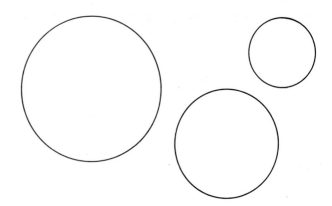

Triangles have three sides.
These are triangles.

Circles have no straight sides.
These are circles.

Look at the shapes below.

1. Write the letters of the shapes that are circles. b, d

2. Write the letters of the shapes that are triangles.

3. Write the letters of the squares.

4. Write the letters of the rectangles that are not squares.

Practice with Names for Shapes

Tell whether each shape is a **rectangle**, a **square**, a **triangle**, or a **circle**.

1.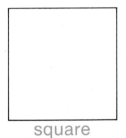

square

2.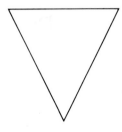

3.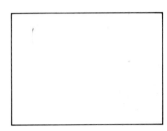

4.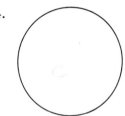

5.

6.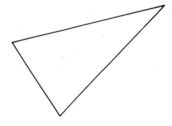

7.

8.

9.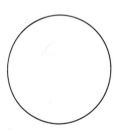

 Review (pp. 179–181)

Write the name of each shape.

1.

2.

3.

4.

5.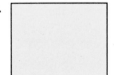

Angles

Sides meet to form an **angle**.
Squares and rectangles have
four angles.

Triangles have three angles.

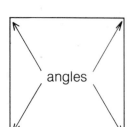

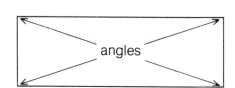

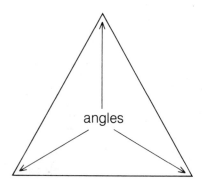

How many angles in each shape?

1.

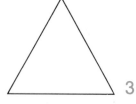

3

2.

3.

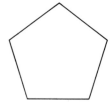

4.

5.

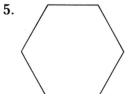

6.

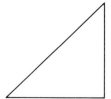

 **Calculate**

7. Ralph bought 4 square rugs for
$6 each and 5 round rugs for
$8 each. How much did he
spend in all?

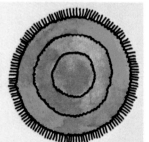

Testing for Right Angles

Step 1
Fold a piece of paper.

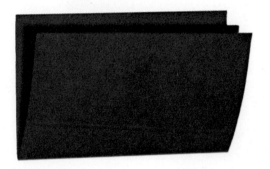

Step 2
Fold again.
Edges must meet exactly.

Mark this corner.
This is a right angle.

Use your right angle. How many right angles in each shape?

1.

3

2.

3.

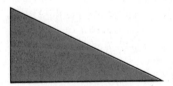

4.

5.

6.

 **Challenge**

7. Draw a triangle with one right angle.

8. Draw a shape that has four right angles.

Line Symmetry

This shape has been folded on the dotted line.

The fold line is a **line of symmetry**. Each half is the same size and shape.

This shape has been folded on the dotted line.

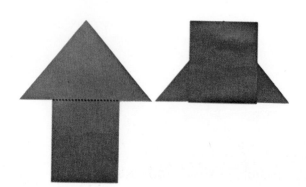

The fold line is **not** a line of symmetry. Each half is **not** the same size and shape.

Is the fold a line of symmetry? Write yes or no.

1.  yes

2.

3.

Can the shape be folded to make a line of symmetry?

4.

5.

6.

More Line Symmetry

Write the letter of the unfolded shape for each folded shape.

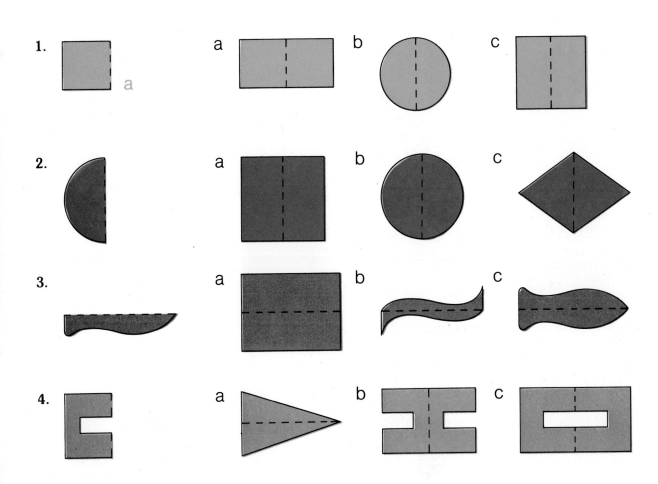

1.   a   b   c

   a

2.   a   b   c

3.   a   b   c

4.   a   b   c

 **Challenge**

5. This letter has a line of symmetry. Write six capital
   letters that have a line of symmetry.

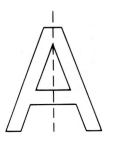

Congruent Shapes

Shapes that have the same
size and shape are **congruent**.

These are congruent.

These are not congruent.

**Write the letter of the shape that is congruent
to the first shape in the row.**

1. 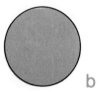   a   b   c

b

2.   a   b   c

3.   a   b 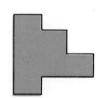   c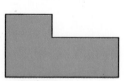

4.   a   b   c

Similar Shapes

Shapes that have the same shape are **similar**.

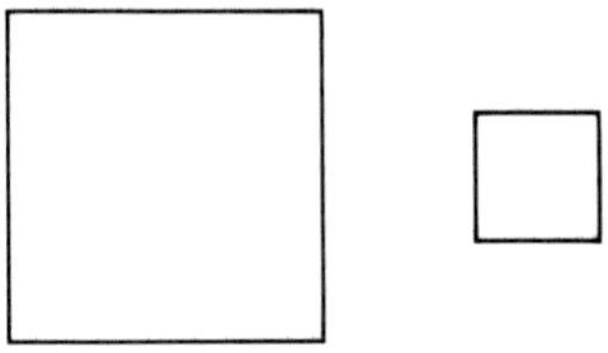

These are similar. 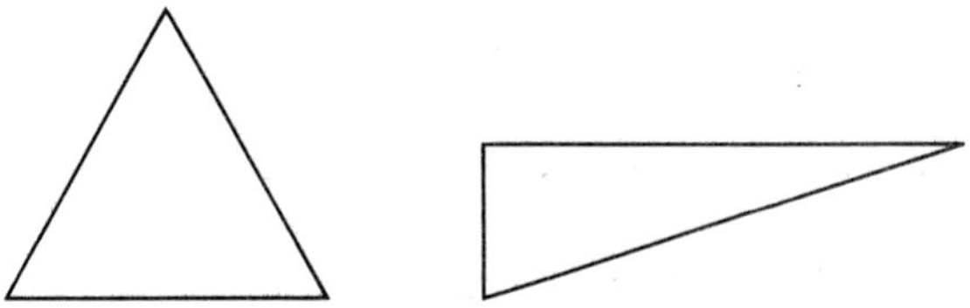   These are not similar.

Are these shapes similar? Write yes or no.

1.   no

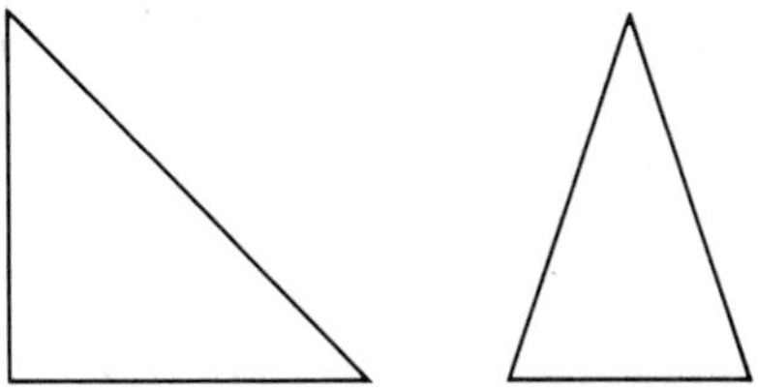

2.

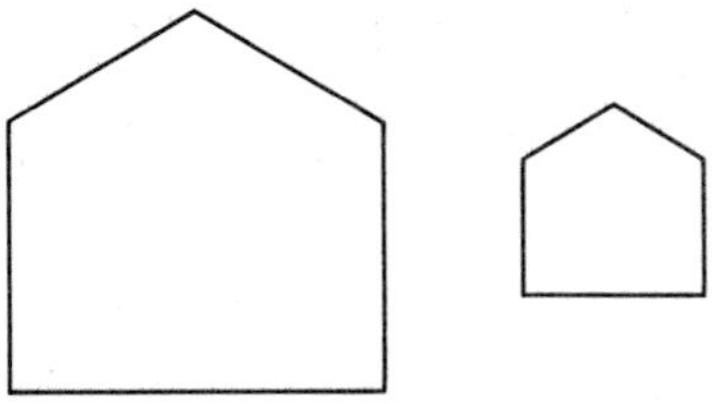

3.

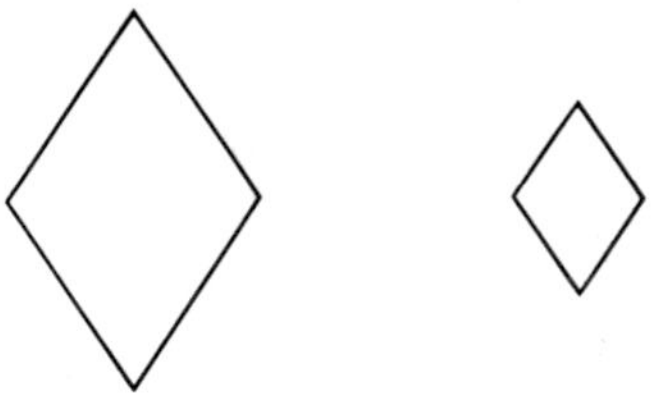

4.

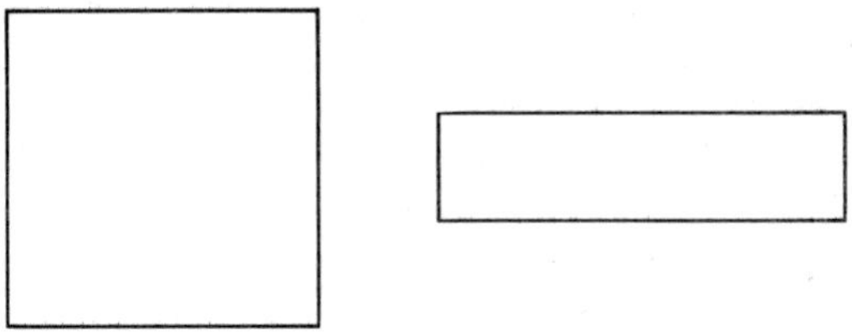

5.

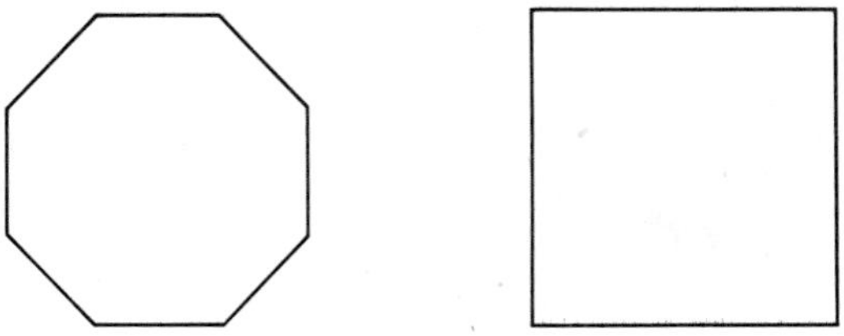

6.

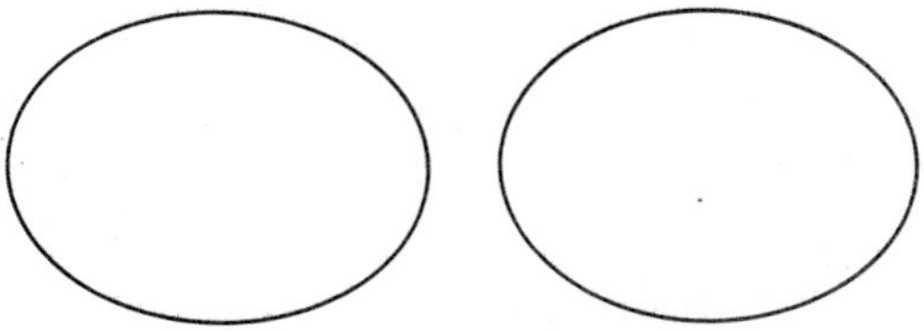

![Calculate] **Calculate**

7. A triangle has sides that measure 213 meters, 425 meters, and 368 meters. What is the distance around the triangle?

Congruence and Similarity

Are these shapes congruent? Write **yes** or **no**.

1. yes

2.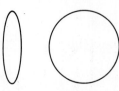

3.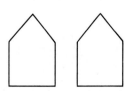

4.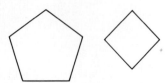

5.

6.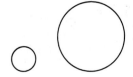

Are these shapes similar? Write **yes** or **no**.

7.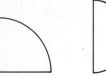

8.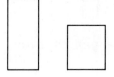

9.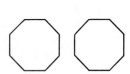

10.

11.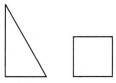

12.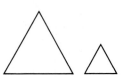

 Challenge

Is each shape divided into congruent parts?
Write **yes** or **no**.

13.

14.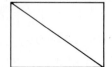

15.

16.

Matching Solid Shapes

Write the letter of the solid shape that is most like the drawing.

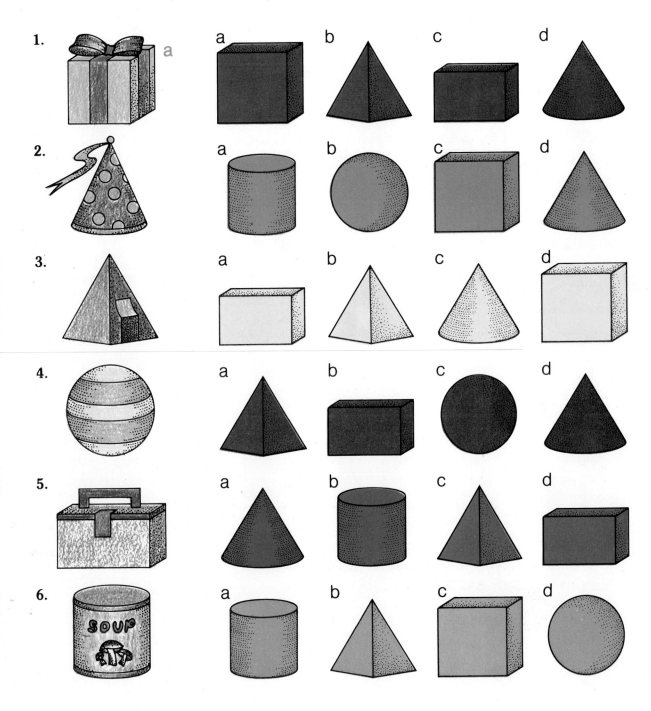

1. a

2.

3.

4.

5.

6.

Solid Shapes and Faces

Each flat surface of a solid is a **face**.
Two faces meet at an **edge**.

This shape has five faces in all.

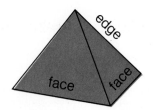

Write the letter of the faces that make each solid shape.

1.  c   a

2. 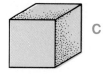   b

3.   c

4.    d

5.   e

Names for Solid Shapes

Here are some solid shapes and their names.

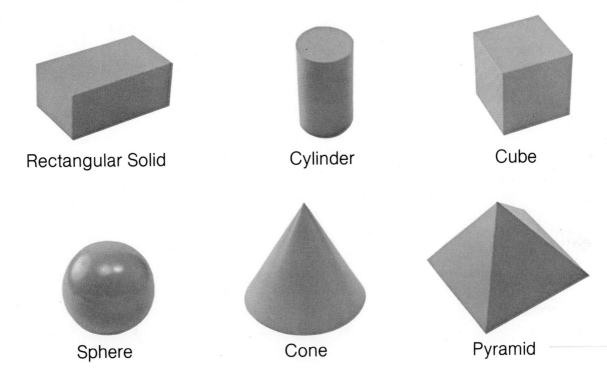

Rectangular Solid   Cylinder   Cube

Sphere   Cone   Pyramid

Write the name of a solid shape to answer each question.

1. The cube has six squares for faces. Which shape has four triangles for faces?   pyramid

2. The cylinder has two circles for faces. Which shape has one circle as a face?

3. The rectangular solid has six faces. Which other shape has six faces?

4. The cube has twelve edges. Which shape has eight edges?

5. Which three shapes have no curved faces or edges?

6. Which shape has no flat faces?

Recognizing Solid Shapes

You can fold this shape to make a cube.

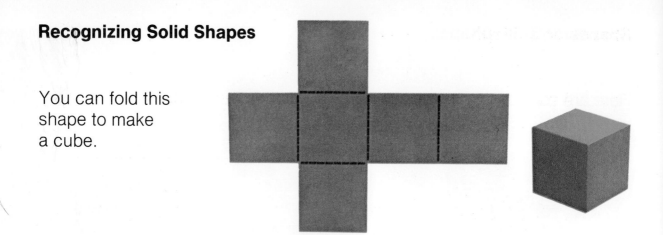

Write the letter of the flat shape that can be used to make the solid shape.

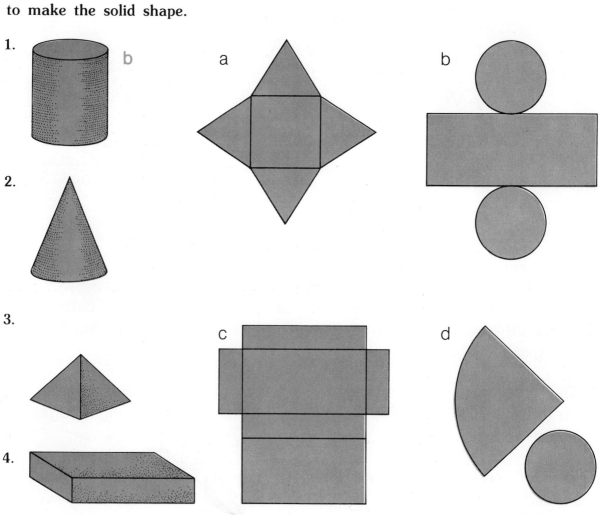

1. b

a

b

2.

3.

c

d

4.

Shapes on a Graph

To name the position of the cube, say that it is 3 over, 2 up.

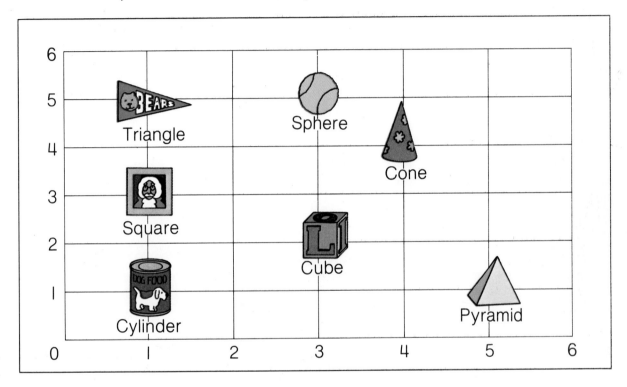

Use the graph. Start at 0. Write the name of the shape or solid.

1. 5 over, I up   pyramid
2. I over, I up
3. 3 over, 5 up

4. I over, 3 up
5. I over, 5 up
6. 4 over, 4 up

 Review   (pp. 179–193)

Write the name of each solid shape.

1.
2.
3.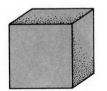
4.

Chapter Review

Write the name of each shape.   (ex. 1–3: p. 181)

1.

2.

3.

How many right angles in each shape?   (ex. 4–5: p. 183)

4.

5.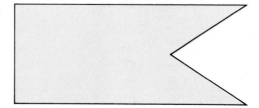

Write the answers.   (ex. 6: p. 186),   (ex. 7: p. 187)

6. Is each pair congruent?
   Write **yes** or **no**.

7. Is each pair similar?
   Write **yes** or **no**.

6a.   6b.   7a.   7b.

Write the name of each solid shape.   (ex. 8–11: p. 191)

8.   9.   10.   11.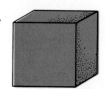

Chapter Test

Write the name of each shape.

1.

2.

3.

How many right angles in each shape?

4.

5.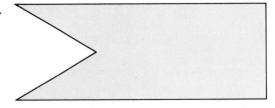

Write the answers.

6. Is each pair congruent?
   Write **yes** or **no**.

7. Is each pair similar?
   Write **yes** or **no**.

6a.   6b.   7a.   7b.

Write the name of each solid shape.

8. 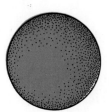   9. 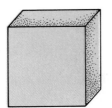   10.    11.

Brush Up

Add.

1.	52 + 30	2.	51 + 83	3.	63 + 44	4.	38 + 25	5.	84 + 32

6.	23 + 152	7.	415 + 284	8.	543 + 128	9.	614 + 175	10.	357 + 265

Subtract.

11.	48 − 9	12.	75 − 52	13.	62 − 36	14.	83 − 21	15.	97 − 8

16.	472 − 241	17.	987 − 146	18.	742 − 270	19.	523 − 108	20.	648 − 521

21.	2475 − 1023	22.	3672 − 1299	23.	5700 − 275	24.	4820 − 2150	25.	6014 − 3275

Multiply.

26.	6 × 2	27.	4 × 4	28.	8 × 3	29.	2 × 9	30.	1 × 8	31.	9 × 3	32.	8 × 5

33.	4 × 5	34.	6 × 3	35.	5 × 5	36.	3 × 8	37.	9 × 4	38.	5 × 6	39.	4 × 9

40.	6 × 1	41.	3 × 7	42.	2 × 8	43.	6 × 4	44.	4 × 3	45.	4 × 8	46.	5 × 7

CHAPTER 9

Fractions and Decimals

Using Fractions at Work

Jane Cunningham is a photographer. She is marking one of her photographs into thirds. If she cuts off $\frac{1}{3}$, she will have $\frac{2}{3}$ left.

Naming Parts of Shapes

You can divide a whole into equal parts.
Equal parts have the same size and the same shape.

Here are some names for equal parts of a whole.

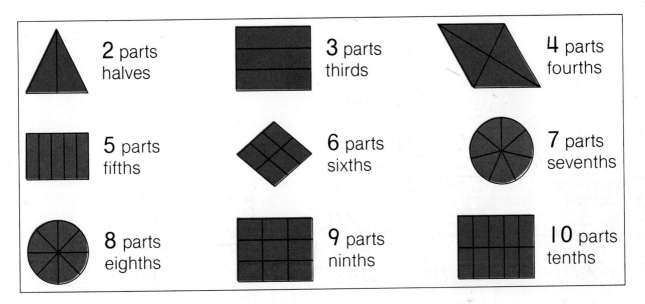

2 parts
halves

3 parts
thirds

4 parts
fourths

5 parts
fifths

6 parts
sixths

7 parts
sevenths

8 parts
eighths

9 parts
ninths

10 parts
tenths

Give the number of parts. Name the kind of parts.

1.  3, thirds

2.

3.

4.

5.

6.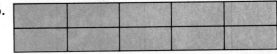

7.

8.

9.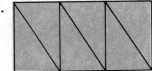

Writing Fractions

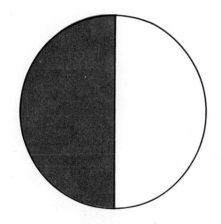

One-half of the circle is shaded.

You can write one-half as a **fraction**.

$\frac{1}{2}$ numerator   (number of shaded parts)
denominator   (total of equal parts)

Write the fraction for the shaded part.

1. 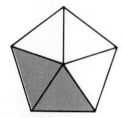 $\frac{4}{6}$

2.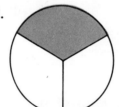

3.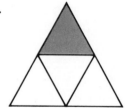

4.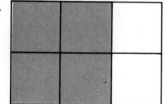

5.

6.

7.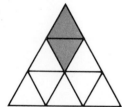

8.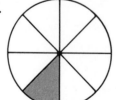

9.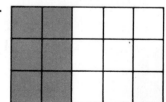

Looking at Halves

Not all halves are equal.

| Paul ate half a melon. | Betty ate half an orange. | Marie ate half a grapefruit. | Mike ate half a plum. |

Use the pictures to answer the questions.

1. Who ate more, Mike or Marie? Marie

2. Who ate more, Marie or Paul?

3. Who ate more, Betty or Marie?

4. Who ate more, Mike or Paul?

5. Who ate more, Paul or Betty?

6. Who ate more, Mike or Betty?

7. Who ate the most?

8. Who ate the least?

 Calculate

Multiply the top and bottom number of each fraction by 5 to make a new fraction.

9. $\frac{3}{4}$

10. $\frac{1}{2}$

11. $\frac{2}{5}$

12. $\frac{1}{6}$

13. $\frac{1}{8}$

Parts of a Group

The whole group has 6 parts.
Each hammer is $\frac{1}{6}$ of the group.

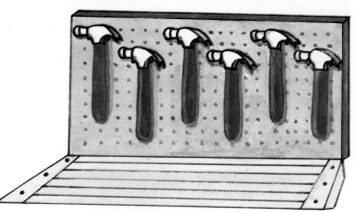

Write the numbers.

1a. How many circles in the group?   7

b. Each circle is $\frac{?}{?}$ of the group? $\frac{1}{7}$

2a. How many triangles in the group?

b. Each triangle is $\frac{?}{?}$ of the group.

3a. How many squares in the group?

b. Each square is $\frac{?}{?}$ of the group.

4a. How many moons in the group?

b. Each moon is $\frac{?}{?}$ of the group.

5a. How many stars in the group?

b. Each star is $\frac{?}{?}$ of the group.

6a. How many diamonds in the group?

b. Each diamond is $\frac{?}{?}$ of the group.

Fractions of a Group

The whole group has 5 parts.

3 are apples. $\frac{3}{5}$ of the group are apples.
2 are bananas. $\frac{2}{5}$ of the group are bananas.

Write the fractions.

1a. $\frac{2}{4}$ of the group are tomatoes.
   b. $\frac{?}{?}$ of the group are peppers. $\frac{2}{4}$

2a. $\frac{3}{7}$ of the group are carrots.
   b. $\frac{?}{?}$ of the group are mushrooms.

3a. $\frac{2}{5}$ of the group are pears.
   b. $\frac{?}{?}$ of the group are grapes.

4a. $\frac{2}{6}$ of the group are pineapples.
   b. $\frac{?}{?}$ of the group are not pineapples.

5a. $\frac{2}{4}$ of the group are cherries.
   b. $\frac{?}{?}$ of the group are not cherries.

6a. $\frac{3}{5}$ of the group are oranges.
   b. $\frac{?}{?}$ of the group are strawberries.

Writing Fractions for Wholes and Groups

Write a fraction to answer each question.

1. What part is red? $\frac{4}{5}$

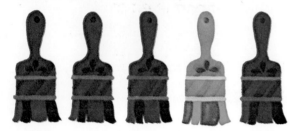

2. What part is yellow?

3. What part is empty?

4. What part is red?

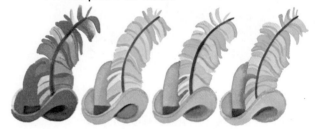

5. What part is red?

6. What part is yellow?

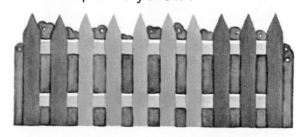

7. What part is green?

8. What part is blue?

Practice Writing Fractions

Answer the questions.

1a. What part is pink? $\frac{2}{6}$
 b. What part is blue?

2a. What part is full?
 b. What part is empty?

3a. What part is orange?
 b. What part is purple?

4a. What part is shaded?
 b. What part is not shaded?

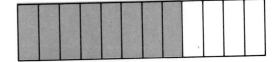

5a. What part is shaded?
 b. What part is not shaded?

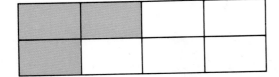

6a. What part is green?
 b. What part is yellow?

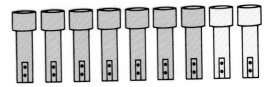

 Review (pp. 199–205)

Write a fraction for each part.

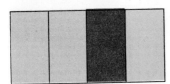

1a. yellow   1b. red

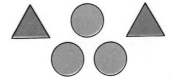

2a. circles   2b. triangles

3a. red   3b. blue

Match Fractions

Write the letter for the picture that matches the fraction.

1. $\frac{7}{10}$ h

2. $\frac{3}{8}$

3. $\frac{1}{2}$

4. $\frac{3}{4}$

5. $\frac{5}{6}$

6. $\frac{1}{3}$

7. $\frac{7}{12}$

8. $\frac{4}{9}$

a

b
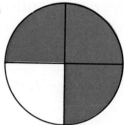

c
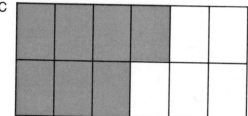

d
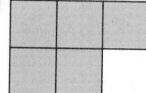

e
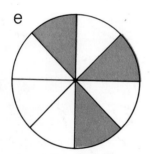

f

g
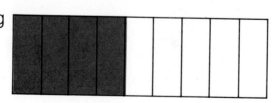

h
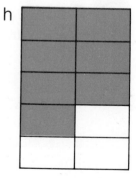

Fraction Pictures

1a. Draw 8 daisies.
 b. Each daisy is $\frac{?}{?}$ of the group. $\frac{1}{8}$
 c. Now put the daisies in 2 rings.
 d. The daisies in one ring are $\frac{?}{?}$ of the total group.

2a. Draw 9 stars.
 b. Each star is $\frac{?}{?}$ of the group.
 c. Now put the stars in 3 rings.
 d. The stars in one ring are $\frac{?}{?}$ of the total group.

3a. Draw 6 cats.
 b. Each cat is $\frac{?}{?}$ of the group.
 c. Now put the cats in 3 rings.
 d. The cats in one ring are $\frac{?}{?}$ of the total group.

4a. Draw 12 fish.
 b. Each fish is $\frac{?}{?}$ of the group.
 c. Now put the fish in 4 groups.
 d. The fish in one group are $\frac{?}{?}$ of the total group.

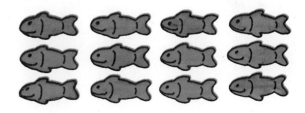

 Challenge

5a. Draw a square.
 b. Divide it to show fourths.

6a. Draw a circle.
 b. Divide it to show halves.

Ordering Fractions

This fraction fence will help you order fractions.

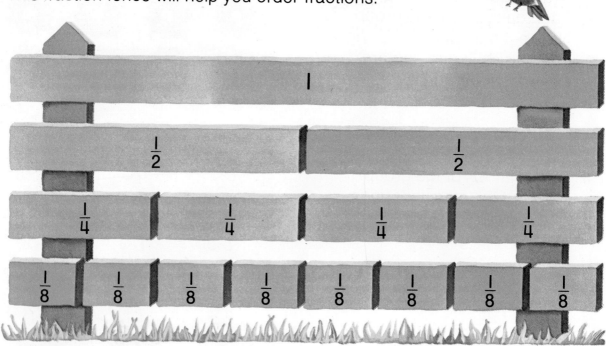

Look at the fraction fence. Which is greater?

1. $\frac{1}{4}$ or $\frac{1}{2}$ $\frac{1}{2}$

2. 1 or $\frac{1}{2}$

3. $\frac{3}{4}$ or $\frac{1}{2}$

4. $\frac{2}{4}$ or $\frac{2}{8}$

5. $\frac{1}{4}$ or $\frac{3}{8}$

6. $\frac{3}{8}$ or $\frac{2}{4}$

7. $\frac{7}{8}$ or 1

8. $\frac{3}{8}$ or 1

9. $\frac{2}{8}$ or $\frac{1}{2}$

10. $\frac{4}{4}$ or $\frac{7}{8}$

Look at the fraction fence. Which is less?

11. $\frac{3}{4}$ or $\frac{7}{8}$ $\frac{3}{4}$

12. $\frac{3}{8}$ or $\frac{3}{4}$

13. $\frac{6}{8}$ or $\frac{2}{4}$

14. 1 or $\frac{3}{4}$

15. $\frac{2}{8}$ or $\frac{3}{4}$

16. $\frac{5}{8}$ or $\frac{1}{2}$

17. $\frac{3}{4}$ or $\frac{4}{8}$

18. $\frac{1}{4}$ or $\frac{3}{8}$

19. 1 or $\frac{6}{8}$

20. $\frac{1}{8}$ or $\frac{1}{2}$

Equal Fractions

Use the fraction fence on page 208.
Equal fractions name the same amount.

$$\frac{2}{8} = \frac{1}{4} \qquad \frac{2}{4} = \frac{1}{2} \qquad \frac{2}{2} = 1$$

Copy and complete.

1. $1 = \frac{?}{4}$ $\frac{4}{4}$

2. $\frac{1}{2} = \frac{?}{4}$

3. $\frac{1}{4} = \frac{?}{8}$

4. $\frac{1}{2} = \frac{?}{8}$

5. $\frac{6}{8} = \frac{?}{4}$

6. $1 = \frac{?}{8}$

7. $\frac{2}{4} = \frac{?}{8}$

8. $\frac{2}{2} = \frac{?}{4}$

9. $\frac{2}{2} = \frac{?}{8}$

10. $1 = \frac{?}{2}$

11. $\frac{1}{4} = \frac{?}{8}$

12. $\frac{2}{8} = \frac{?}{4}$

13. $\frac{4}{4} = \frac{?}{8}$

14. $\frac{3}{4} = \frac{?}{8}$

15. $\frac{8}{8} = \frac{?}{2}$

16. $\frac{1}{2} = \frac{?}{4}$

17. $\frac{2}{2} = \frac{?}{8}$

18. $\frac{4}{4} = \frac{?}{2}$

19. $\frac{4}{8} = \frac{?}{2}$

 Challenge

20. Sandra bicycled for $\frac{3}{4}$ of an hour. Sun Lee bicycled for $\frac{4}{8}$ of an hour. Who spent more time bicycling?

21. Dan read $\frac{1}{3}$ of his book. Jerry read $\frac{4}{6}$ of his book. Who read more?

Mixed Numbers

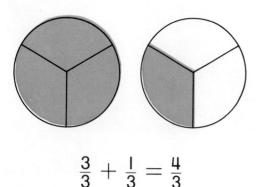

$$\frac{3}{3} + \frac{1}{3} = \frac{4}{3}$$

$\frac{4}{3} = 1$ whole and $\frac{1}{3}$ of a whole

$\frac{4}{3} = 1\frac{1}{3}$

$1\frac{1}{3}$ is a **mixed number**.

$1\frac{1}{3}$ is read *one and one-third.*

Write a fraction and a mixed number for the shaded parts.

1. 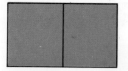 $\frac{3}{2}, 1\frac{1}{2}$

2.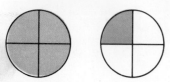

3.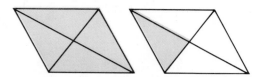

4.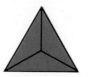

 Challenge

Write a fraction and a mixed number for the shaded parts.

5.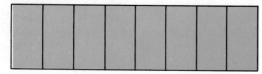

Decimals

Tenths may be written as **decimals**.
Remember the zero and the decimal point.

Four-tenths is red.

$\frac{4}{10}$ or 0.4 is red.

zero → ← decimal
ones   point

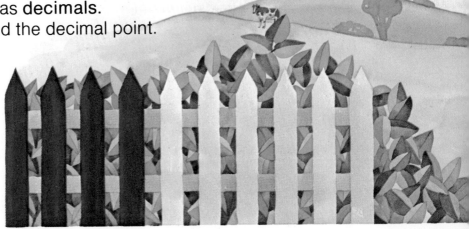

Write the fraction and the decimal.

1. Five-tenths is red. $\frac{5}{10}$, 0.5

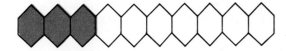

2. Six-tenths is red.

3. Three-tenths is red.

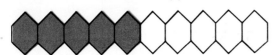

4. One-tenth is red.

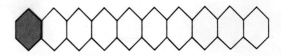

5. Nine-tenths is red.

6. Eight-tenths is red.

7. Seven-tenths is red.

8. Two-tenths is red.

Writing Decimals for Fractions

Write each fraction as a decimal.

1. $\frac{4}{10}$ 0.4   2. $\frac{7}{10}$ 3. $\frac{8}{10}$ 4. $\frac{1}{10}$ 5. $\frac{6}{10}$ 6. $\frac{9}{10}$

7. $\frac{8}{10}$ 8. $\frac{3}{10}$ 9. $\frac{0}{10}$ 10. $\frac{5}{10}$ 11. $\frac{2}{10}$ 12. $\frac{4}{10}$

13. three-tenths   14. eight-tenths   15. five-tenths

16. four-tenths   17. one-tenth   18. six-tenths

 Challenge

Use the chart. Copy and complete.

19a. $\frac{2}{5} = \frac{?}{10}$ $\frac{4}{10}$ 19b. $\frac{2}{5} = 0.\boxed{?}$ 20a. $\frac{3}{5} = \frac{?}{10}$ 20b. $\frac{3}{5} = 0.\boxed{?}$

21a. $\frac{4}{5} = \frac{?}{10}$ 21b. $\frac{4}{5} = 0.\boxed{?}$ 22a. $\frac{1}{5} = \frac{?}{10}$ 22b. $\frac{1}{5} = 0.\boxed{?}$

Decimals on a Number Strip

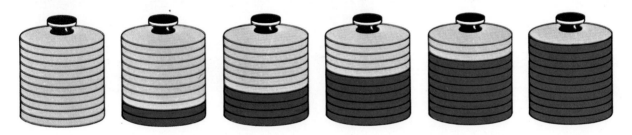

Which is greater? Use the number strip.

1. 0.3 or 0.7   0.7   **2.** 0.8 or 0.5   **3.** 0.3 or 0.4   **4.** 0.2 or 0.5

5. 0.9 or 0.6   **6.** 0.1 or 0.3   **7.** 1.0 or 0.9   **8.** 0.0 or 0.7

Put these in order from least to greatest.

9. 0.3, 0.7, 0.2, 0.9   **10.** 0.3, 0.6, 0.2, 0.8

11. 0.8, 0.1, 0.4, 0.5   **12.** 0.7, 0.4, 0.1, 0.3

13. 0.2, 0.9, 0.6, 0   **14.** 0.9, 0.5, 0.1, 0.7

Write the missing tenths.

15. .▢, 0.4, 0.5   **16.** 0.6, .▢, 0.8   **17.** 0.7, 0.8, ▢

18. 0.1, 0.3, .▢, 0.7, .▢   **19.** 0.7, 0.8, .▢, .▢   **20.** 0.2, 0.4, 0.6, .▢, .▢

Decimals Greater Than One

$1\frac{3}{10}$ or 1.3

Mixed numbers can be written as decimals.

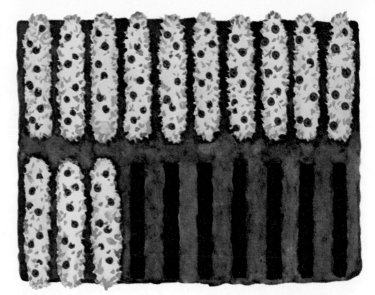

Write each mixed number as a decimal.

1. $4\frac{7}{10}$ 4.7

2. $2\frac{5}{10}$

3. $8\frac{1}{10}$

4. $1\frac{3}{10}$

5. $3\frac{8}{10}$

6. $5\frac{2}{10}$

7. $1\frac{3}{10}$

8. $3\frac{7}{10}$

9. $1\frac{4}{10}$

10. $9\frac{9}{10}$

11. $2\frac{6}{10}$

Which is greater?

12. 2.3 or 2.5

13. 5.6 or 5.1

14. 3.9 or 3.7

15. 8.0 or 8.6

16. 4.5 or 5.4

17. 7.1 or 6.8

18. 2.7 or 3.1

19. 9.0 or 7.9

20. 0.8 or 1.2

21. 3.1 or 2.9

22. 4.1 or 4.7

23. 5.0 or 5.9

 Review (pp. 199–214)

Put these in order from least to greatest.

1. $\frac{6}{8}, \frac{3}{8}, \frac{5}{8}, \frac{1}{8}$

2. 0.3, 0.7, 0.5, 1.2

Adding Decimals

When you add decimals, remember to line up the decimal points.

0.2	0.9	3.4	1.5
+ 0.4	+ 0.4	+ 6.1	+ 2.8
0.6	1.3	9.5	4.3

Add.

1. 4.2
   + 0.7
   4.9

2. 0.3
   + 0.5

3. 0.6
   + 0.3

4. 2.1
   + 3.6

5. 0.3
   + 0.5

6. 0.6
   + 0.9

7. 0.8
   + 0.3

8. 3.4
   + 1.3

9. 2.9
   + 0.4

10. 0.6
    + 0.2

11. 4.8
    + 3.5

12. 0.6
    + 0.6

13. 3.4
    + 5.8

14. 0.7
    + 0.6

15. 4.5
    + 2.3

16. 0.8
    + 0.5

17. 2.5
    + 1.9

18. 4.8
    + 0.3

 Calculate

19. One week Paul skated 1.7, 2.6, 1.3, 1.4, 1.5, 2.1, and 1.9 kilometers. How many kilometers did he skate?

Subtracting Decimals

```
        3  15
  6.9    4̸.5̸
- 3.4  - 2.8
  3.5    1.7
```

When you subtract decimals, remember to line up the decimal points.

Subtract.

1. 0.8 − 0.3 **0.5**	2. 0.7 − 0.1	3. 0.6 − 0.3	4. 0.5 − 0.2	5. 0.9 − 0.6	6. 0.8 − 0.4
7. 3.6 − 1.2	8. 6.7 − 2.5	9. 4.9 − 2.3	10. 9.7 − 6.6	11. 7.5 − 3.3	12. 8.8 − 5.6
13. 3.1 − 1.5	14. 5.2 − 2.7	15. 6.3 − 0.5	16. 7.0 − 1.9	17. 2.6 − 0.7	18. 1.4 − 0.8

 Challenge

19. Ricardo had 3.5 meters of rope. He used 1.2 meters to make a leash for his dog. How much rope did he have left?

20. Ricardo's father bought 7.0 meters of fence for the backyard. If he used 5.9 meters, how many meters of fence did he have left?

Map Problems

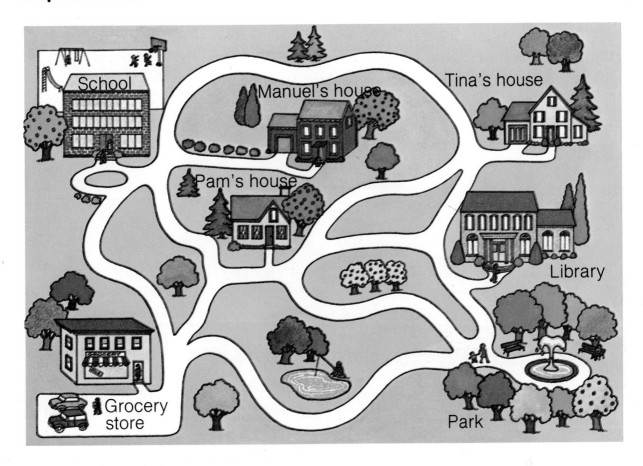

Add or subtract to solve each problem.

1. Pam walked 0.5 kilometers to the grocery store. Then she walked 1.5 kilometers to school. How far did she walk in all? 2 kilometers

2. Manuel walked 0.4 kilometers to school. Then he rode 1.5 kilometers to the grocery store. How much farther did he ride than walk?

3. Pam walked 1.8 kilometers to the park. Then she rode 2.5 kilometers to the grocery store. How much farther did she ride than walk?

4. Tina walked 0.8 kilometers to the library. Then she walked 0.5 kilometers to the park. How far did she walk in all?

Chapter Review

Write a fraction or mixed number for the part
that is shaded.   (ex. 1–2: p. 200),   (ex. 3: p. 203),   (ex. 4–5: p. 210)

1.

2.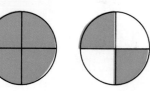

3.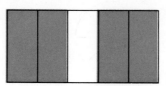

4.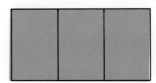

5.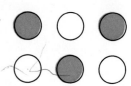

Write decimals for these.   (ex. 6–11: p. 212),   (ex. 12–17: p. 214)

6. $\dfrac{3}{10}$ 7. $\dfrac{6}{10}$ 8. $\dfrac{5}{10}$ 9. $\dfrac{1}{10}$ 10. $\dfrac{4}{10}$ 11. $\dfrac{2}{10}$

12. $3\dfrac{9}{10}$ 13. $8\dfrac{7}{10}$ 14. $6\dfrac{1}{10}$ 15. $9\dfrac{6}{10}$ 16. $7\dfrac{5}{10}$ 17. $1\dfrac{3}{10}$

Put these in order from least to greatest.   (ex. 18–21: p. 213)

18. 0.8, 0.4, 0.3, 0.1   19. 0.3, 0.0, 0.8, 0.5

20. 0.2, 0.8, 0.7, 0.5   21. 0.1, 0.4, 1.0, 0.6

Add or subtract.   (ex. 22–24: p. 215),   (ex. 25–27: p. 216)

22. $\begin{array}{r} 2.1 \\ +\,3.6 \\ \hline \end{array}$
23. $\begin{array}{r} 2.5 \\ +\,1.9 \\ \hline \end{array}$
24. $\begin{array}{r} 0.6 \\ +\,0.4 \\ \hline \end{array}$
25. $\begin{array}{r} 2.7 \\ -\,0.4 \\ \hline \end{array}$
26. $\begin{array}{r} 0.9 \\ -\,0.5 \\ \hline \end{array}$
27. $\begin{array}{r} 8.4 \\ -\,2.9 \\ \hline \end{array}$

Chapter Test

Write a fraction or mixed number for the part that is shaded.

1.

2.

3.

4.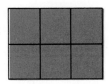

5.

Write decimals for these.

6. $\frac{9}{10}$ 7. $\frac{7}{10}$ 8. $\frac{2}{10}$ 9. $\frac{5}{10}$ 10. $\frac{8}{10}$ 11. $\frac{1}{10}$

12. $6\frac{7}{10}$ 13. $2\frac{3}{10}$ 14. $4\frac{1}{10}$ 15. $8\frac{4}{10}$ 16. $1\frac{6}{10}$ 17. $9\frac{9}{10}$

Put these in order from least to greatest.

18. 0.7, 0.9, 0.4, 0.2

19. 0.4, 0.1, 0.0, 0.9

20. 0.2, 0.5, 1.0, 0.6

21. 0.5, 0.8, 1.3, 0.4

Add or subtract.

22. 3.6
  + 0.3

23. 2.5
  + 6.2

24. 0.4
  + 0.1

25. 4.6
  − 2.1

26. 0.9
  − 0.2

27. 7.3
  − 2.7

Brush Up

Multiply.

1. 1×2 2. 2×8 3. 5×7 4. 3×7 5. 4×10

6. 4×3 7. 3×6 8. 5×4 9. 2×4 10. 8×3

11. 6×2 12. 5×9 13. 3×5 14. 5×10 15. 7×4

16. 7×10 17. 3×5 18. 3×3 19. 4×7 20. 0×9

21. $\begin{array}{r} 8 \\ \times 4 \\ \hline \end{array}$ 22. $\begin{array}{r} 4 \\ \times 6 \\ \hline \end{array}$ 23. $\begin{array}{r} 9 \\ \times 5 \\ \hline \end{array}$ 24. $\begin{array}{r} 2 \\ \times 9 \\ \hline \end{array}$ 25. $\begin{array}{r} 5 \\ \times 8 \\ \hline \end{array}$ 26. $\begin{array}{r} 8 \\ \times 3 \\ \hline \end{array}$ 27. $\begin{array}{r} 3 \\ \times 6 \\ \hline \end{array}$

28. $\begin{array}{r} 10 \\ \times 2 \\ \hline \end{array}$ 29. $\begin{array}{r} 2 \\ \times 4 \\ \hline \end{array}$ 30. $\begin{array}{r} 4 \\ \times 2 \\ \hline \end{array}$ 31. $\begin{array}{r} 4 \\ \times 8 \\ \hline \end{array}$ 32. $\begin{array}{r} 1 \\ \times 0 \\ \hline \end{array}$ 33. $\begin{array}{r} 3 \\ \times 9 \\ \hline \end{array}$ 34. $\begin{array}{r} 5 \\ \times 5 \\ \hline \end{array}$

35. $\begin{array}{r} 5 \\ \times 4 \\ \hline \end{array}$ 36. $\begin{array}{r} 7 \\ \times 2 \\ \hline \end{array}$ 37. $\begin{array}{r} 1 \\ \times 1 \\ \hline \end{array}$ 38. $\begin{array}{r} 5 \\ \times 6 \\ \hline \end{array}$ 39. $\begin{array}{r} 4 \\ \times 9 \\ \hline \end{array}$ 40. $\begin{array}{r} 0 \\ \times 3 \\ \hline \end{array}$ 41. $\begin{array}{r} 4 \\ \times 4 \\ \hline \end{array}$

Write the numbers.

42. 2 tens 43. 6 tens 44. 4 hundreds

45. 8 thousands 46. 1 hundred 47. 5 thousands

Add.

48. $16 + 4$ 49. $28 + 3$ 50. $35 + 2$ 51. $40 + 3$ 52. $22 + 8$

53. $14 + 6$ 54. $54 + 4$ 55. $15 + 8$ 56. $12 + 7$ 57. $41 + 5$

CHAPTER 10

Multiplication

Using Multiplication at Work

Peter O'Malley is a roofer. He needs 9 shingles for each square meter of roof. He multiplies 9×8 to find how many shingles he needs to cover a section of roof that measures 8 square meters. He needs 72 shingles to cover the section of roof.

Practicing Multiplication

Find the products.

1. 8×4 32   2. 5×3 3. 5×4 4. 1×7 5. 5×5

6. 4×6 7. 4×4 8. 2×6 9. 7×5 10. 5×6

11. 6×5 12. 6×1 13. 9×2 14. 5×2 15. 1×3

16. 7×4 17. 1×4 18. 9×3 19. 10×3 20. 3×8

21. 3×2 22. 7×2 23. 3×7 24. 10×6 25. 4×9

Multiply. Remember, any number times 0 is 0.

26. $\begin{array}{r} 5 \\ \times\ 0 \\ \hline \end{array}$ 27. $\begin{array}{r} 4 \\ \times\ 0 \\ \hline \end{array}$ 28. $\begin{array}{r} 10 \\ \times\ 8 \\ \hline \end{array}$

29. $\begin{array}{r} 2 \\ \times\ 0 \\ \hline \end{array}$ 30. $\begin{array}{r} 10 \\ \times\ 2 \\ \hline \end{array}$ 31. $\begin{array}{r} 6 \\ \times\ 0 \\ \hline \end{array}$

32. $\begin{array}{r} 10 \\ \times\ 7 \\ \hline \end{array}$ 33. $\begin{array}{r} 7 \\ \times\ 0 \\ \hline \end{array}$ 34. $\begin{array}{r} 0 \\ \times\ 5 \\ \hline \end{array}$

35. $\begin{array}{r} 0 \\ \times\ 9 \\ \hline \end{array}$ 36. $\begin{array}{r} 10 \\ \times\ 1 \\ \hline \end{array}$ 37. $\begin{array}{r} 8 \\ \times\ 0 \\ \hline \end{array}$

 Calculate
Find each answer.

38. $(4631 - 4625) \times 3$ 39. $(8756 - 8749) \times 4$ 40. $(6082 - 6078) \times 5$

Multiplying by 6

Put the edge of a ruler along each dotted line. Complete a multiplication fact for the drawing above the ruler.

$1 \times 6 = 6$

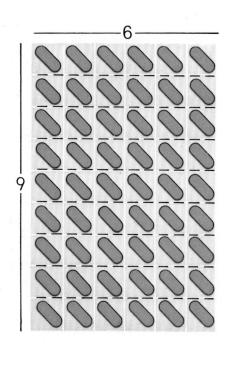

1. 1×6 6
2. 2×6
3. 3×6
4. 4×6
5. 5×6
6. 6×6
7. 7×6
8. 8×6
9. 9×6

Find the products.

10. $\begin{array}{r} 6 \\ \times 4 \\ \hline 24 \end{array}$	11. $\begin{array}{r} 6 \\ \times 6 \\ \hline \end{array}$	12. $\begin{array}{r} 5 \\ \times 6 \\ \hline \end{array}$	13. $\begin{array}{r} 6 \\ \times 7 \\ \hline \end{array}$	14. $\begin{array}{r} 6 \\ \times 0 \\ \hline \end{array}$	15. $\begin{array}{r} 8 \\ \times 6 \\ \hline \end{array}$	16. $\begin{array}{r} 6 \\ \times 6 \\ \hline \end{array}$
17. $\begin{array}{r} 4 \\ \times 6 \\ \hline \end{array}$	18. $\begin{array}{r} 3 \\ \times 6 \\ \hline \end{array}$	19. $\begin{array}{r} 10 \\ \times 6 \\ \hline \end{array}$	20. $\begin{array}{r} 9 \\ \times 6 \\ \hline \end{array}$	21. $\begin{array}{r} 1 \\ \times 6 \\ \hline \end{array}$	22. $\begin{array}{r} 6 \\ \times 5 \\ \hline \end{array}$	23. $\begin{array}{r} 7 \\ \times 6 \\ \hline \end{array}$

24. 6×10
25. 8×6
26. 3×6
27. 6×6
28. 9×6

Write a fact for each product. Use 6 as one of the factors.

29. 12
30. 24
31. 18
32. 0
33. 6
34. 42

35. 48
36. 54
37. 36
38. 30
39. 42
40. 60

Multiplying by 7

Put the edge of a ruler along each dotted line. Complete a multiplication fact for the drawing above the ruler.

$$1 \times 7 = 7$$

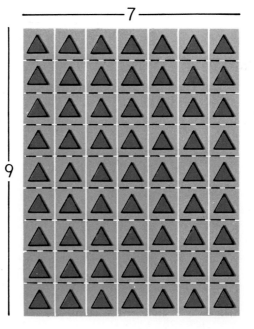

1. 1×7 7
2. 2×7
3. 3×7
4. 4×7
5. 5×7
6. 6×7
7. 7×7
8. 8×7
9. 9×7

Multiply.

10. $\begin{array}{r} 7 \\ \times 6 \\ \hline 42 \end{array}$
11. $\begin{array}{r} 7 \\ \times 2 \\ \hline \end{array}$
12. $\begin{array}{r} 8 \\ \times 7 \\ \hline \end{array}$
13. $\begin{array}{r} 7 \\ \times 1 \\ \hline \end{array}$
14. $\begin{array}{r} 7 \\ \times 7 \\ \hline \end{array}$
15. $\begin{array}{r} 3 \\ \times 7 \\ \hline \end{array}$
16. $\begin{array}{r} 10 \\ \times 7 \\ \hline \end{array}$

17. $\begin{array}{r} 7 \\ \times 8 \\ \hline \end{array}$
18. $\begin{array}{r} 7 \\ \times 7 \\ \hline \end{array}$
19. $\begin{array}{r} 7 \\ \times 0 \\ \hline \end{array}$
20. $\begin{array}{r} 10 \\ \times 7 \\ \hline \end{array}$
21. $\begin{array}{r} 7 \\ \times 9 \\ \hline \end{array}$
22. $\begin{array}{r} 5 \\ \times 7 \\ \hline \end{array}$
23. $\begin{array}{r} 7 \\ \times 3 \\ \hline \end{array}$

24. 1×7
25. 8×7
26. 6×7
27. 7×4
28. 7×9

 Challenge

Complete these facts.

29. $? \times 8 = 56$
30. $7 \times ? = 28$
31. $? \times 7 = 42$
32. $? \times 9 = 63$

Multiplying by 6 and 7

Multiply.

1. 6×8 48   2. 1×6 3. 5×7 4. 7×4 5. 9×7

6. 7×6 7. 7×2 8. 6×1 9. 0×7 10. 3×6

11. 7×3 12. 4×7 13. 6×6 14. 6×10 15. 7×10

16. 9×6 17. 6×10 18. 7×1 19. 6×4 20. 8×6

21. 3×7 22. 6×3 23. 0×6 24. 7×5 25. 1×7

26. 2×6 27. 8×7 28. 7×9 29. 6×7 30. 10×6

31. 7×8 32. 2×7 33. 6×5 34. 4×6 35. 6×2

36. 6×9 37. 5×6 38. 10×7 39. 7×0 40. 7×7

41. A garden has 6 rows of tomato plants. There are 8 plants in each row. How many tomato plants in all?

42. There are 7 rows of bean plants with 6 plants in each row. How many bean plants in all?

43. There are 4 rows of corn plants with 7 plants in each row. How many corn plants in all?

Multiplying by 8

Put the edge of a ruler along each dotted line. Complete a multiplication fact for the drawing above the ruler.

$$1 \times 8 = 8$$

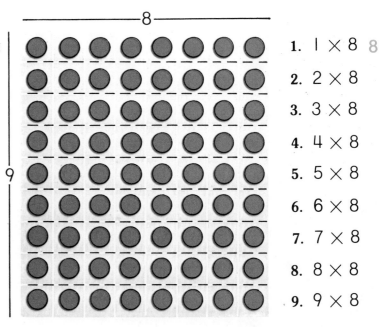

1. 1×8 8
2. 2×8
3. 3×8
4. 4×8
5. 5×8
6. 6×8
7. 7×8
8. 8×8
9. 9×8

Find the products.

10.	11.	12.	13.	14.	15.	16.
8	2	8	3	8	8	8
$\times 4$	$\times 8$	$\times 5$	$\times 8$	$\times 7$	$\times 1$	$\times 6$
32						

17.	18.	19.	20.	21.	22.	23.
8	6	7	8	8	10	4
$\times 8$	$\times 8$	$\times 8$	$\times 9$	$\times 0$	$\times 8$	$\times 8$

24. 8×5 25. 8×3 26. 8×8 27. 10×8 28. 9×8

Write a fact for each product. Use 8 as one of the factors.

29. 40   30. 24   31. 0   32. 16   33. 64   34. 72   35. 8

36. 32   37. 80   38. 56   39. 64   40. 48   41. 32   42. 56

Multiplying by 9

Multiply.

1. 9×9 81
2. 5×9
3. 9×7
4. 2×9

5. 9×6
6. 3×9
7. 4×9
8. 9×8

Crack the code to find the answer.

Why did Johnny take a ruler to bed?

Code	n	w	p	h	s	t	e	o	l	g
	9	18	27	36	45	54	63	72	81	90

9. $\begin{array}{r} 9 \\ \times 6 \\ \hline \end{array}$
10. $\begin{array}{r} 8 \\ \times 9 \\ \hline \end{array}$
11. $\begin{array}{r} 5 \\ \times 9 \\ \hline \end{array}$
12. $\begin{array}{r} 9 \\ \times 7 \\ \hline \end{array}$
13. $\begin{array}{r} 7 \\ \times 9 \\ \hline \end{array}$
14. $\begin{array}{r} 9 \\ \times 4 \\ \hline \end{array}$
15. $\begin{array}{r} 9 \\ \times 8 \\ \hline \end{array}$

16. $\begin{array}{r} 2 \\ \times 9 \\ \hline \end{array}$
17. $\begin{array}{r} 9 \\ \times 9 \\ \hline \end{array}$
18. $\begin{array}{r} 9 \\ \times 8 \\ \hline \end{array}$
19. $\begin{array}{r} 1 \\ \times 9 \\ \hline \end{array}$
20. $\begin{array}{r} 10 \\ \times 9 \\ \hline \end{array}$
21. $\begin{array}{r} 4 \\ \times 9 \\ \hline \end{array}$
22. $\begin{array}{r} 9 \\ \times 7 \\ \hline \end{array}$

23. $\begin{array}{r} 9 \\ \times 5 \\ \hline \end{array}$
24. $\begin{array}{r} 9 \\ \times 9 \\ \hline \end{array}$
25. $\begin{array}{r} 7 \\ \times 9 \\ \hline \end{array}$
26. $\begin{array}{r} 9 \\ \times 3 \\ \hline \end{array}$
27. $\begin{array}{r} 6 \\ \times 9 \\ \hline \end{array}$

28. The answer is

__ __   __ __ __   __ __ __   __ __ __ __

9.   10.   11.   12.   13.   14.   15.   16.   17.   18.   19.   20.

__ __   __ __ __ __ __

21.   22.   23.   24.   25.   26.   27.

Practicing Multiplication

Find the products.

1.	2.	3.	4.	5.	6.	7.
9	3	9	4	3	7	7
× 8	× 6	× 5	× 7	× 8	× 6	× 9
72						

8.	9.	10.	11.	12.	13.	14.
5	6	3	4	5	7	9
× 8	× 8	× 7	× 9	× 6	× 7	× 9

15.	16.	17.	18.	19.	20.	21.
6	5	7	8	6	8	8
× 6	× 7	× 8	× 8	× 9	× 4	× 9

22. 7 × 4   23. 5 × 8   24. 4 × 6   25. 7 × 6   26. 4 × 9

27. 8 × 7   28. 8 × 5   29. 4 × 7   30. 6 × 5   31. 0 × 8

32. 9 × 2   33. 7 × 1   34. 5 × 5   35. 3 × 9   36. 8 × 3

37. Ann and Maria go sledding
3 times. Each time they
sled for 2 hours. How many
hours do they sled in all?

 Review   (pp. 223–229)

1.	2.	3.	4.	5.	6.
7	8	8	8	7	7
× 6	× 7	× 8	× 9	× 7	× 9

Multiplication Chart

×	0	1	2	3	4	5	6	7	8	9	10
0	0	0	0	0	0	0	0	0	0	0	0
1	0	1	2	3	4	5	6	7	8	9	10
2	0	2	4	6	8	10	12	14	16	18	20
3	0	3	6	9	12	15	18	21	24	27	30
4	0	4	8	12	16	20	24	28	32	36	40
5	0	5	10	15	20	25	30	35	40	45	50
6	0	6	12	18	24	30	36	42	48	54	60
7	0	7	14	21	28	35	42	49	56	63	70
8	0	8	16	24	32	40	48	56	64	72	80
9	0	9	18	27	36	45	54	63	72	81	90
10	0	10	20	30	40	50	60	70	80	90	100

Use the table. Write as many different facts as you can for each product.

1. 27 $3 \times 9 = 27, 9 \times 3 = 27$

2. 12

3. 20

4. 40

5. 63

6. 56

7. 36

8. 24

9. 16

10. 18

11. 72

12. 54

13. 21

14. 28

15. 30

16. 32

17. 15

18. 42

19. 14

20. 45

21. 10

22. 48

Parade Problems

Solve each problem.

1. 7 drummers march in a row. There are 6 rows of drummers. How many drummers march?
$6 \times 7 = 42$

2. 5 people hold the strings for each giant balloon. There are 8 giant balloons. How many people hold strings?

3. There are 4 horse riders in each row. There are 9 rows of horse riders. How many horse riders in all?

4. There are 6 clowns on each float. There are 6 floats. How many clowns in all?

 Challenge

Find the answers to these problems.

5. A horse can learn 1 new trick in 3 weeks. How long will it take to teach him 8 tricks?

6. It takes 4 people 4 months to make one giant balloon. How long would it take 2 people to make the balloon?

Adding and Multiplying Two-Digit Numbers

If you can add, then you can multiply.

Step 1 Add ones.	Step 2 Add tens.	Step 1 Multiply ones.	Step 2 Multiply tens.
42 42 + 42 ――― 6	42 42 + 42 ――― 126	42 × 3 ――― 6	42 × 3 ――― 126

Multiply. Check the first row by adding.

1. 31   31
    × 2 + 31
    ――   ――
    62   62

2. 24
    × 2
    ――

3. 32
    × 3
    ――

4. 20
    × 4
    ――

5. 34
    × 2
    ――

6. 14
    × 2
    ――

7. 30
    × 3
    ――

8. 11
    × 7
    ――

9. 21
    × 3
    ――

10. 34
     × 2
     ――

11. 12
     × 3
     ――

12. 13
     × 3
     ――

13. 11
     × 9
     ――

14. 31
     × 4
     ――

15. 51
     × 6
     ――

16. 90
     × 5
     ――

17. 71
     × 8
     ――

18. 70
     × 3
     ――

19. 12
     × 4
     ――

20. 20
     × 3
     ――

21. 33
     × 2
     ――

22. 21
     × 7
     ――

23. 40
     × 6
     ――

Practicing Multiplication

Add and multiply.

1a. 62 62 + 62 186	**1b.** 62 × 3	**2a.** 44 + 44	**2b.** 44 × 2	**3a.** 43 43 + 43	**3b.** 43 × 3
4a. 21 21 21 + 21	**4b.** 21 × 4	**5a.** 50 50 + 50	**5b.** 50 × 3	**6a.** 32 32 32 + 32	**6b.** 32 × 4

Multiply.

7. 64 × 2	**8.** 22 × 3	**9.** 53 × 3	**10.** 72 × 3	**11.** 23 × 3	**12.** 84 × 2
13. 52 × 4	**14.** 91 × 5	**15.** 60 × 3			
16. 93 × 3	**17.** 61 × 7	**18.** 82 × 4			

19. An orchard has 55 rows of trees with 8 trees in each row. How many trees in all?

20. Juanita can pick 6 apples in one minute. How many apples can she pick in 25 minutes?

Multiply and Add Puzzle

4 times 3, plus 2 equals 14.

	×3	+2
4	12	14

4 × 3   12 + 2

Copy the tables. Fill in the missing numbers.

1.

	×3	+2
6	18	20
3		
4		

2.

	×2	+1
2		
3		
5		

3.

	×4	+4
0		
5		
7		

4.

	×5	+3
6		
0		
8		

5.

	×6	+2
3		
9		
4		

6.

	×3	+5
5		
2		
6		

7.

	×8	+1
10		
7		
6		

8.

	×4	+6
2		
9		
4		

9.

	×7	+3
7		
4		
5		

Trading Ones in Multiplication

Step 1
Multiply ones.
Trade 10 ones for 1 ten.

Step 2
Multiply tens.
Add tens from trade.

Check
by adding.

$$
\begin{array}{r}
\overset{1}{26} \\
\times\ 3 \\
\hline
8
\end{array}
$$

$3 \times 6 = 18$
$18 = 1$ ten 8 ones

$$
\begin{array}{r}
\overset{1}{26} \\
\times\ 3 \\
\hline
78
\end{array}
$$

Think:
3 ones $\times$ 2 tens = 6 tens
6 tens + 1 ten = 7 tens

$$
\begin{array}{r}
\overset{1}{26} \\
26 \\
+\ 26 \\
\hline
78
\end{array}
$$

Multiply. Check the first row by adding.

1. $\begin{array}{r} 18 \\ \times\ 4 \\ \hline 72 \end{array}$
2. $\begin{array}{r} 15 \\ \times\ 3 \\ \hline \end{array}$
3. $\begin{array}{r} 17 \\ \times\ 4 \\ \hline \end{array}$
4. $\begin{array}{r} 14 \\ \times\ 5 \\ \hline \end{array}$
5. $\begin{array}{r} 12 \\ \times\ 6 \\ \hline \end{array}$

6. $\begin{array}{r} 19 \\ \times\ 2 \\ \hline \end{array}$
7. $\begin{array}{r} 28 \\ \times\ 3 \\ \hline \end{array}$
8. $\begin{array}{r} 14 \\ \times\ 4 \\ \hline \end{array}$
9. $\begin{array}{r} 13 \\ \times\ 6 \\ \hline \end{array}$
10. $\begin{array}{r} 23 \\ \times\ 4 \\ \hline \end{array}$

11. $\begin{array}{r} 36 \\ \times\ 2 \\ \hline \end{array}$
12. $\begin{array}{r} 14 \\ \times\ 7 \\ \hline \end{array}$
13. $\begin{array}{r} 26 \\ \times\ 3 \\ \hline \end{array}$
14. $\begin{array}{r} 38 \\ \times\ 2 \\ \hline \end{array}$
15. $\begin{array}{r} 12 \\ \times\ 7 \\ \hline \end{array}$

16. $\begin{array}{r} 13 \\ \times\ 7 \\ \hline \end{array}$
17. $\begin{array}{r} 13 \\ \times\ 5 \\ \hline \end{array}$
18. $\begin{array}{r} 19 \\ \times\ 2 \\ \hline \end{array}$

19. Dr. Espinoza helps 47 people
each week. How many people
can she help in 2 weeks?

More Trading

Sometimes you trade.

No trading.   Trading.

$$\begin{array}{r} 42 \\ \times\ \ 3 \\ \hline 126 \end{array}$$
$$\begin{array}{r} 1 \\ 14 \\ \times\ \ 3 \\ \hline 42 \end{array}$$

Find the products.

1. $\begin{array}{r} 59 \\ \times\ 6 \\ \hline 354 \end{array}$
2. $\begin{array}{r} 17 \\ \times\ 3 \\ \hline \end{array}$
3. $\begin{array}{r} 12 \\ \times\ 4 \\ \hline \end{array}$

4. $\begin{array}{r} 14 \\ \times\ 7 \\ \hline \end{array}$
5. $\begin{array}{r} 27 \\ \times\ 3 \\ \hline \end{array}$
6. $\begin{array}{r} 17 \\ \times\ 5 \\ \hline \end{array}$
7. $\begin{array}{r} 19 \\ \times\ 3 \\ \hline \end{array}$
8. $\begin{array}{r} 38 \\ \times\ 2 \\ \hline \end{array}$
9. $\begin{array}{r} 20 \\ \times\ 5 \\ \hline \end{array}$

10. $\begin{array}{r} 54 \\ \times\ 3 \\ \hline \end{array}$
11. $\begin{array}{r} 45 \\ \times\ 3 \\ \hline \end{array}$
12. $\begin{array}{r} 35 \\ \times\ 5 \\ \hline \end{array}$
13. $\begin{array}{r} 43 \\ \times\ 4 \\ \hline \end{array}$
14. $\begin{array}{r} 32 \\ \times\ 5 \\ \hline \end{array}$
15. $\begin{array}{r} 26 \\ \times\ 2 \\ \hline \end{array}$

16. $\begin{array}{r} 28 \\ \times\ 4 \\ \hline \end{array}$
17. $\begin{array}{r} 22 \\ \times\ 8 \\ \hline \end{array}$
18. $\begin{array}{r} 37 \\ \times\ 4 \\ \hline \end{array}$
19. $\begin{array}{r} 55 \\ \times\ 6 \\ \hline \end{array}$
20. $\begin{array}{r} 70 \\ \times\ 2 \\ \hline \end{array}$
21. $\begin{array}{r} 42 \\ \times\ 5 \\ \hline \end{array}$

Review   (pp. 223–236)

1. $\begin{array}{r} 7 \\ \times\ 8 \\ \hline \end{array}$
2. $\begin{array}{r} 32 \\ \times\ 3 \\ \hline \end{array}$
3. $\begin{array}{r} 82 \\ \times\ 3 \\ \hline \end{array}$
4. $\begin{array}{r} 19 \\ \times\ 5 \\ \hline \end{array}$
5. $\begin{array}{r} 38 \\ \times\ 4 \\ \hline \end{array}$
6. $\begin{array}{r} 56 \\ \times\ 8 \\ \hline \end{array}$

Kit Problems

Multiply to solve each problem.

1. There are 7 parts in each toy car kit. How many parts in 23 kits? 161

2. There are 9 parts in each airplane kit. How many parts in 41 kits?

3. There are 5 parts in each kite kit. How many parts in 43 kits?

4. There are 8 parts in each sailboat kit. How many parts in 31 kits?

5. There are 9 parts in each lamp kit. How many parts in 50 kits?

6. There are 4 parts in each table kit. How many parts in 45 kits?

 Challenge

7. It takes 4 minutes to cut out the pieces for a kite. It takes 5 minutes to put the pieces together. How long does it take to make 34 kites?

Adding and Multiplying Hundreds

$132 + 132 + 132 = \boxed{?}$

You can add or multiply
to solve this problem.

Add ones.   Multiply ones.
Add tens.   Multiply tens.
Add hundreds.   Multiply hundreds.

```
  132
  132                 132
+ 132               ×   3
  396                 396
```

Find the products. Check the first row by adding.

1. 211 × 3 <u> </u> 633	2. 321 × 2	3. 700 × 4	4. 111 × 5	5. 455 × 1
6. 413 × 2	7. 500 × 3	8. 568 × 1	9. 121 × 4	10. 231 × 2
11. 432 × 2	12. 212 × 3	13. 220 × 4	14. 400 × 3	15. 657 × 0
16. 324 × 2	17. 600 × 2	18. 312 × 3	19. 222 × 4	20. 332 × 2

Multiplying Three Digits by One Digit

Step 1
Multiply ones.
Trade 10 ones for 1 ten.

$$\begin{array}{r} \overset{1}{4}37 \\ \times\quad 2 \\ \hline 4 \end{array}$$

Step 2
Multiply tens.
Add tens from trade.

$$\begin{array}{r} \overset{1}{4}37 \\ \times\quad 2 \\ \hline 74 \end{array}$$

Step 3
Multiply hundreds.

$$\begin{array}{r} \overset{1}{4}37 \\ \times\quad 2 \\ \hline 874 \end{array}$$

Multiply. Check the first row by adding.

1. $\begin{array}{r} 148 \\ \times\quad 2 \\ \hline 296 \end{array}$
2. $\begin{array}{r} 125 \\ \times\quad 3 \\ \hline \end{array}$
3. $\begin{array}{r} 115 \\ \times\quad 5 \\ \hline \end{array}$
4. $\begin{array}{r} 137 \\ \times\quad 2 \\ \hline \end{array}$
5. $\begin{array}{r} 236 \\ \times\quad 2 \\ \hline \end{array}$

6. $\begin{array}{r} 337 \\ \times\quad 2 \\ \hline \end{array}$
7. $\begin{array}{r} 116 \\ \times\quad 4 \\ \hline \end{array}$
8. $\begin{array}{r} 208 \\ \times\quad 3 \\ \hline \end{array}$
9. $\begin{array}{r} 129 \\ \times\quad 2 \\ \hline \end{array}$
10. $\begin{array}{r} 226 \\ \times\quad 2 \\ \hline \end{array}$

11. $\begin{array}{r} 127 \\ \times\quad 3 \\ \hline \end{array}$
12. $\begin{array}{r} 305 \\ \times\quad 4 \\ \hline \end{array}$
13. $\begin{array}{r} 114 \\ \times\quad 6 \\ \hline \end{array}$
14. $\begin{array}{r} 300 \\ \times\quad 7 \\ \hline \end{array}$
15. $\begin{array}{r} 118 \\ \times\quad 5 \\ \hline \end{array}$

16. $\begin{array}{r} 600 \\ \times\quad 3 \\ \hline \end{array}$
17. $\begin{array}{r} 425 \\ \times\quad 3 \\ \hline \end{array}$
18. $\begin{array}{r} 112 \\ \times\quad 9 \\ \hline \end{array}$
19. $\begin{array}{r} 400 \\ \times\quad 2 \\ \hline \end{array}$
20. $\begin{array}{r} 316 \\ \times\quad 3 \\ \hline \end{array}$

 Calculate

Multiply from left to right.

21. $8 \times 2 \times 3 \times 6 \times 7$

22. $6 \times 5 \times 5 \times 8 \times 4 \times 6 \times 3$

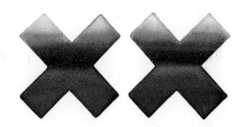

Practicing Multiplication

Remember these?

No trading.	Trading ones.	No trading.	Trading ones.
32 × 3 —— 96	17 × 4 —— 68	134 × 2 —— 268	114 × 6 —— 684

Multiply.

1. 8
× 6
——
48

2. 7
× 5

3. 4
× 6

4. 8
× 3

5. 6
× 7

6. 7
× 7

7. 9
× 6

8. 8
× 8

9. 16
× 5

10. 14
× 4

11. 12
× 8

12. 36
× 2

13. 28
× 3

14. 24
× 7

15. 28
× 3

16. 15
× 4

17. 46
× 3

18. 141
× 2

19. 122
× 3

20. 221
× 4

21. 438
× 2

22. 214
× 7

Multiplying Money

$$\begin{array}{r} \overset{1}{27}¢ \\ \times\ 2 \\ \hline 54¢ \end{array} \qquad \begin{array}{r} \overset{1}{\$3.16} \\ \times\ \ 3 \\ \hline \$9.48 \end{array}$$

Multiply. Remember to use . and $ in your answer.

1. $\begin{array}{r} \$4.29 \\ \times\ \ \ 2 \\ \hline \$8.58 \end{array}$
   2. $\begin{array}{r} 17¢ \\ \times\ 3 \\ \hline \end{array}$
   3. $\begin{array}{r} 39¢ \\ \times\ 2 \\ \hline \end{array}$
   4. $\begin{array}{r} 17¢ \\ \times\ 4 \\ \hline \end{array}$
   5. $\begin{array}{r} 16¢ \\ \times\ 5 \\ \hline \end{array}$

6. $\begin{array}{r} \$1.21 \\ \times\ \ \ 3 \\ \hline \end{array}$
   7. $\begin{array}{r} \$2.14 \\ \times\ \ \ 2 \\ \hline \end{array}$
   8. $\begin{array}{r} \$1.15 \\ \times\ \ \ 3 \\ \hline \end{array}$
   9. $\begin{array}{r} \$2.36 \\ \times\ \ \ 2 \\ \hline \end{array}$
   10. $\begin{array}{r} \$3.28 \\ \times\ \ \ 3 \\ \hline \end{array}$

11. $\begin{array}{r} \$1.48 \\ \times\ \ \ 2 \\ \hline \end{array}$
   12. $\begin{array}{r} \$1.09 \\ \times\ \ \ 3 \\ \hline \end{array}$
   13. $\begin{array}{r} \$1.23 \\ \times\ \ \ 4 \\ \hline \end{array}$
   14. $\begin{array}{r} \$1.00 \\ \times\ \ \ 5 \\ \hline \end{array}$
   15. $\begin{array}{r} \$1.14 \\ \times\ \ \ 6 \\ \hline \end{array}$

 Challenge

16. Larry and Ann bought 3 sandwiches at 75¢ each and 4 oranges at 15¢ each. How much did they spend?

Chapter Review

Find the products.   (ex. 1–5: p. 224),   (ex. 6–10: p. 225),   (ex. 11–17: p. 227),   (ex. 18–25: p. 228)

1. 3×6 2. 5×6 3. 6×4 4. 6×8 5. 4×6

6. 7×6 7. 7×7 8. 2×7 9. 9×7 10. 8×7

11. 7×8 12. 5×8 13. 8×4 14. 8×9 15. 8×8

16. 8×6 17. 8×3 18. 9×4 19. 5×9 20. 9×2

21. 7×9 22. 9×9 23. 9×8 24. 6×9 25. 9×1

Multiply.   (ex. 26–30: p. 232),   (ex. 31–35: p. 235),   (ex. 36–40: p. 239)

26.
$$\begin{array}{r} 34 \\ \times\ 2 \\ \hline \end{array}$$

27.
$$\begin{array}{r} 20 \\ \times\ 3 \\ \hline \end{array}$$

28.
$$\begin{array}{r} 11 \\ \times\ 6 \\ \hline \end{array}$$

29.
$$\begin{array}{r} 32 \\ \times\ 4 \\ \hline \end{array}$$

30.
$$\begin{array}{r} 10 \\ \times\ 5 \\ \hline \end{array}$$

31.
$$\begin{array}{r} 12 \\ \times\ 6 \\ \hline \end{array}$$

32.
$$\begin{array}{r} 16 \\ \times\ 4 \\ \hline \end{array}$$

33.
$$\begin{array}{r} 19 \\ \times\ 2 \\ \hline \end{array}$$

34.
$$\begin{array}{r} 26 \\ \times\ 3 \\ \hline \end{array}$$

35.
$$\begin{array}{r} 14 \\ \times\ 7 \\ \hline \end{array}$$

36.
$$\begin{array}{r} 326 \\ \times\ 2 \\ \hline \end{array}$$

37.
$$\begin{array}{r} 116 \\ \times\ 4 \\ \hline \end{array}$$

38.
$$\begin{array}{r} 114 \\ \times\ 5 \\ \hline \end{array}$$

39.
$$\begin{array}{r} 438 \\ \times\ 2 \\ \hline \end{array}$$

40.
$$\begin{array}{r} 218 \\ \times\ 3 \\ \hline \end{array}$$

Multiply.   (ex. 41–50: p. 241)

41.
$$\begin{array}{r} 16¢ \\ \times\ 5 \\ \hline \end{array}$$

42.
$$\begin{array}{r} 38¢ \\ \times\ 2 \\ \hline \end{array}$$

43.
$$\begin{array}{r} 17¢ \\ \times\ 4 \\ \hline \end{array}$$

44.
$$\begin{array}{r} \$1.13 \\ \times\ 6 \\ \hline \end{array}$$

45.
$$\begin{array}{r} \$1.24 \\ \times\ 3 \\ \hline \end{array}$$

46.
$$\begin{array}{r} 25¢ \\ \times\ 3 \\ \hline \end{array}$$

47.
$$\begin{array}{r} 18¢ \\ \times\ 9 \\ \hline \end{array}$$

48.
$$\begin{array}{r} 11¢ \\ \times\ 9 \\ \hline \end{array}$$

49.
$$\begin{array}{r} \$4.32 \\ \times\ 8 \\ \hline \end{array}$$

50.
$$\begin{array}{r} \$2.65 \\ \times\ 3 \\ \hline \end{array}$$

Chapter Test

Find the products.

1. 3×6
2. 9×6
3. 6×8
4. 4×6
5. 0×6

6. 2×7
7. 5×7
8. 7×4
9. 7×7
10. 7×9

11. 8×6
12. 8×8
13. 5×8
14. 8×7
15. 8×9

Multiply.

16.
$$\begin{array}{r} 30 \\ \times\ 3 \\ \hline \end{array}$$

17.
$$\begin{array}{r} 21 \\ \times\ 4 \\ \hline \end{array}$$

18.
$$\begin{array}{r} 64 \\ \times\ 2 \\ \hline \end{array}$$

19.
$$\begin{array}{r} 11 \\ \times\ 7 \\ \hline \end{array}$$

20.
$$\begin{array}{r} 22 \\ \times\ 2 \\ \hline \end{array}$$

21.
$$\begin{array}{r} 18 \\ \times\ 3 \\ \hline \end{array}$$

22.
$$\begin{array}{r} 24 \\ \times\ 4 \\ \hline \end{array}$$

23.
$$\begin{array}{r} 316 \\ \times\ 2 \\ \hline \end{array}$$

24.
$$\begin{array}{r} 111 \\ \times\ 5 \\ \hline \end{array}$$

25.
$$\begin{array}{r} 718 \\ \times\ 2 \\ \hline \end{array}$$

Multiply.

26.
$$\begin{array}{r} 27¢ \\ \times\ 2 \\ \hline \end{array}$$

27.
$$\begin{array}{r} 15¢ \\ \times\ 3 \\ \hline \end{array}$$

28.
$$\begin{array}{r} 16¢ \\ \times\ 5 \\ \hline \end{array}$$

29.
$$\begin{array}{r} \$1.14 \\ \times\ 4 \\ \hline \end{array}$$

30.
$$\begin{array}{r} \$1.26 \\ \times\ 2 \\ \hline \end{array}$$

Brush Up

Add or subtract.

1. 253
   $+ 467$

2. 457
   $- 120$

3. 1049
   $+ 6652$

4. 4996
   $- 2834$

5. 986
   $- 477$

6. 1659
   $+ 3426$

7. 890
   $- 677$

8. 239
   $+ 195$

9. 4327
   $- 1018$

10. 659
    $+ 343$

11. 8.9
    $- 1.4$

12. 0.5
    $+ 0.4$

13. 1.6
    $+ 3.2$

14. 5.7
    $- 1.9$

15. 8.5
    $- 4.6$

Multiply.

16. 4×8

17. 9×3

18. 6×5

19. 2×7

20. 7×7

21. 5×8

22. 3×7

23. 8×6

24. 5×9

25. 9×4

26. 64
    $\times 3$

27. 300
    $\times 5$

28. 863
    $\times 6$

29. $1.24
    $\times 8$

30. $2.72
    $\times 2$

Write decimals for these.

31. $\frac{1}{10}$

32. $3\frac{1}{10}$

33. $\frac{5}{10}$

34. $2\frac{4}{10}$

35. $\frac{8}{10}$

36. $2\frac{3}{10}$

Put these in order from least to greatest.

37. 0.6, 0.7, 0.1, 0.5

38. 0.9, 0.4, 1.0, 0.2

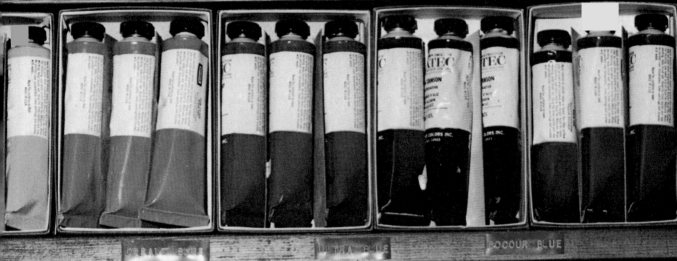

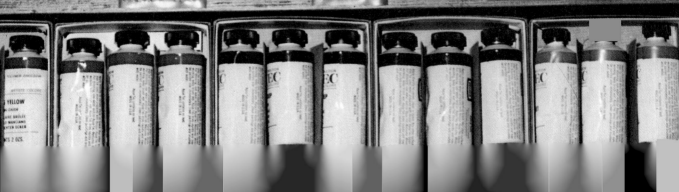

CHAPTER 11

Division

Using Division at Work

Carlos Escobar is a paper hanger. He has 10 rolls of wallpaper. He needs about 5 rolls for one room of a house. He divides 10 ÷ 5 to find how many rooms he can paper with the rolls he has. He has enough wallpaper for about 2 rooms.

Equal Groups

Write the answers.

1. There are 10 apples in all.
   a. How many apples on
      each tree?   5
   b. How many trees? 2

2. There are 12 flowers in all.
   a. How many flowers in
      each vase? 4
   b. How many vases?

3. There are 15 turtles in all.
   a. How many turtles on
      each rock?
   b. How many rocks?

4. There are 8 wheels in all.
   a. How many wheels on
      each bicycle?
   b. How many bicycles?

5. There are 15 birds in all.
   a. How many birds in
      each nest?
   b. How many nests?

Finding the Number of Groups

You have 12 crayons. You put 4 crayons in each group. How many groups do you make?

12 crayons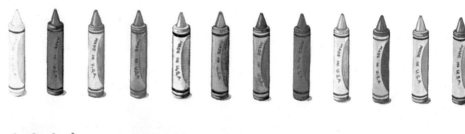

Groups of 4

You make 3 groups.

Use markers or pieces of paper. Write the answers.

1. Take 15 markers.
   Put 5 in each group.
   How many groups do you make? 3

2. Take 16 markers.
   Put 4 in each group.
   How many groups do you make?

3. Take 16 markers.
   Put 8 in each group.
   How many groups do you make?

4. Take 20 markers.
   Put 5 in each group.
   How many groups do you make?

5. Take 14 markers.
   Put 7 in each group.
   How many groups do you make?

6. Take 20 markers.
   Put 4 in each group.
   How many groups do you make?

Finding the Number in Each Group

You have 12 tops. You have 3 friends. You want
to give each friend a fair share of tops. How many
tops in each fair share?

12 tops

Make 3 fair shares.

Each friend gets 4 tops.

Use markers or pieces of paper. Write the answers.

1. Take 18 markers.
   Make 3 fair shares.
   How many in each fair share?   6

2. Take 20 markers.
   Make 5 fair shares.
   How many in each fair share?

3. Take 10 markers.
   Make 2 fair shares.
   How many in each fair share?

4. Take 12 markers.
   Make 6 fair shares.
   How many in each fair share?

5. Take 16 markers.
   Make 4 fair shares.
   How many in each fair share?

6. Take 14 markers.
   Make 7 fair shares.
   How many in each fair share?

Division Facts

Divide 12 into 3 fair shares.

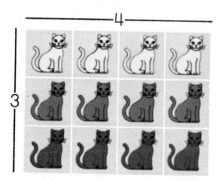

division fact

$$\begin{array}{r} 4 \\ 3\overline{)12} \end{array}$$

divisor   quotient

There are 3 fair shares.
There are 4 in each fair share.

Answer the question. Then write a division fact.
Make a drawing or use markers if you need help.

1. Divide 12 into 2 fair shares.
   How many in each fair share? 6 $2\overline{)12}$ with 6 above

2. Divide 18 into 3 fair shares.
   How many in each fair share?

3. Divide 18 into 6 fair shares.
   How many in each fair share?

4. Divide 20 into 5 fair shares.
   How many in each fair share?

5. Divide 20 into 2 fair shares.
   How many in each fair share?

Write a division fact.

6. There are 5 in each fair share.
   How many fair shares in 20?

7. There are 10 in each fair share.
   How many fair shares in 20?

8. There are 4 in each fair share.
   How many fair shares in 16?

9. There are 8 in each fair share.
   How many fair shares in 16?

Division Problems

Dan the storekeeper puts everything into equal groups.

He has 14 apples and 2 baskets. How many apples can he put in each basket?

number of apples in each basket ⌐

number of baskets → $2\overline{)14}$ ⌐7

number of apples ⌐

Use the pictures. Write a division fact.

1. How many oranges in each bag?

$$3\overline{)18}\,^{6}$$

2. How many lightbulbs in each box?

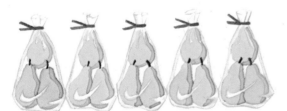

3. How many pears in each bag?

4. How many bars of soap in each package?

Division Facts for 2

You can write
two division
facts for
this drawing.

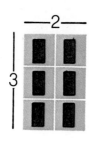

$$3 \overline{)6} ^{2} \leftarrow \begin{array}{l}\text{number in}\\\text{each row}\end{array}$$

$$2 \overline{)6} ^{3} \leftarrow \begin{array}{l}\text{number of}\\\text{rows}\end{array}$$

Write two division facts for each drawing.

1.
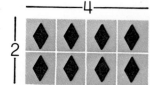

$$2 \overline{)8} ^{4} \qquad 4 \overline{)8} ^{2}$$

2.
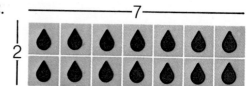

3.
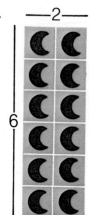

4.
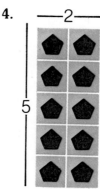

5.
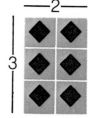

6.

7.
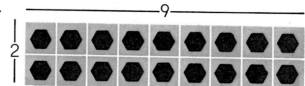

Practicing Division Facts for 2

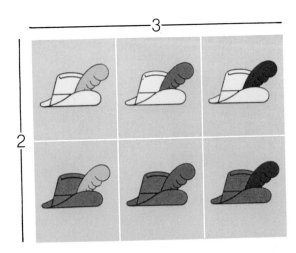

You can write two division facts and two multiplication facts for the drawing.

$$\begin{array}{r} 2 \\ \times\ 3 \\ \hline 6 \end{array} \qquad \begin{array}{r} 3 \\ \times\ 2 \\ \hline 6 \end{array} \qquad 2\overline{)6} \qquad 3\overline{)6}$$

Write two multiplication and two division facts for each drawing.

1.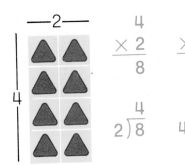

$$\begin{array}{r} 4 \\ \times\ 2 \\ \hline 8 \end{array} \qquad \begin{array}{r} 2 \\ \times\ 4 \\ \hline 8 \end{array}$$

$$2\overline{)8} \qquad 4\overline{)8}$$

2.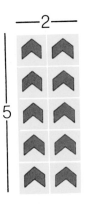

3.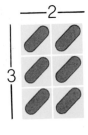

Multiply or divide.

4a. 2×7 4b. $2\overline{)14}$ 5a. 2×2 5b. $2\overline{)4}$

6a. 2×3 6b. $2\overline{)6}$ 7a. 2×4 7b. $2\overline{)8}$

8a. 2×8 8b. $2\overline{)16}$ 9a. 2×0 9b. $2\overline{)0}$

10a. 2×9 10b. $2\overline{)18}$ 11a. 2×6 11b. $2\overline{)12}$

12a. 2×5 12b. $2\overline{)10}$ 13a. 2×1 13b. $2\overline{)2}$

Division Facts for 3

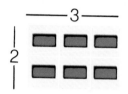

You can write division facts two ways.

$$3\overline{)6} \quad \begin{array}{c} 2 \end{array} \qquad 6 \div 3 = 2$$

Both mean six divided by three equals two.

Write four division facts for each drawing.

1.

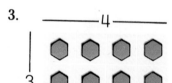

$$3\overline{)27} \qquad 9\overline{)27}$$

$$27 \div 3 = 9$$
$$27 \div 9 = 3$$

2.

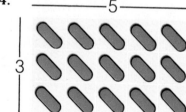

3.

4.

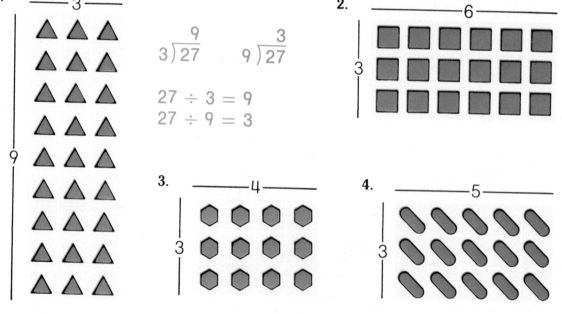

5.

6.

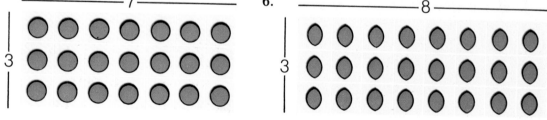

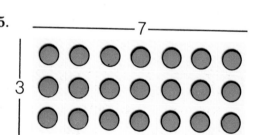

Practicing Division Facts for 2 and 3

Divide.

1. $3\overline{)12}$ (answer: 4)   2. $2\overline{)0}$ 3. $3\overline{)24}$ 4. $2\overline{)14}$ 5. $3\overline{)18}$

6. $2\overline{)8}$ 7. $3\overline{)9}$ 8. $2\overline{)16}$ 9. $3\overline{)21}$ 10. $2\overline{)18}$

11. $3\overline{)15}$ 12. $2\overline{)12}$ 13. $3\overline{)27}$ 14. $2\overline{)10}$ 15. $3\overline{)6}$

Divide.

16. $3 \div 3$ 17. $12 \div 2$ 18. $15 \div 3$ 19. $16 \div 2$ 20. $6 \div 3$

21. $2 \div 2$ 22. $21 \div 3$ 23. $18 \div 2$ 24. $12 \div 3$ 25. $6 \div 2$

26. $18 \div 3$ 27. $14 \div 2$ 28. $6 \div 3$ 29. $10 \div 2$ 30. $24 \div 3$

 Challenge
Find the answers by dividing.

31. Miguel has 12 toy animals. He gives an equal number to 3 children. How many does each child get?

32. Carol has 18 toy animals. She gives an equal number to 6 children. How many does each child get?

Division Facts for 4

Write two division facts for each drawing.

1.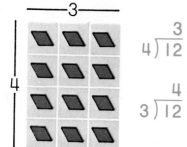

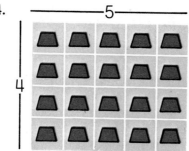

$$\begin{array}{r} 3 \\ 4\overline{)12} \end{array}$$

$$\begin{array}{r} 4 \\ 3\overline{)12} \end{array}$$

2.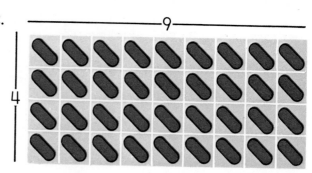

3.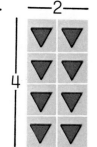

4.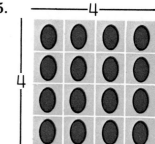

5.

6.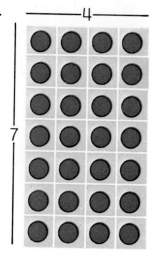

7.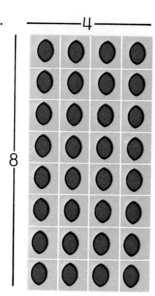

8.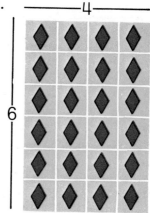

Practicing Division Facts for 2, 3, and 4

You can multiply to check division.

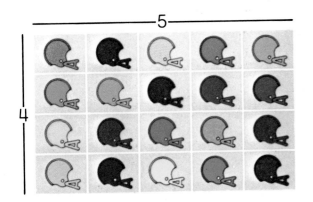

Divide.

$$4\overline{)20}^{5}$$

Check.

$$\begin{array}{r} 4 \\ \times\, 5 \\ \hline 20 \end{array}$$

Divide. Check your answers by multiplying.

1. $4\overline{)24}^{6}$ 2. $3\overline{)18}$ 3. $2\overline{)12}$ 4. $4\overline{)16}$ 5. $3\overline{)12}$

6. $2\overline{)8}$ 7. $3\overline{)27}$ 8. $3\overline{)9}$ 9. $2\overline{)6}$ 10. $2\overline{)16}$

11. $36 \div 4$ 12. $14 \div 2$ 13. $15 \div 3$ 14. $28 \div 4$ 15. $18 \div 2$

16. $16 \div 4$ 17. $21 \div 3$ 18. $8 \div 4$ 19. $20 \div 4$ 20. $8 \div 2$

21. $24 \div 3$ 22. $10 \div 2$ 23. $32 \div 4$ 24. $27 \div 3$ 25. $12 \div 4$

 Calculate

Work each problem from left to right.

26. $6 \times 5 \div 6 \times 7 \div 5$

27. $7 \times 8 \div 8 \times 3 \div 7$

28. $9 \times 9 \div 9 \times 2 \div 2$

29. $4 \times 5 \div 5 \times 4 \div 8$

Division Facts for 5

Write two division facts for each drawing.

1.
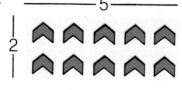

$$10 \div 2 = 5$$
$$10 \div 5 = 2$$

2.
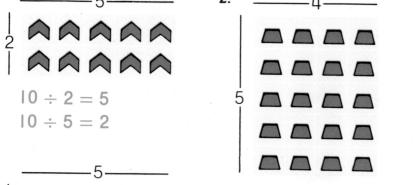

3.
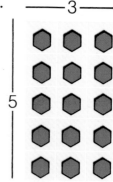

4.
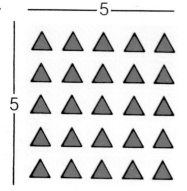

5.
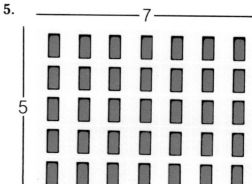

6.
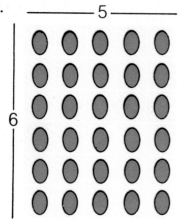

7.
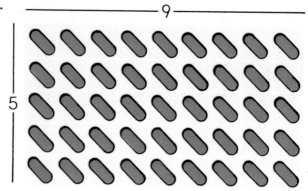

Division with 3, 4, and 5

Divide.

1. $4\overline{)24}$ → 6   2. $3\overline{)6}$ 3. $5\overline{)30}$ 4. $3\overline{)18}$ 5. $4\overline{)16}$

6. $3\overline{)21}$ 7. $5\overline{)45}$ 8. $4\overline{)28}$ 9. $3\overline{)3}$ 10. $5\overline{)25}$

11. $4\overline{)36}$ 12. $5\overline{)5}$ 13. $5\overline{)15}$ 14. $3\overline{)12}$ 15. $4\overline{)20}$

16. $27 \div 3$ 17. $35 \div 5$ 18. $12 \div 4$ 19. $8 \div 4$ 20. $15 \div 3$

21. $36 \div 4$ 22. $16 \div 4$ 23. $40 \div 5$ 24. $10 \div 5$ 25. $9 \div 3$

26. $32 \div 4$ 27. $4 \div 4$ 28. $24 \div 3$ 29. $27 \div 3$ 30. $20 \div 5$

31. $16 \div 4$ 32. $25 \div 5$

33. Alan has 28 photographs. If he puts 4 photographs on each page of his photo album, how many pages will he use?

 Review (pp. 247–259)

1. $2\overline{)16}$ 2. $3\overline{)27}$ 3. $3\overline{)18}$ 4. $28 \div 4$ 5. $35 \div 5$

0 and I in Division

When you divide any number by I,
the quotient is the same as the number.

$$1\overline{)4} \quad \text{quotient}$$

$$53 \div 1 = 53 \quad \text{quotient}$$

When you divide 0 by any number,
the quotient is 0.

$$0 \div 3 = 0 \qquad 23\overline{)0}$$

Divide.

1. $0 \div 5$ 0   2. $3 \div 1$ 3. $5 \div 1$ 4. $0 \div 6$ 5. $4 \div 1$

6. $7 \div 1$ 7. $9 \div 1$ 8. $0 \div 3$ 9. $12 \div 1$ 10. $0 \div 8$

11. $0 \div 2$ 12. $27 \div 1$ 13. $13 \div 1$ 14. $0 \div 1$ 15. $1 \div 1$

16. $1\overline{)2}$ 17. $1\overline{)8}$ 18. $1\overline{)0}$ 19. $14\overline{)0}$ 20. $12\overline{)0}$

21. $6\overline{)0}$ 22. $1\overline{)15}$ 23. $1\overline{)36}$ 24. $1\overline{)10}$ 25. $1\overline{)0}$

26. Linda has 6 plants. She
puts I plant in each pot.
How many pots does she need?

Division Facts for 6

$$6\overline{)36}^{\,6} \qquad 6\overline{)42}^{\,7} \qquad 6\overline{)48}^{\,8} \qquad 6\overline{)54}^{\,9}$$

Divide.

1. $6\overline{)42}^{\,7}$ 2. $6\overline{)12}$ 3. $6\overline{)24}$ 4. $6\overline{)48}$ 5. $6\overline{)18}$

6. $6\overline{)54}$ 7. $6\overline{)18}$ 8. $6\overline{)42}$ 9. $6\overline{)6}$ 10. $6\overline{)30}$

11. $6\overline{)36}$ 12. $6\overline{)42}$ 13. $6\overline{)0}$ 14. $6\overline{)48}$ 15. $6\overline{)24}$

16. $30 \div 6$ 17. $48 \div 6$ 18. $12 \div 6$ 19. $54 \div 6$ 20. $0 \div 6$

21. $6 \div 6$ 22. $24 \div 6$ 23. $42 \div 6$ 24. $36 \div 6$ 25. $18 \div 6$

26. Carl planted 54 trees. He put 6 trees in each row. How many rows did he plant?

27. Aline planted 36 bean plants. She put 6 plants in each row. How many rows did she plant?

Practicing Division Facts with 4, 5, and 6

Divide.

1. $18 \div 6$ 3   2. $12 \div 4$ 3. $45 \div 5$ 4. $6 \div 6$ 5. $28 \div 4$

6. $30 \div 6$ 7. $48 \div 6$ 8. $36 \div 4$ 9. $24 \div 4$ 10. $24 \div 6$

11. $42 \div 6$ 12. $35 \div 5$ 13. $8 \div 4$ 14. $40 \div 5$ 15. $32 \div 4$

16. $6\overline{)48}$ 17. $5\overline{)25}$ 18. $5\overline{)30}$ 19. $4\overline{)16}$ 20. $6\overline{)0}$

21. $6\overline{)36}$ 22. $5\overline{)15}$ 23. $6\overline{)12}$ 24. $4\overline{)20}$ 25. $6\overline{)54}$

26. $4\overline{)24}$ 27. $5\overline{)35}$ 28. $4\overline{)32}$ 29. $6\overline{)42}$ 30. $6\overline{)18}$

 Challenge

To find a product, multiply. To find a factor, divide.
Copy and complete these charts.

	Factor	Factor	Product
31.	?	4	24
32.	3	9	?
33.	5	?	35
34.	?	6	18
35.	1	?	7
36.	?	2	14

	Factor	Factor	Product
37.	3	?	21
38.	4	9	?
39.	?	7	35
40.	?	2	16
41.	4	8	?
42.	?	5	40

Multiplying and Dividing by 7

Multiplying by 7 can help you divide by 7.

$$7 \times 7 = 49 \qquad 49 \div 7 = 7$$

$$7 \times 8 = 56 \qquad 56 \div 7 = 8$$

$$7 \times 9 = 63 \qquad 63 \div 7 = 9$$

Find the products.

1. 5×7 35
2. 7×1
3. 2×7
4. 8×7
5. 7×0
6. 7×3
7. 7×6
8. 10×7
9. 4×7
10. 7×7
11. 9×7
12. 7×8
13. 7×2
14. 1×7
15. 7×5

Divide.

16. $7\overline{)42}$
17. $7\overline{)49}$
18. $7\overline{)35}$
19. $7\overline{)14}$
20. $7\overline{)7}$

21. $7\overline{)56}$
22. $7\overline{)63}$
23. $7\overline{)21}$
24. $7\overline{)28}$
25. $7\overline{)0}$

26. $63 \div 7$
27. $49 \div 7$
28. $0 \div 7$
29. $56 \div 7$
30. $7 \div 1$

Practicing Division Facts with 5, 6, and 7

Divide. Check the first row by multiplying.

1. $42 \div 7$ 6
2. $25 \div 5$
3. $14 \div 7$
4. $49 \div 7$
5. $36 \div 6$

6. $56 \div 7$
7. $42 \div 6$
8. $30 \div 5$
9. $56 \div 7$
10. $24 \div 6$

11. $63 \div 7$
12. $54 \div 6$
13. $21 \div 7$
14. $18 \div 6$
15. $20 \div 5$

16. $28 \div 7$
17. $48 \div 6$
18. $30 \div 6$
19. $35 \div 5$
20. $40 \div 5$

21. $15 \div 5$
22. $10 \div 5$
23. $45 \div 9$
24. $12 \div 6$
25. $14 \div 7$

Write a multiplication fact and a division fact for each number.

26. 56 $7 \times 8 = 56, 56 \div 8 = 7$
27. 12
28. 14
29. 21

30. 42
31. 30
32. 35
33. 63
34. 36
35. 40

36. 54
37. 20
38. 49

39. 18
40. 24
41. 48

 Challenge

42. There are 7 days in a week. Joe drinks 3 glasses of juice each day. How many glasses of juice does he drink in a week?

Division Facts for 8

$64 \div 8 = 8$

$72 \div 8 = 9$

Divide.

1. $48 \div 8$ 6
2. $32 \div 8$
3. $16 \div 8$
4. $0 \div 8$
5. $72 \div 8$
6. $24 \div 8$
7. $64 \div 8$
8. $40 \div 8$
9. $56 \div 8$
10. $72 \div 8$

Divide.

11. $8\overline{)16}$
12. $8\overline{)24}$
13. $8\overline{)56}$
14. $8\overline{)8}$
15. $8\overline{)32}$

16. $8\overline{)48}$
17. $8\overline{)40}$
18. $8\overline{)72}$
19. $8\overline{)64}$
20. $8\overline{)0}$

21. There are 35 children practicing for the music program. They sing in 5 equal groups. How many children in each group?

22. 72 chairs are needed for the program. The chairs are set up in 9 equal rows. How many chairs in each row?

Division Facts for 9

$$9\overline{)81}$$ with quotient 9

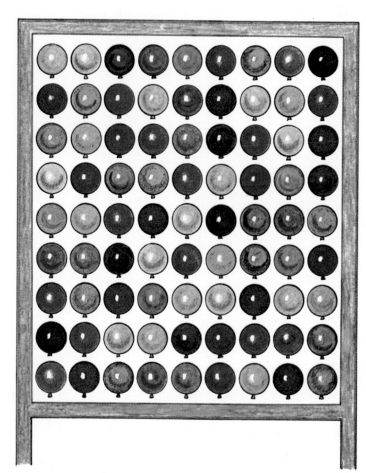

Divide.

1. $9\overline{)72}$ (with 8 written above)
2. $9\overline{)45}$
3. $9\overline{)18}$
4. $9\overline{)81}$
5. $9\overline{)27}$

6. $9\overline{)54}$
7. $9\overline{)9}$
8. $9\overline{)36}$
9. $9\overline{)63}$
10. $9\overline{)18}$

11. $45 \div 9$
12. $81 \div 9$
13. $0 \div 9$
14. $72 \div 9$
15. $9 \div 9$

16. $18 \div 9$
17. $54 \div 9$
18. $63 \div 9$
19. $36 \div 9$
20. $27 \div 9$

Practicing Division

Divide.

1. $54 \div 9$ 6
2. $12 \div 3$
3. $10 \div 5$

4. $16 \div 2$
5. $36 \div 4$
6. $28 \div 4$

7. $45 \div 5$
8. $36 \div 6$
9. $21 \div 7$

10. $42 \div 6$
11. $18 \div 2$
12. $24 \div 8$

13. $27 \div 3$
14. $45 \div 9$
15. $16 \div 4$

16. $15 \div 5$
17. $18 \div 6$
18. $81 \div 9$

19. $9 \div 3$
20. $48 \div 8$
21. $24 \div 4$

22. $20 \div 5$
23. $12 \div 6$
24. $72 \div 8$

25. $35 \div 7$
26. $32 \div 8$
27. $48 \div 6$

28. $28 \div 7$
29. $20 \div 5$
30. $49 \div 7$

31. $56 \div 8$
32. $30 \div 6$
33. $36 \div 9$

34. $16 \div 8$
35. $40 \div 5$
36. $56 \div 7$

 Review (pp. 247–267)

1. $3\overline{)24}$
2. $6\overline{)48}$
3. $7\overline{)49}$
4. $8\overline{)56}$
5. $9\overline{)63}$

Camping Problems

Divide to solve these problems.

1. 45 people come to Camp Keegan. 5 people stay in each cabin. How many cabins?   9

2. 4 people can use one canoe. There are 32 people. How many canoes do they need?

3. The hikers walked 18 kilometers in 3 hours. How far did they walk each hour?

4. 7 hikers brought 21 sandwiches. How many sandwiches for each?

5. Paula can swim across the lake in 8 minutes. How many times can she swim across the lake in 24 minutes?

6. It costs $9 a day to stay at Camp Keegan. Jack pays $54. How many days does he stay?

7. Campers sit by the fire and each tells 2 ghost stories. They tell 18 stories in all. How many campers are there?

8. There are 6 players on each ball team. There are 36 players. How many teams?

Add and Divide Puzzle

Step 1
Add 4 to
each number.

$10 + 4 = 14$

Step 2
Divide that
number by 2.

$14 \div 2 = 7$

	+4	÷2
10	14	7
12	16	8
16	20	10

Copy and complete these puzzles.

1.

	+2	÷4
14	16	4
30		
22		

2.

	+6	÷3
21		
9		
12		

3.

	+4	÷8
12		
28		
52		

4.

	+5	÷5
25		
15		
45		

5.

	+8	÷2
10		
18		
14		

6.

	+1	÷9
62		
8		
26		

7.

	+4	÷7
52		
17		
45		

8.

	+3	÷6
33		
21		
39		

9.

	+5	÷3
22		
13		
16		

Division with Remainders

$3\overline{)23}$ You cannot make 3 fair shares with 2 tens,
so trade 2 tens 3 ones for 23 ones. Then divide.

$$\begin{array}{r} 7\ r2 \\ 3\overline{)23} \end{array}$$

You get 7 ones in each share
and 2 left over.

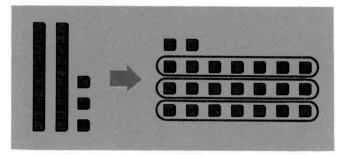

Use markers or pieces of paper. Write the answers.

1. Take 18 markers.
   Make 7 fair shares.
   a. How many in each share?   2
   b. How many left over?   4

2. Take 11 markers.
   Make 2 fair shares.
   a. How many in each share?
   b. How many left over?

3. Take 16 markers.
   Make 5 fair shares.
   a. How many in each share?
   b. How many left over?

4. Take 24 markers.
   Make 5 fair shares.
   a. How many in each share?
   b. How many left over?

5. Take 10 markers.
   Make 3 fair shares.
   a. How many in each share?
   b. How many left over?

6. Take 17 markers.
   Make 5 fair shares.
   a. How many in each share?
   b. How many left over?

7. Take 22 markers.
   Make 6 fair shares.
   a. How many in each share?
   b. How many left over?

8. Take 16 markers.
   Make 3 fair shares.
   a. How many in each share?
   b. How many left over?

Finding Remainders

A multiplication table can help you divide.

To find $3\overline{)20}$, think:

$$\begin{array}{c} 6 \\ 3\overline{)18} \end{array} \text{ and } \begin{array}{c} 7 \\ 3\overline{)21}, \end{array}$$

so the answer to $3\overline{)20}$
must be 6 with a **remainder**.

×	1	2	3	4	5	6	7	8	9
2	2	4	6	8	10	12	14	16	18
3	3	6	9	12	15	18	21	24	27

quotient $\begin{array}{c} \text{6 r2} \quad \text{remainder} \\ 3\overline{)20} \\ \underline{-18} \quad 6 \times 3 = 18 \\ 2 \end{array}$

divisor

First find the quotient 6.
Then multiply: $6 \times 3 = 18$.
Then subtract: $20 - 18 = 2$.
2 is the remainder.

**Use the multiplication table. Divide. Remember,
the remainder must be less than the divisor.**

1. $\begin{array}{c} \text{4 r1} \\ 2\overline{)9} \end{array}$ 2. $3\overline{)7}$ 3. $2\overline{)19}$ 4. $3\overline{)11}$ 5. $2\overline{)15}$

6. $3\overline{)17}$ 7. $2\overline{)7}$ 8. $2\overline{)13}$ 9. $3\overline{)25}$ 10. $2\overline{)17}$

11. $3\overline{)13}$ 12. $3\overline{)14}$ 13. $2\overline{)11}$ 14. $3\overline{)23}$ 15. $3\overline{)5}$

16. $3\overline{)10}$ 17. $2\overline{)5}$ 18. $3\overline{)22}$ 19. $3\overline{)20}$ 20. $2\overline{)25}$

21. $2\overline{)19}$ 22. $3\overline{)28}$ 23. $3\overline{)16}$ 24. $2\overline{)21}$ 25. $3\overline{)26}$

More Division with Remainders

The remainder must be less than the divisor.

$$\begin{array}{r} 8 \text{ r2} \\ 4\overline{)34} \\ -32 \\ \hline 2 \end{array}$$

Divide.

1. $4\overline{)14}$ **3 r2**   2. $5\overline{)16}$ 3. $4\overline{)21}$ 4. $5\overline{)18}$ 5. $5\overline{)22}$

6. $4\overline{)10}$ 7. $5\overline{)11}$ 8. $5\overline{)19}$ 9. $4\overline{)15}$ 10. $5\overline{)24}$

11. $4\overline{)27}$ 12. $5\overline{)26}$ 13. $4\overline{)19}$ 14. $5\overline{)36}$ 15. $4\overline{)30}$

16. $5\overline{)32}$ 17. $4\overline{)13}$ 18. $5\overline{)37}$ 19. $5\overline{)21}$ 20. $4\overline{)19}$

 Calculate

Work each problem from left to right.

21. $18 \div 9 \times 6 \div 4 \times 5$ 22. $12 \div 4 \times 3 \times 3 \div 9$

23. $7 \times 5 \div 1 \div 7 \times 4$ 24. $7 \times 6 \div 2 \div 3 \times 1$

25. $6 \times 6 \div 9 \times 7 \div 2$ 26. $6 \times 4 \div 3 \times 5 \div 2$

Two-Digit Quotients

$2\overline{)68}$ There are enough tens to make equal groups.

Step 1
Divide tens.
Multiply. Subtract.

$$\begin{array}{r} 3 \\ 2\overline{)68} \\ -6 \\ \hline 0 \end{array}$$ 3 tens × 2 = 6 tens

Step 2
Bring down ones.

$$\begin{array}{r} 3 \\ 2\overline{)68} \\ -6 \\ \hline 08 \end{array}$$

Step 3
Divide ones.
Multiply. Subtract.

$$\begin{array}{r} 34 \\ 2\overline{)68} \\ -6 \\ \hline 08 \\ -8 \\ \hline 0 \end{array}$$ 4 × 2 = 8

This is 6 tens and 8 ones divided into 2 equal parts.

Divide.

1. $6\overline{)60}$ (10)

2. $4\overline{)84}$

3. $3\overline{)36}$

4. $5\overline{)55}$

5. $3\overline{)63}$

6. $2\overline{)80}$

7. $7\overline{)77}$

8. $2\overline{)64}$

9. $4\overline{)88}$

10. $3\overline{)60}$

11. $2\overline{)84}$

12. $9\overline{)99}$

13. $5\overline{)50}$

14. $2\overline{)86}$

15. $3\overline{)30}$

Two-Digit Quotients with Remainders

Step 1
Divide tens. Multiply.
Subtract. Bring down ones.

$$
\begin{array}{r}
1 \\
5\overline{)69} \\
-5 \\
\hline
19
\end{array}
$$

Step 2
Divide ones.
Multiply. Subtract.

$$
\begin{array}{r}
13 \\
5\overline{)69} \\
-5 \\
\hline
19 \\
-15 \\
\hline
4
\end{array}
$$

Step 3
Write the
remainder.

$$
\begin{array}{r}
13\ r4 \\
5\overline{)69} \\
-5 \\
\hline
19 \\
-15 \\
\hline
4
\end{array}
$$

Divide.

1. 27 r2
   3)83

2. 2)37

3. 3)41

4. 5)62

5. 3)44

6. 2)35

7. 5)73

8. 3)47

9. 4)54

10. 7)94

11. 3)71

12. 2)59

13. 6)73

14. 5)76

15. 4)37

16. 4)89

17. 3)52

18. 2)97

19. 6)85

20. 5)82

21. 5)77

22. 2)31

23. 6)91

24. 7)82

25. 4)47

26. 2)61

27. 5)59

28. 8)93

29. 6)67

30. 7)87

More Quotients with Remainders

Divide.

1. 7)83 $\overset{\text{I I r6}}{}$

2. 2)27

3. 3)41

4. 5)68

5. 4)59

6. 2)31

7. 6)93

8. 4)75

9. 5)83

10. 6)74

11. 3)79

12. 8)95

13. 6)85

14. 4)66

15. 2)49

16. 7)81

17. 2)63

18. 5)82

19. 2)33

20. 3)86

21. 7)97

22. 5)77

23. 3)41

24. 4)47

25. 7)82

26. 6)43

27. 5)81

 Challenge

Divide to solve these problems.

28. Larry buys 4 blue pencils for 28¢ and 6 red pencils for 48¢. Which pencils cost more?

29. Julie buys 7 green pencils for 63¢ and 8 orange pencils for 64¢. Which pencils cost more?

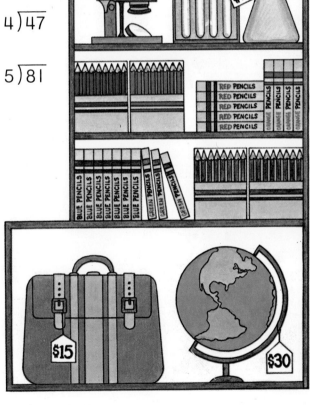

Divide. (ex. 1–2: p. 252), (ex. 3–5: p. 254),
(ex. 6–8: p. 256), (ex. 9–10: p. 258), (ex. 11–15: p. 260)

1. $2\overline{)8}$ 2. $2\overline{)18}$ 3. $3\overline{)27}$ 4. $3\overline{)24}$ 5. $3\overline{)15}$

6. $4\overline{)28}$ 7. $4\overline{)16}$ 8. $4\overline{)24}$ 9. $5\overline{)40}$ 10. $5\overline{)35}$

11. $0 \div 4$ 12. $3 \div 1$ 13. $5 \div 1$ 14. $0 \div 8$ 15. $0 \div 1$

Divide. (ex. 16–17: p. 261), (ex. 18–20: p. 263),
(ex. 21–25: p. 265), (ex. 26–30: p. 266)

16. $6\overline{)30}$ 17. $6\overline{)18}$ 18. $7\overline{)35}$ 19. $7\overline{)14}$ 20. $7\overline{)63}$

21. $64 \div 8$ 22. $32 \div 8$ 23. $56 \div 8$ 24. $16 \div 8$ 25. $48 \div 8$

26. $18 \div 9$ 27. $81 \div 9$ 28. $45 \div 9$ 29. $72 \div 9$ 30. $36 \div 9$

Divide. (ex. 31–35: p. 271), (ex. 36–40: p. 273),
(ex. 41–45: p. 274)

31. $3\overline{)13}$ 32. $2\overline{)7}$ 33. $2\overline{)11}$ 34. $3\overline{)20}$ 35. $2\overline{)17}$

36. $2\overline{)84}$ 37. $5\overline{)50}$ 38. $3\overline{)36}$ 39. $4\overline{)88}$ 40. $5\overline{)55}$

41. $5\overline{)59}$ 42. $8\overline{)95}$ 43. $6\overline{)71}$ 44. $3\overline{)47}$ 45. $7\overline{)84}$

Chapter Test

Divide.

1. $2\overline{)14}$ 2. $4\overline{)20}$ 3. $5\overline{)25}$ 4. $3\overline{)18}$ 5. $5\overline{)15}$

6. $36 \div 4$ 7. $0 \div 6$ 8. $21 \div 3$ 9. $0 \div 8$ 10. $8 \div 1$

Divide.

11. $6\overline{)12}$ 12. $6\overline{)24}$ 13. $8\overline{)32}$ 14. $8\overline{)48}$ 15. $9\overline{)81}$

16. $63 \div 7$ 17. $56 \div 7$ 18. $54 \div 9$ 19. $32 \div 8$ 20. $18 \div 6$

Divide.

21. $2\overline{)9}$ 22. $3\overline{)17}$ 23. $2\overline{)13}$ 24. $2\overline{)15}$ 25. $3\overline{)11}$

26. $2\overline{)64}$ 27. $3\overline{)36}$ 28. $6\overline{)84}$ 29. $6\overline{)64}$ 30. $8\overline{)91}$

or subtract.

1. $\begin{array}{r} 82 \\ + 9 \\ \hline \end{array}$ 2. $\begin{array}{r} 65 \\ + 38 \\ \hline \end{array}$ 3. $\begin{array}{r} 48 \\ + 38 \\ \hline \end{array}$ 4. $\begin{array}{r} 367 \\ + 254 \\ \hline \end{array}$ 5. $\begin{array}{r} 159 \\ + 436 \\ \hline \end{array}$

6. $\begin{array}{r} 73 \\ - 6 \\ \hline \end{array}$ 7. $\begin{array}{r} 55 \\ - 27 \\ \hline \end{array}$ 8. $\begin{array}{r} 80 \\ - 53 \\ \hline \end{array}$ 9. $\begin{array}{r} 745 \\ - 228 \\ \hline \end{array}$ 10. $\begin{array}{r} 304 \\ - 175 \\ \hline \end{array}$

Multiply or divide.

11. $\begin{array}{r} 8 \\ \times 3 \\ \hline \end{array}$ 12. $\begin{array}{r} 7 \\ \times 8 \\ \hline \end{array}$ 13. $\begin{array}{r} 9 \\ \times 4 \\ \hline \end{array}$ 14. $\begin{array}{r} 6 \\ \times 5 \\ \hline \end{array}$ 15. $\begin{array}{r} 8 \\ \times 8 \\ \hline \end{array}$

16. $\begin{array}{r} 20 \\ \times 4 \\ \hline \end{array}$ 17. $\begin{array}{r} 14 \\ \times 5 \\ \hline \end{array}$ 18. $\begin{array}{r} 119 \\ \times 2 \\ \hline \end{array}$ 19. $\begin{array}{r} 127 \\ \times 3 \\ \hline \end{array}$ 20. $\begin{array}{r} 113 \\ \times 4 \\ \hline \end{array}$

21. $4\overline{)24}$ 22. $6\overline{)42}$ 23. $5\overline{)45}$ 24. $9\overline{)63}$ 25. $8\overline{)56}$

26. $2\overline{)15}$ 27. $5\overline{)34}$ 28. $3\overline{)63}$ 29. $2\overline{)83}$ 30. $7\overline{)97}$

Write the name of each shape.

31.    32. 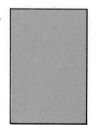   33. 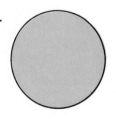   34.

CHAPTER 12

Measurement

Using Measurement at Work

Tom Simon works in a fabric store. A customer needs 3 meters of material to make a skirt and 2 meters to make a matching blouse. Tom adds 3 meters + 2 meters to find how many meters of material to cut in all. Tom cuts a piece of material 5 meters long.

Measuring to the Nearest Centimeter

The line is 1 **centimeter** long.
You can write **cm** for centimeter.

⊢——⊣
1 cm

The ribbon is about 6 centimeters long.

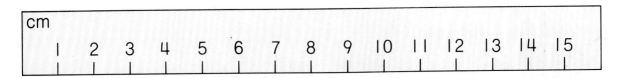

Make a careful guess. Then measure each object to the nearest centimeter.

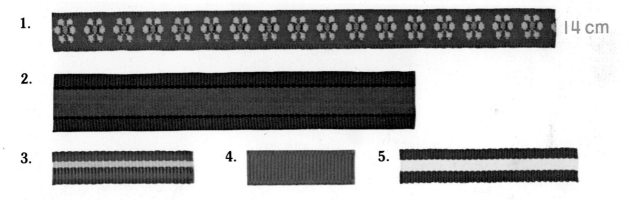

1. 14 cm

2.

3.   4.   5.

Measure these. Write the lengths in centimeters.

6.    7.

8. 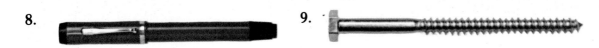   9.

Meters

There are 100 cm in a **meter**.
You can write **m** for meter.

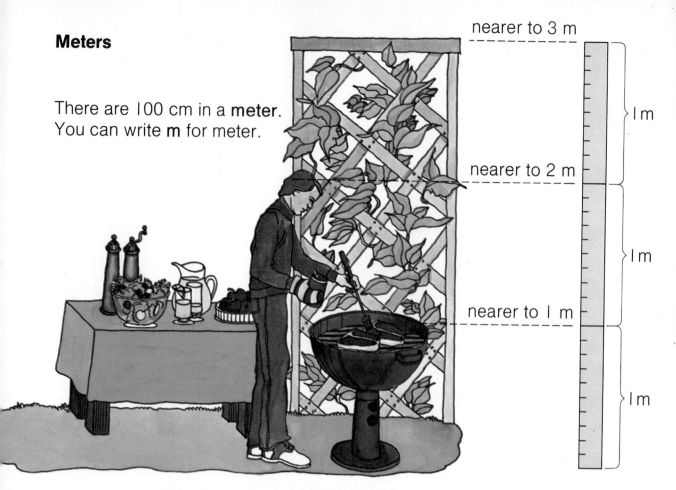

nearer to 3 m

1 m

nearer to 2 m

1 m

nearer to 1 m

1 m

Which are more than a meter?
Which are less than a meter? Write the answers.

1. your arm   less

2. your foot

3. a ladder

4. a door's height

5. a car

6. a book

7. the length of the chalkboard

8. the length of your classroom

Calculate

Add. Which answer is greater?

9a. 15 cm + 6 cm + 23 cm + 33 cm + 19 cm
b. 26 cm + 7 cm + 48 cm + 5 cm + 17 cm

Graphing Heights

Bar graphs are used to show and compare information.

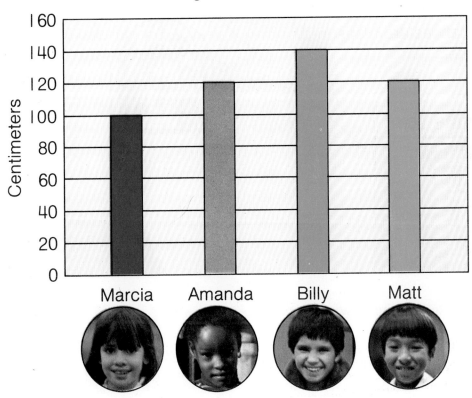

Heights of Four Children

Use the bar graph to answer these questions.

1. Is any child 160 cm tall? no

2. Who is the tallest person?

3. Which child is 120 cm tall?

4. Which child is 140 cm tall?

5. How much taller than Amanda is Billy?

6. How much taller than Marcia is Amanda?

7. Is the tallest person taller than 150 cm?

8. How much taller than Matt is Billy?

Kilometers

There are 1000 meters in a **kilometer**.
You can write **km** for kilometer.
You could walk 1 km
in about 10 minutes.
Long distances are measured
in kilometers.

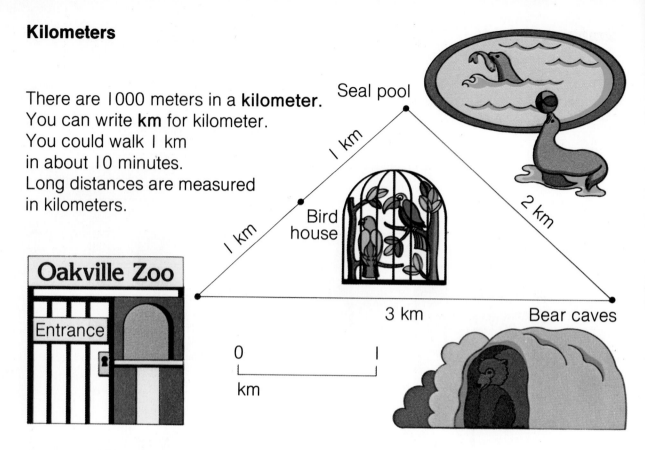

Seal pool

1 km

1 km

2 km

Bird house

3 km

Bear caves

Oakville Zoo

Entrance

0   1

km

Use the map to find the answers.

1. How many kilometers from the entrance to the bear caves?   3 km

2. How many kilometers from the bear caves to the seal pool?

3. How many kilometers from the seal pool to the bird house?

4. How many kilometers in a round trip around the zoo?

 Challenge

Would you use centimeters, meters, or kilometers to measure these?

5. the length of your bedroom

6. the width of a stamp

7. the length of a bus

8. the distance between two cities

Perimeter

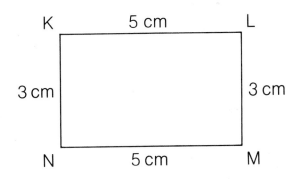

K   5 cm   L

3 cm   3 cm

N   5 cm   M

The **perimeter** of a shape is the distance around it. To find the perimeter of a shape, add the lengths of its sides.

$$3 \text{ cm} + 5 \text{ cm} + 3 \text{ cm} + 5 \text{ cm} = 16 \text{ cm}$$

The perimeter is 16 cm.

Measure the length of each side to the nearest centimeter. Add to find the perimeter.

1.

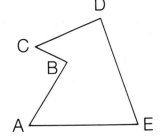

1a. X to Y   3 cm
  b. Y to Z
  c. Z to X
  d. Perimeter is ▨ cm.

2.

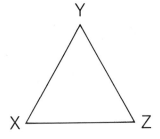

2a. A to B
  b. B to C
  c. C to D
  d. D to E
  e. E to A
  f. Perimeter is ▨ cm.

3.

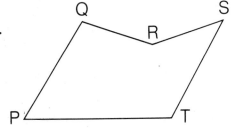

3a. P to Q
  b. Q to R
  c. R to S
  d. S to T
  e. T to P
  f. Perimeter is ▨ cm.

Perimeter Problems

The lengths of the sides have been measured for you.
Find the perimeters.

1.
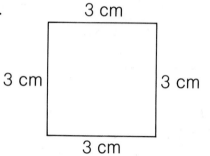

3 cm

3 cm   3 cm

3 cm

12 cm

2.
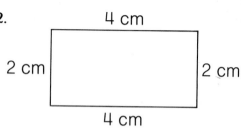

4 cm

2 cm   2 cm

4 cm

3.
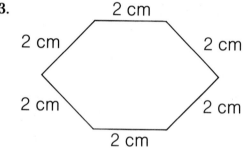

2 cm

2 cm   2 cm

2 cm   2 cm

2 cm

4.
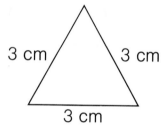

3 cm   3 cm

3 cm

5.
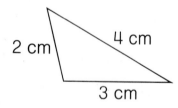

2 cm   4 cm

3 cm

6.
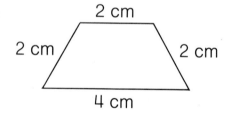

2 cm

2 cm   2 cm

4 cm

 Challenge

Find the answer.

7. Sarah's bedroom is square. Each
   side of the room is 10 meters long.
   What is the perimeter of her bedroom?

Area

The **area** of a surface is measured
in square units. One square unit
is a **square centimeter** or
square cm.

This rectangle has 2 rows of
square centimeters. Each row
has 4 square centimeters.

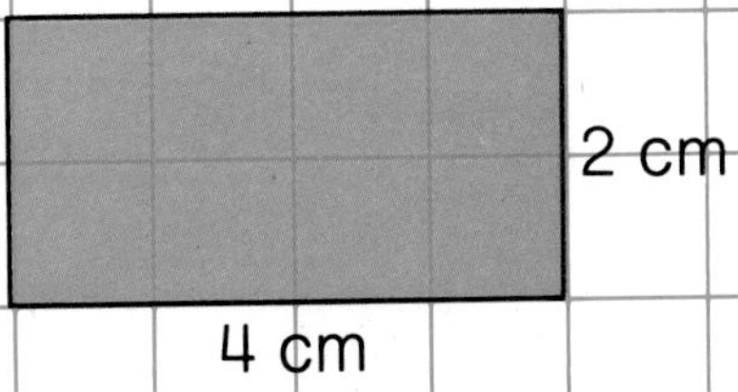

☐ I square centimeter

2 cm

4 cm

The area is
8 square cm.

Find the area of each surface.
Write your answer in square centimeters.

1.

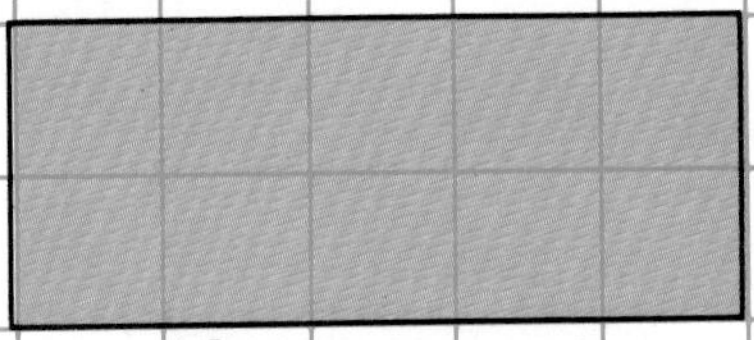

10 square cm

2.

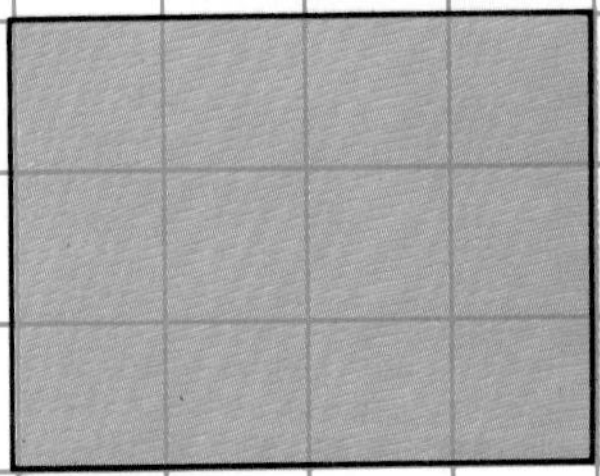

3.

4.

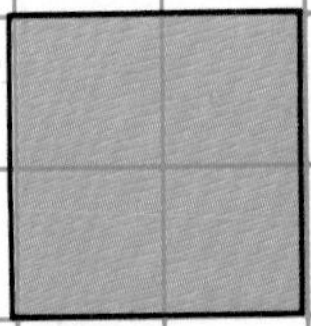

5.

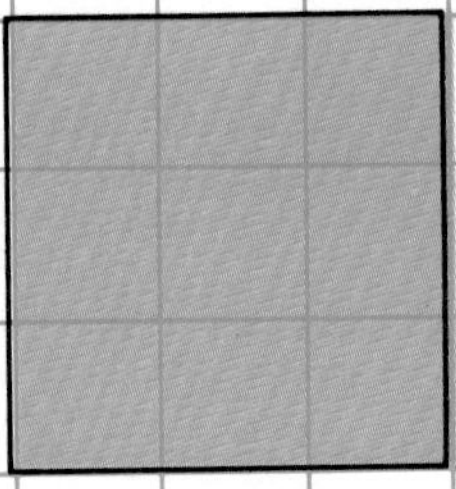

6.

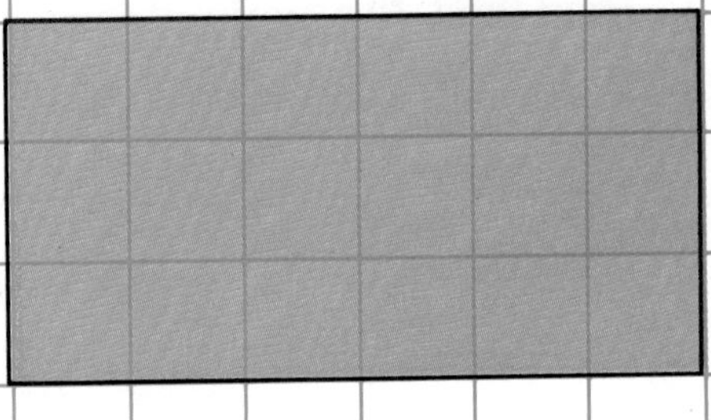

Volume

This is a **cubic centimeter** or **cubic cm**.
Cubic centimeters are used to measure
volume.

The volume is 8 cubic cm.

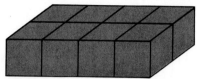

How many cubic centimeters?

1.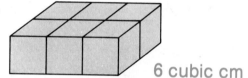

6 cubic cm

2.

3.

4.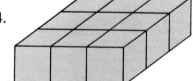

 Review   (pp. 281–288)

Measure the length of each side to the nearest centimeter.
Then find the perimeter.

1.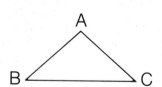

2.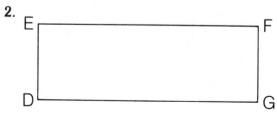

Grams and Kilograms

A paper clip weighs about
I **gram (g)**.

There are I000 grams
in I kilogram.

A book weighs about
I **kilogram (kg)**.

Would you use grams or kilograms to measure the weights?

1.  grams

2.

3.

4.

5.

6.

Choosing Grams or Kilograms

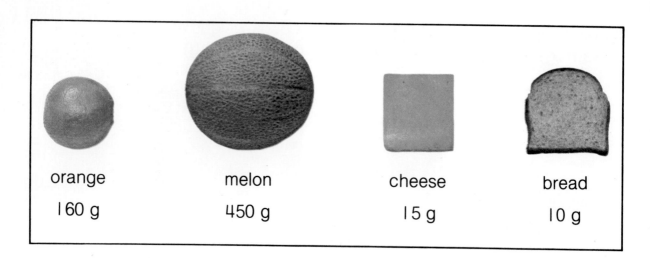

orange	melon	cheese	bread
160 g	450 g	15 g	10 g

Use the pictures. Add or subtract to find the answers.

1. How much more does the melon weigh than the orange?   290 g

2. How much do 2 oranges weigh?

3. You make a sandwich with 2 pieces of bread and 3 slices of cheese. How much does it weigh?

4. You order about a kilogram (1000 grams) of melons. How many melons will you get?

Choose the best answer.

5. A telephone weighs about 2 g, 20 g, or 2 kg.

6. A cat weighs about 5 g, 5 kg, or 50 kg.

7. An egg weighs about 50 g, 5 kg, or 50 kg.

8. 2 loaves of bread weigh about 1 g, 1 kg, or 10 kg.

9. A piece of chalk weighs about 10 g, 1 kg, or 10 kg.

10. A nickel weighs about 5 g, 500 g, or 5 kg.

Liters

A cubic centimeter holds 1 **milliliter (ml)** of liquid. There are 1000 milliliters in 1 **liter (ℓ)** of liquid.

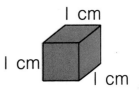

1 cm
1 cm
1 cm

250 ml

500 ml

30 ml

Add or subtract to find the answers.

1. Walt has a liter of milk. He uses 500 milliliters to make soup. How much is left?
   500 ml

2. Teresa has a liter of juice. She drinks 800 milliliters. How much is left?

3. There were 2 liters of soup. After dinner there are only 500 milliliters left. How much soup was served at dinner?

4. Linda has 300 milliliters of milk. She needs a liter for her recipe. How much more does she need?

 Challenge

5. Bryan has 585 milliliters orange juice, 420 milliliters apple juice, and a punch bowl that holds 1 liter. Will all the juice fit in the bowl? If not, how much will be left over?

Temperature in Degrees Celsius

Temperature can be measured in **degrees Celsius (°C).** Each mark on this thermometer stands for 2 degrees.

37° Celsius is written 37°C.

Use the thermometer.
What temperature is shown
for each of these?

1. hot summer day   32°C

2. body temperature

3. cool fall day

4. temperature indoors

5. water boils

6. water freezes

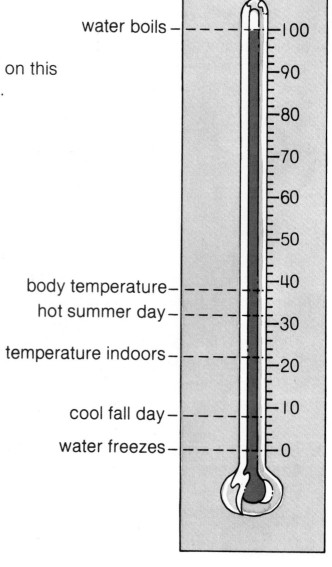

Choose the best answer.

7. A nice spring day would be about 15°C or 50°C.

8. A cold winter day would be about 30°C or 3°C.

9. You want to make ice cubes. What temperature do you need, 0°C or 10°C?

10. Which air temperature is more comfortable, 14°C or 40°C?

Measuring to the Nearest Inch

This line is **I inch** long.
You can write **in.** for inch.

$\vdash$————$\dashv$
I in.

The crayon is about 3 in. long.

in.						
	1	2	3	4	5	6

Make a careful guess. Then measure each object to the nearest inch.

1.

4 in.

2.

3.

4.

5.

6.

7.

Feet, Yards, and Miles

These units are also used
to measure length.

1 foot (ft)	= 12 inches
1 yard (yd)	= 3 feet
1 yard	= 36 inches
1 mile (mi)	= 1760 yards
1 mile	= 5280 feet

Write more or less to answer these.

1. Is your arm more or less than a foot long?   more

2. Is your arm more or less than a yard long?

3. Is a car more or less than 2 yards long?

4. Is a penny more or less than an inch wide?

5. Is a loaf of bread more or less than a yard long?

6. Is it more or less than a mile from your bedroom to the kitchen?

7. Is a pencil more or less than a foot long?

8. Is a tree more or less than a mile high?

9. Is a tree more or less than a yard high?

10. Are your fingers more or less than an inch long?

Cups, Pints, and Quarts

You can use these units to measure liquids.

| I pint (pt) = 2 cups |
| I quart (qt) = 2 pints |
| I quart = 4 cups |

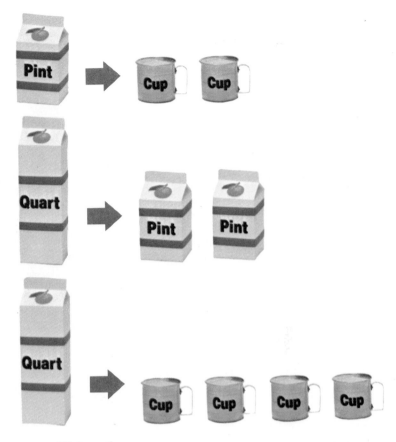

Use the table at the top of the page. Write the answers.

1. Carol has 2 quarts of juice. She drinks 2 cups. How many cups does she have left?   6 cups

2. Warren has I quart of water. He drinks 3 cups. How much does he have left?

3. Phil has 2 pints of soup. How many quarts is that?

4. Laura has 6 cups of milk. How many pints is that?

5. Paul has 7 cups of milk. Is that more or less than 2 quarts?

6. Melissa has 5 pints of juice. Is that more or less than 2 quarts?

 **Review**   (pp. 281–295)

1. 100 cm = ⬚ m

2. 6 ft = ⬚ yd

3. 2 ft = ⬚ in.

Cups, Pints, Quarts, and Gallons

Gallons are also used
to measure liquids.

I gallon (gal) = 4 quarts I gallon = 8 pints I gallon = 16 cups

Use the table at the top of the page. Write the answers.

1. Before the party there was a gallon of orange juice. The guests drank 3 quarts of juice. How much juice was left?   I quart

2. To make fruit punch you need 4 quarts orange juice, 3 quarts grape juice, and I quart lemonade. How many gallons is that?

3. Each guest at the party drinks I cup of juice. How many guests will I gallon serve?

4. Karen wants to make 2 gallons of fruit punch. She has 6 quarts. How many more quarts does she need?

5. Is I gallon more or less than 18 cups?

6. Is 7 quarts more or less than 2 gallons?

Ounces, Pounds, and Tons

Ounces, pounds, and **tons**
are used to measure weight.

| I pound (lb) = I6 ounces (oz) |
| I ton (T) = 2000 pounds |

8 ounces   60 pounds   2 tons

Choose the best answer.

1. This book weighs about
   2 oz, 2 lb, or 20 lb.   2 lb

2. A canary weighs about
   6 lb, 6 oz, or 6 tons.

3. A small car weighs about
   I00 lb, I00 oz, or I ton.

4. A loaf of bread weighs about
   I6 oz, I6 lb, or I60 oz.

5. A hamburger weighs about
   40 oz, 4 oz, or 4 lb.

6. A dog weighs about 40 oz,
   40 lb, or 400 lb.

 Challenge

7. A baby elephant weighs 200 lb.
   How many baby elephants
   weigh a ton?

8. A small seal weighs 500 lb.
   How many small seals weigh
   a ton?

Graphing Weight

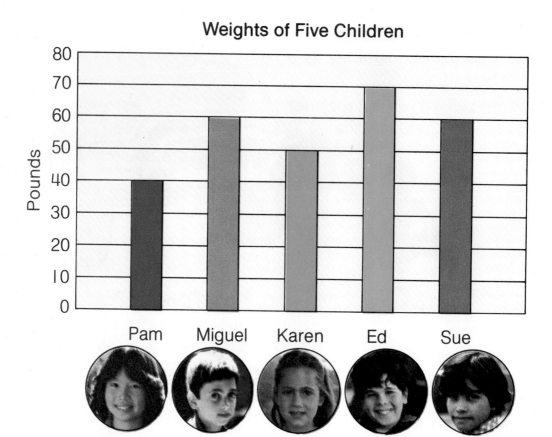

Weights of Five Children

Pounds

80
70
60
50
40
30
20
10
0

Pam   Miguel   Karen   Ed   Sue

Use the bar graph to find the answers.

1. The scale on this bar graph shows weight from ⬚ pounds to ⬚ pounds.   0, 80

2. How much does Miguel weigh?

3. How much does Ed weigh?

4. How much does Karen weigh?

5. How much more does Ed weigh than Miguel?

6. How much more does Ed weigh than Karen?

7. How much do the girls weigh together?

8. How much do the boys weigh together?

Temperature in Degrees Fahrenheit

Temperature can be measured in
degrees Fahrenheit (°F). Each mark
on this thermometer stands for
2 degrees.

70 degrees Fahrenheit
is written 70°F.

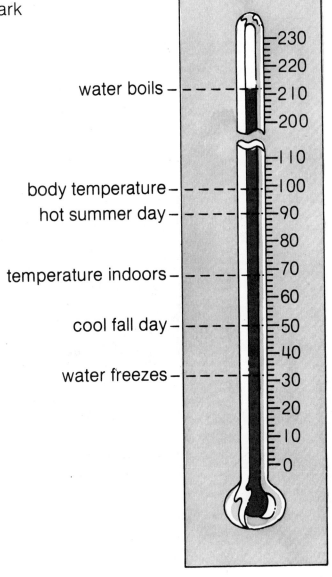

**Use the thermometer.
What temperature is shown
for each of these?**

1. water boils   212°F

2. temperature indoors

3. hot summer day

4. body temperature

5. water freezes

6. cool fall day

 Calculate

7. Find the average of these temperatures:
   30°F, 32°F, 40°F, 46°F. (Hint: Add. Then divide by 4.)

Chapter Review

Measure these. Write the lengths in centimeters.   (ex. 1–2: p. 281)

1.

2.

Choose the best answer.   (ex. 3: p. 282),   (ex. 4: p. 284),   (ex. 5–6: p. 289)

3. The door is 3 centimeters, 3 meters, or 30 meters high.

4. The road is 150 centimeters, 15 meters, or 15 kilometers long.

5. A nickel weighs about 5 grams, 500 grams, or 5 kilograms.

6. A dog weighs about 3 grams, 30 grams, or 30 kilograms.

Measure these. Write the lengths in inches.   (ex. 7–8: p. 293)

7.

8.

Choose the best answer.   (ex. 9–10: p. 294),   (ex. 11: p. 296),   (ex. 12: p. 297)

9. A pencil is about 6 inches, 6 feet, or 60 inches long.

10. The road is 9 yards, 9 feet, or 9 miles long.

11. You would drink 2 cups, 2 quarts, or 2 gallons of milk with dinner.

12. A sandwich weighs about 4 pounds, 50 ounces, or 4 ounces.

Chapter Test

Measure these. Write the lengths in centimeters.

1.

2.

Choose the best answer.

3. Jim walks 1 kilometer, 100 centimeters, or 1 meter to school.

4. The room is 12 meters, 120 centimeters, or 120 meters long.

5. A pencil weighs about 60 grams, 600 grams, or 6 grams.

6. A cat weighs about 5 grams, 50 grams, or 5 kilograms.

Measure these. Write the lengths in inches.

7.

8.

Choose the best answer.

9. This book weighs about 2 pounds, 2 ounces, or 20 pounds.

10. An apple weighs about 4 ounces, 4 pounds, or 40 ounces.

11. The child is 5 inches, 50 inches, or 5 yards high.

12. The rug is 9 inches, 9 feet, or 900 yards long.

Brush Up

Add, subtract, multiply, or divide.

1. 37
    + 23

2. 49
    + 94

3. 278
    + 36

4. 654
    + 355

5. 496
    + 489

6. 45
    − 9

7. 50
    − 34

8. 768
    − 458

9. 532
    − 346

10. 800
     − 291

11. 9
     × 7

12. 7
     × 8

13. 39
     × 2

14. 15
     × 4

15. 128
     × 3

16. 8)42

17. 5)45

18. 6)42

19. 4)84

20. 5)76

21. 93¢
     − 24¢

22. 58¢
     − 27¢

23. $4.18
     − 2.11

24. $3.25
     − 1.85

25. $6.00
     − 3.50

Which is greater?

26. 4376 or 4637

27. $\frac{3}{4}$ or $\frac{3}{8}$

28. $\frac{1}{4}$ or $\frac{1}{2}$

29. 0.3 or 0.2

Measure the length of each side to the nearest centimeter.
Add to find the perimeter.

30a. A to B
  b. B to C
  c. C to D
  d. D to A
  e. Perimeter is ▯ cm.

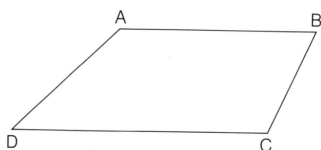

Extra Practice

Set 1 For use after pages 9–13.
Add or subtract.

1. $\begin{array}{r} 2 \\ + 4 \\ \hline \end{array}$
2. $\begin{array}{r} 14 \\ - 6 \\ \hline \end{array}$
3. $\begin{array}{r} 9 \\ + 6 \\ \hline \end{array}$
4. $\begin{array}{r} 11 \\ - 7 \\ \hline \end{array}$
5. $\begin{array}{r} 4 \\ + 8 \\ \hline \end{array}$
6. $\begin{array}{r} 4 \\ - 2 \\ \hline \end{array}$

7. $\begin{array}{r} 10 \\ - 5 \\ \hline \end{array}$
8. $\begin{array}{r} 12 \\ - 6 \\ \hline \end{array}$
9. $\begin{array}{r} 8 \\ + 2 \\ \hline \end{array}$
10. $\begin{array}{r} 10 \\ - 9 \\ \hline \end{array}$
11. $\begin{array}{r} 6 \\ + 4 \\ \hline \end{array}$
12. $\begin{array}{r} 16 \\ - 9 \\ \hline \end{array}$

13. $8 + 8$
14. $13 - 8$
15. $3 + 2$
16. $7 - 4$
17. $5 + 7$
18. $16 - 7$
19. $9 + 4$
20. $8 - 3$
21. $8 + 5$
22. $18 - 9$

Set 2 For use after pages 17–18.
Add or subtract.

1. $7 + 3 + 6$
2. $8 + 1 + 5$
3. $2 + 6 + 8$
4. $5 + 7 + 1$
5. $3 + 7 + 3$
6. $2 + 3 + 6$
7. $1 + 6 + 4$
8. $5 + 2 + 8$
9. $(6 + 4) - 3$
10. $(11 - 5) + 2$
11. $8 + (1 + 9)$
12. $9 - (11 - 8)$

Set 3 For use after pages 22–25.
Add or subtract.

1. $\begin{array}{r} 60 \\ + 20 \\ \hline \end{array}$
2. $\begin{array}{r} 40 \\ + 30 \\ \hline \end{array}$
3. $\begin{array}{r} 50 \\ + 10 \\ \hline \end{array}$
4. $\begin{array}{r} 80 \\ - 70 \\ \hline \end{array}$
5. $\begin{array}{r} 70 \\ - 60 \\ \hline \end{array}$
6. $\begin{array}{r} 90 \\ - 30 \\ \hline \end{array}$

7. $\begin{array}{r} 21 \\ + 43 \\ \hline \end{array}$
8. $\begin{array}{r} 14 \\ + 32 \\ \hline \end{array}$
9. $\begin{array}{r} 33 \\ + 16 \\ \hline \end{array}$
10. $\begin{array}{r} 71 \\ + 4 \\ \hline \end{array}$
11. $\begin{array}{r} 52 \\ + 23 \\ \hline \end{array}$
12. $\begin{array}{r} 72 \\ + 15 \\ \hline \end{array}$

13. $\begin{array}{r} 88 \\ - 45 \\ \hline \end{array}$
14. $\begin{array}{r} 75 \\ - 22 \\ \hline \end{array}$
15. $\begin{array}{r} 43 \\ - 12 \\ \hline \end{array}$
16. $\begin{array}{r} 28 \\ - 13 \\ \hline \end{array}$
17. $\begin{array}{r} 36 \\ - 15 \\ \hline \end{array}$
18. $\begin{array}{r} 55 \\ - 22 \\ \hline \end{array}$

Set 4   For use after pages 31–34.
Copy and complete.

1. 58 = ▢ tens ▢ ones

2. 96 = ▢ tens ▢ ones

3. 77 = ▢ tens ▢ ones

4. 42 = ▢ tens ▢ ones

5. 35 = ▢ tens ▢ ones

6. 29 = ▢ tens ▢ ones

Write the number that is greater.

7. 48 or 52   8. 24 or 28   9. 36 or 34   10. 89 or 98

11. 64 or 43   12. 42 or 24   13. 25 or 52   14. 34 or 43

15. 55 or 77   16. 21 or 19   17. 27 or 32   18. 18 or 81

19. 54 or 45   20. 32 or 23   21. 43 or 34   22. 56 or 65

Set 5   For use after pages 35–37.
Round to the nearest ten.

1. 27   2. 43   3. 56   4. 78   5. 92   6. 88   7. 12

8. 24   9. 51   10. 16   11. 39   12. 45   13. 62   14. 8

Set 6   For use after pages 38–40.
Write the numbers.

1. 7 hundreds 9 tens 6 ones

2. 7 hundreds 1 ten 3 ones

3. 5 hundreds 2 tens 8 ones

4. 4 hundreds 8 ones

Write the sums.

5.	6.	7.	8.	9.	10.
200	800	600	300	500	900
60	40	50	30	80	20
+ 3	+ 7	+ 9	+ 3	+ 6	+ 1

Set 7 For use after pages 40–42.

Answer the questions.

1. Use the number 781.
   a. What is the total value of the digit 8?
   b. What is the total value of the digit 7?
   c. What is the total value of the digit 1?

2. Use the number 346.
   a. What is the total value of the digit 3?
   b. What is the total value of the digit 6?
   c. What is the total value of the digit 4?

Set 8 For use after pages 43–44.

Order these numbers. Use > for is greater than and < for is less than.

1. 500 ◯ 700
2. 485 ◯ 475
3. 380 ◯ 382
4. 506 ◯ 526
5. 438 ◯ 483
6. 640 ◯ 604
7. 658 ◯ 586
8. 792 ◯ 927

Set 9 For use after pages 45–47.

Answer the questions.

1. Use the number 1673.
   a. What is the total value of the digit 7?
   b. What is the total value of the digit 1?
   c. What is the total value of the digit 6?

2. Use the number 9765.
   a. What is the total value of the digit 5?
   b. What is the total value of the digit 9?
   c. What is the total value of the digit 7?

Set 10 For use after pages 48–49.

Find the rule and the next number.

1. 35, 40, 45, 50, ☐
2. 3, 6, 9, 12, ☐
3. 20, 18, 16, 14, ☐
4. 4, 8, 12, 16, ☐

Set 11 For use after pages 55–57.
Add.

1. 15
   + 83

2. 53
   + 14

3. 81
   + 13

4. 64
   + 25

5. 29
   + 30

6. 77
   + 22

7. 231
   + 425

8. 152
   + 501

9. 184
   + 210

10. 435
   + 241

11. 873
   + 114

12. 789
   + 210

13. 6053 + 424

14. 22 + 657

15. 3124 + 2023

16. 663 + 1124

17. 8342 + 1346

18. 18 + 961

19. 4322 + 4675

20. 781 + 1218

21. 2423 + 4375

22. 34 + 843

23. 3729 + 4160

24. 523 + 4366

Set 12 For use after pages 60–64.
Add and trade.

1. 56
   + 15

2. 45
   + 36

3. 74
   + 18

4. 67
   + 27

5. 58
   + 24

6. 39
   + 29

7. 29
   + 17

8. 25
   + 16

9. 36
   + 28

10. 47
   + 14

11. 55
   + 28

12. 48
   + 25

13. 14
    36
   + 22

14. 36
    16
   + 13

15. 25
    13
   + 5

16. 34
    16
   + 7

17. 16
    25
   + 4

18. 47
    15
   + 11

Set 13 For use after pages 65–67.
Add.

1. 261
   + 193

2. 375
   + 244

3. 281
   + 365

4. 370
   + 241

5. 566
   + 262

6. 462
   + 181

7. 344
   + 260

8. 753
   + 153

9. 291
   + 346

10. 461
   + 358

11. 592
   + 136

12. 363
   + 274

Set 14 For use after pages 68–75.

Find the sums.

1. 296 + 515	2. 219 + 195	3. 189 + 237	4. 639 + 177	5. 556 + 464	6. 782 + 239

7. 192
   316
 + 215

8. 154
    45
 + 423

9. 348
   184
 + 18

10. 259
    136
 + 222

11. 765
    54
 + 389

12. 309
   262
 + 487

13. 456 + 157   14. 696 + 344   15. 288 + 767   16. 749 + 292

Set 15 For use after pages 76–81.

Add.

1. 3654
 + 2358

2. 6734
 + 378

3. 5795
 + 2965

4. 4629
 + 2593

5. 1532
 + 7889

6. 4965
   8734
 + 189

7. 8609
    394
 + 236

8. 6728
   1364
 + 1566

9. 7099
    347
 + 806

10. 5365
    1465
 + 1557

11. 1459 + 2663   12. 2947 + 3265   13. 8836 + 1195

14. 7028 + 2999   15. 3658 + 2673   16. 9549 + 786

17. 5367 + 2854   18. 4289 + 393   19. 5473 + 2748

Set 16 For use after pages 82–85.

Add.

1. $6.41
 + 2.39

2. $7.28
 + 1.56

3. $4.33
 + 0.45

4. $5.62
 + 3.26

5. $4.89
 + 1.89

6. $4.28
 + 3.87

7. $7.08
 + 3.72

8. $5.95
 + 0.26

9. $1.94
 + 5.66

10. $5.72
 + 1.39

Set 17 For use after pages 91–92.
Find the differences.

1. 68	2. 75	3. 98	4. 43	5. 87	6. 64
− 43	− 33	− 76	− 21	− 65	− 30

7. 36 − 24   8. 71 − 20   9. 54 − 32   10. 83 − 52   11. 47 − 25

12. 24 − 12   13. 46 − 31   14. 73 − 51   15. 52 − 21   16. 97 − 83

Set 18 For use after pages 93–99.
Are there enough ones to subtract? Write **yes** or **no**.
Do not subtract.

1. 42	2. 95	3. 77	4. 86	5. 19	6. 32
− 13	− 24	− 36	− 49	− 5	− 13

Subtract. Add to check.

7. 52	8. 40	9. 56	10. 24	11. 63	12. 50
− 28	− 25	− 17	− 15	− 47	− 26

13. 56	14. 90	15. 34	16. 44	17. 70	18. 68
− 39	− 12	− 19	− 28	− 45	− 39

19. 67 − 19   20. 71 − 36   21. 65 − 36   22. 42 − 26   23. 83 − 64

Set 19 For use after pages 100–101.
Subtract. Check the first row.

1. 957	2. 261	3. 382	4. 574	5. 763	6. 541
− 418	− 148	− 123	− 238	− 127	− 333

7. 622	8. 783	9. 692	10. 471	11. 653	12. 355
− 414	− 234	− 467	− 252	− 436	− 218

Set 20 For use after pages 104–105.
Subtract. Check the first row.

1. 439
   − 142

2. 726
   − 334

3. 538
   − 256

4. 636
   − 441

5. 716
   − 321

6. 519
   − 225

7. 537
   − 256

8. 446
   − 151

9. 739
   − 286

10. 455
    − 192

11. 967
    − 374

12. 843
    − 260

Set 21 For use after pages 108–111.
Subtract. Check the first row.

1. 466
   − 287

2. 513
   − 296

3. 486
   − 197

4. 371
   − 182

5. 923
   − 748

6. 728
   − 239

7. 500
   − 126

8. 700
   − 174

9. 604
   − 256

10. 503
    − 296

11. 900
    − 748

12. 505
    − 267

13. 403 − 145

14. 500 − 145

15. 801 − 258

16. 302 − 136

Set 22 For use after pages 112–113.
Subtract.

1. 4757
   − 2368

2. 3942
   − 1888

3. 5615
   − 2736

4. 3608
   − 1709

5. 2793
   − 1834

Set 23 For use after pages 114–117.
Subtract. Check the first row.

1. $6.43
   − 3.61

2. $1.92
   − 0.89

3. $4.44
   − 3.06

4. $0.86
   − 0.47

5. $3.09
   − 1.29

6. $5.26 − $3.46

7. $4.00 − $2.67

8. $7.36 − $1.47

9. $8.15 − $0.97

10. $3.49 − $2.73

11. $6.83 − $4.95

Set 24   For use after pages 123–125.
Write the time shown on each clock.

1.

2.

3.

Set 25   For use after page 126.
**Use the calendar on page 126. Write the date
for each day.**

1. the second Monday

2. the fourth Saturday

3. the first Sunday

4. the third Thursday

5. the third Sunday

6. the fifth Monday

Set 26   For use after pages 127–129.
Write the total amounts.

1.

2.

3.

4.

Set 27   For use after pages 135–138.

Find the sums. Write a multiplication fact for each problem.

1. $6 + 6 + 6 + 6$

2. $2 + 2 + 2 + 2 + 2 + 2$

3. $7 + 7 + 7 + 7 + 7$

4. $8 + 8 + 8$

Find the sums. Write a multiplication fact if you can.

5.	6.	7.	8.	9.	10.	11.
9	5	2	3	6	1	4
9	5	2	3	5	1	4
9	5	2	3	4	1	4
9	+ 4	2	+ 3	6	+ 1	8
+ 9		+ 2		+ 6		+ 3

Set 28   For use after pages 149–154.

Find the products.

1.	2.	3.	4.	5.	6.	7.
6	7	9	4	5	6	8
× 2	× 3	× 2	× 4	× 3	× 5	× 3

8. 9×4 9. 5×2 10. 6×3 11. 7×5 12. 8×5 13. 2×2

14. 7×2 15. 5×5 16. 2×4 17. 4×3 18. 9×5 19. 7×4

20. 4×5 21. 9×3 22. 8×2 23. 8×4 24. 6×4 25. 3×3

Set 29   For use after pages 155–159.

Find the products.

1.	2.	3.	4.	5.	6.	7.
9	8	10	5	6	10	4
× 0	× 1	× 6	× 0	× 1	× 4	× 0

8. 1×3 9. 8×4 10. 4×6 11. 5×4 12. 3×3 13. 4×7

14. 0×8 15. 5×5 16. 9×5 17. 6×0 18. 7×2 19. 3×9

Set 30 For use after pages 165–168.

Read each problem. Then answer the questions about it.

1. You have $5.00. You buy a book for $1.95. How much do you have left?
   a. What is the question?
   b. What are the important facts?

2. A zoo has 12 white bears, 8 brown bears, and 5 black bears. How many bears in all?
   a. What is the question?
   b. What are the important facts?

Decide what to do. Write add, subtract, or multiply for each problem.

3. Newspapers cost ■ each. How much do ▲ newspapers cost?

4. You have ■ blue pencils and ▲ green pencils. How many pencils is that?

5. You swim for ■ hours a day for ▲ days. How many hours do you swim in all?

6. You have ■ red marbles and ▲ black marbles. You give away the red ones. How many marbles do you have left?

Set 31 For use after pages 169–171.

Read each problem. Then answer the questions about it.

1. You have 9 post cards. Each one costs 15¢. You buy 5 more. How many post cards do you have now?
   a. What is the question?
   b. Will you add, subtract, or multiply?
   c. What numbers do you need?
   d. What number is not needed?
   e. Solve the problem.

2. One Saturday 8 people went fishing. 5 people each caught 2 fish. How many fish did they catch in all?
   a. What is the question?
   b. Will you add, subtract, or multiply?
   c. What numbers do you need?
   d. What number is not needed?
   e. Solve the problem.

Set 32   For use after pages 179–183.

Tell whether each shape is a **rectangle**, a **square**,
a **triangle**, or a **circle**.

1.   2.   3.   4.

How many angles in each shape?

5.   6. 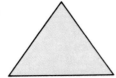   7.

Set 33   For use after pages 186–188.
Write the answers.

1. Is each pair congruent?
   Write **yes** or **no**.

2. Is each pair similar?
   Write **yes** or **no**.

1a.   1b.   2a.   2b.

Set 34   For use after pages 189–191.
Tell whether each shape is a **cube**, a **cone**, a **pyramid**,
or a **cylinder**.

1.   2.   3. 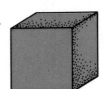   4.

Set 35 For use after pages 204–205.

Write the fraction for the shaded part.

1.

2.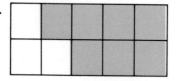

3.

4.

Write the fractions.

5a. $\frac{2}{4}$ of the group are squares.

b. $\frac{?}{?}$ of the group are circles.

6a. $\frac{1}{5}$ of the group are circles.

b. $\frac{?}{?}$ of the group are stars.

Set 36 For use after pages 208–210.

Which fraction is greater? Use the fraction fence on page 208 if you need help.

1. $\frac{2}{8}$ or $\frac{1}{2}$

2. 1 or $\frac{1}{2}$

3. $\frac{6}{8}$ or 1

4. $\frac{5}{8}$ or $\frac{1}{2}$

5. $\frac{7}{8}$ or $\frac{3}{4}$

6. $\frac{3}{8}$ or $\frac{4}{4}$

7. $\frac{3}{4}$ or $\frac{4}{8}$

8. $\frac{1}{4}$ or $\frac{3}{8}$

9. 1 or $\frac{3}{4}$

10. $\frac{3}{4}$ or $\frac{5}{8}$

Copy and complete.

11. $\frac{2}{4} = \frac{?}{8}$

12. $\frac{2}{8} = \frac{?}{4}$

13. $\frac{1}{2} = \frac{?}{8}$

14. $1 = \frac{?}{2}$

15. $\frac{1}{2} = \frac{?}{4}$

16. $\frac{3}{4} = \frac{?}{8}$

17. $1 = \frac{?}{8}$

18. $\frac{6}{8} = \frac{?}{4}$

19. $\frac{1}{4} = \frac{?}{8}$

20. $1 = \frac{?}{4}$

Set 37 For use after pages 211–212.
Write each fraction as a decimal.

1. $\frac{5}{10}$ 2. $\frac{7}{10}$ 3. $\frac{9}{10}$ 4. $\frac{2}{10}$ 5. $\frac{8}{10}$ 6. $\frac{4}{10}$ 7. $\frac{6}{10}$

8. three-tenths   9. two-tenths   10. six-tenths

11. seven-tenths   12. one-tenth   13. four-tenths

Set 38 For use after pages 213–214.
Which is greater?

1. 9.0 or 9.5   2. 2.9 or 2.7   3. 4.6 or 4.1   4. 5.6 or 6.5

5. 7.1 or 6.9   6. 2.8 or 3.2   7. 0.9 or 1.1   8. 6.5 or 5.9

9. 1.5 or 0.8   10. 3.6 or 4.2   11. 3.4 or 4.3   12. 3.1 or 2.3

Write each mixed number as a decimal.

13. $6\frac{1}{10}$ 14. $7\frac{3}{10}$ 15. $1\frac{5}{10}$ 16. $8\frac{9}{10}$ 17. $7\frac{6}{10}$

18. $4\frac{2}{10}$ 19. $9\frac{8}{10}$ 20. $1\frac{1}{10}$ 21. $3\frac{6}{10}$ 22. $5\frac{7}{10}$

Set 39 For use after pages 215–217.
Add or subtract.

1. 2.1   2. 3.4   3. 1.6   4. 1.4   5. 3.5   6. 2.7
  + 0.8   + 1.6   + 3.3   + 1.9   + 0.8   + 1.1

7. 5.6   8. 7.9   9. 8.5   10. 3.9   11. 3.0   12. 7.5
  − 2.2   − 6.1   − 5.4   − 0.4   − 1.6   − 4.6

13. 4.3   14. 2.7   15. 7.8   16. 6.3   17. 5.8   18. 3.4
   + 1.8   + 3.4   + 0.5   − 5.7   − 4.7   − 2.6

Set 40   For use after pages 224–227.
Find the products.

1. 3 × 6	2. 5 × 7	3. 4 × 8	4. 1 × 7	5. 8 × 7	6. 6 × 6	7. 3 × 8
8. 5 × 6	9. 9 × 8	10. 2 × 7	11. 1 × 8	12. 4 × 6	13. 3 × 7	14. 6 × 8

15. 1×6 16. 4×7 17. 9×7 18. 2×8 19. 5×8 20. 9×6

21. 6×7 22. 2×6 23. 7×8 24. 8×6 25. 8×8 26. 0×8

Set 41   For use after pages 228–231.
Find the products.

1. 3 × 9	2. 6 × 9	3. 1 × 9	4. 5 × 9	5. 9 × 9	6. 5 × 9	7. 8 × 9

8. 2×9 9. 4×9 10. 2×6 11. 3×7 12. 5×6 13. 7×7

14. 6×8 15. 7×9 16. 6×6 17. 3×8 18. 7×6 19. 2×8

Set 42   For use after pages 232–233.
Multiply. Check the first row by adding.

1. 34 × 2	2. 13 × 3	3. 40 × 5	4. 41 × 4	5. 20 × 6	6. 11 × 7
7. 14 × 2	8. 12 × 4	9. 24 × 2	10. 41 × 5	11. 13 × 2	12. 60 × 5
13. 44 × 2	14. 21 × 2	15. 33 × 3	16. 24 × 2	17. 23 × 3	18. 30 × 6
19. 11 × 6	20. 12 × 3	21. 21 × 4	22. 34 × 2	23. 43 × 3	24. 53 × 2

Set 43   For use after pages 234–237.
Multiply. Check the first row by adding.

1. 25 $\times$ 2	2. 16 $\times$ 3	3. 13 $\times$ 4	4. 24 $\times$ 5	5. 34 $\times$ 3	6. 42 $\times$ 5
7. 56 $\times$ 3	8. 36 $\times$ 4	9. 72 $\times$ 8	10. 43 $\times$ 6	11. 54 $\times$ 3	12. 68 $\times$ 2
13. 45 $\times$ 5	14. 57 $\times$ 3	15. 62 $\times$ 5	16. 48 $\times$ 2	17. 19 $\times$ 3	18. 55 $\times$ 5

Set 44   For use after page 238.
Multiply. Check the first row by adding.

1. 212 $\times$ 4	2. 301 $\times$ 7	3. 411 $\times$ 2	4. 310 $\times$ 6	5. 602 $\times$ 3	6. 521 $\times$ 4
7. 813 $\times$ 2	8. 224 $\times$ 2	9. 231 $\times$ 3	10. 422 $\times$ 4	11. 311 $\times$ 6	12. 713 $\times$ 3

Set 45   For use after pages 239–241.
Multiply.

1. 117 $\times$ 2	2. 124 $\times$ 3	3. 409 $\times$ 4	4. 313 $\times$ 4	5. 205 $\times$ 3	6. 315 $\times$ 2
7. 226 $\times$ 2	8. 504 $\times$ 3	9. 519 $\times$ 2	10. 223 $\times$ 4	11. 512 $\times$ 7	12. 203 $\times$ 8
13. $1.35 $\times$ 2	14. $2.29 $\times$ 3	15. $1.06 $\times$ 7	16. $4.19 $\times$ 2	17. $3.08 $\times$ 3	
18. $2.07 $\times$ 3	19. $3.14 $\times$ 3	20. $3.27 $\times$ 2	21. $1.13 $\times$ 5	22. $4.26 $\times$ 2	

Set 46   For use after pages 247–249.

Use markers or pieces of paper. Write the answers.

1. Take 16 markers.
Put 4 in each group.
How many groups do you make?

2. Take 12 markers.
Put 3 in each group.
How many groups do you make?

3. Take 15 markers.
Make 5 fair shares.
How many in each fair share?

4. Take 20 markers.
Make 4 fair shares.
How many in each fair share?

5. Take 12 markers.
Make 4 fair shares.
How many in each fair share?

6. Take 18 markers.
Make 6 fair shares.
How many in each fair share?

Set 47   For use after pages 256–260.

Divide.

1. $3\overline{)24}$ 2. $4\overline{)4}$ 3. $3\overline{)12}$ 4. $2\overline{)4}$ 5. $4\overline{)16}$

6. $5\overline{)45}$ 7. $3\overline{)3}$ 8. $4\overline{)36}$ 9. $1\overline{)4}$ 10. $5\overline{)30}$

11. $10 \div 5$ 12. $18 \div 3$ 13. $0 \div 2$ 14. $28 \div 4$ 15. $18 \div 2$

16. $0 \div 8$ 17. $6 \div 3$ 18. $40 \div 5$ 19. $9 \div 1$ 20. $35 \div 5$

Set 48   For use after pages 265–269.

Divide.

1. $6\overline{)42}$ 2. $7\overline{)21}$ 3. $6\overline{)18}$ 4. $8\overline{)24}$ 5. $9\overline{)18}$

6. $6\overline{)6}$ 7. $7\overline{)35}$ 8. $9\overline{)36}$ 9. $7\overline{)49}$ 10. $6\overline{)54}$

11. $48 \div 8$ 12. $54 \div 9$ 13. $40 \div 8$ 14. $12 \div 6$ 15. $45 \div 9$

16. $81 \div 9$ 17. $36 \div 6$ 18. $32 \div 8$ 19. $56 \div 7$ 20. $72 \div 9$

21. $30 \div 6$ 22. $28 \div 7$ 23. $18 \div 9$ 24. $63 \div 7$ 25. $56 \div 8$

Set 49 For use after pages 270–272.

Use markers or pieces of paper. Write the answers.

1. Take 23 markers.
   Make 7 fair shares.
   a. How many in each share?
   b. How many left over?

2. Take 13 markers.
   Make 2 fair shares.
   a. How many in each share?
   b. How many left over?

3. Take 19 markers.
   Make 5 fair shares.
   a. How many in each share?
   b. How many left over?

4. Take 25 markers.
   Make 8 fair shares.
   a. How many in each share?
   b. How many left over?

Divide.

5. $8\overline{)33}$

6. $5\overline{)49}$

7. $2\overline{)17}$

8. $3\overline{)23}$

9. $4\overline{)22}$

10. $6\overline{)39}$

11. $7\overline{)37}$

12. $9\overline{)20}$

13. $4\overline{)35}$

14. $8\overline{)61}$

15. $7\overline{)44}$

16. $5\overline{)37}$

17. $4\overline{)25}$

18. $6\overline{)19}$

19. $7\overline{)24}$

Set 50 For use after page 273.

Divide.

1. $3\overline{)63}$

2. $4\overline{)88}$

3. $2\overline{)28}$

4. $5\overline{)65}$

5. $3\overline{)93}$

6. $6\overline{)66}$

7. $4\overline{)56}$

8. $2\overline{)84}$

9. $5\overline{)70}$

10. $4\overline{)48}$

Set 51 For use after pages 274–275.

Divide.

1. $3\overline{)73}$

2. $2\overline{)85}$

3. $4\overline{)91}$

4. $3\overline{)64}$

5. $5\overline{)74}$

6. $6\overline{)67}$

7. $4\overline{)55}$

8. $3\overline{)47}$

9. $5\overline{)66}$

10. $2\overline{)47}$

Set 52   For use after pages 281–284.

Measure these. Write the lengths in centimeters.

1.

2.

Set 53   For use after pages 285–286.

Find the perimeters.

1.

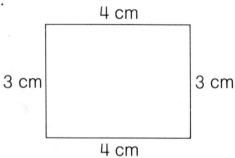

4 cm

3 cm   3 cm

4 cm

2.

5 cm   5 cm

4 cm

Set 54   For use after pages 289–292.

Use the pictures on page 290. Add or subtract to find the answers.

1. How much do 2 pieces of cheese weigh?

2. How much more does the orange weigh than the bread?

Use the pictures on page 291. Add or subtract to find the answers.

3. You have a liter of milk. You need 500 milliliters to make pudding. How much milk is left?

4. You have 200 milliliters of milk. You need a liter for a recipe. How much more milk do you need?

Set 55   For use after pages 295–299.

Write more or less to answer these.

1. Is 3 cups more or less than I quart?

2. Is 24 ounces more or less than I pound?

Enrichment

Set 1   For use after page 8.

In a magic square, the sum of each column, row, and diagonal is the same. In this magic square, the magic sum is 18.

5	4	9
10	6	2
3	8	7

Copy and complete each magic square. First find the magic sum. Then add and subtract to fill in the empty squares.

1.

4	3	8
9		
2		

2.

3	2	7
	4	

3.

	8	7
	6	
5		

Set 2   For use after page 13.

The numbers 0, 2, 4, 6, 8, 10, . . . are **even numbers**. The numbers 1, 3, 5, 7, 9, 11, . . . are **odd numbers**.

Copy each number. Tell whether it is odd (O) or even (E).

1. 43   2. 22   3. 18   4. 20   5. 35   6. 51   7. 64

Set 3   For use after page 21.

The sum of two even numbers is an even number.
The sum of two odd numbers is an even number.
The sum of an odd number and an even number is an odd number.

Copy each problem. Do not add. Tell whether the sum is odd (O) or even (E).

1. $13 + 4$ 2. $10 + 12$ 3. $15 + 3$ 4. $3 + 5 + 7$ 5. $2 + 6 + 8$

Set 4 For use after page 23.

The difference between two even numbers is an even number. The difference between two odd numbers is an even number. The difference between an odd number and an even number is an odd number.

Copy each problem. Do not subtract. Tell whether the difference is odd (O) or even (E).

1. $22 - 10$ 2. $43 - 13$ 3. $16 - 7$ 4. $34 - 21$ 5. $77 - 65$

6. $36 - 22$ 7. $88 - 15$ 8. $59 - 36$ 9. $48 - 27$ 10. $15 - 9$

Set 5 For use after page 35.

1. Begin with 4. Count by tens to 54. Write the words for each number.

2. Begin with 7. Count by tens to 87. Write the words for each number.

3. What number is 10 more than 35?

4. What number is 10 less than 66?

Set 6 For use after page 40.

Name the place for the digit 0.

1. 120   2. 110   3. 101   4. 107   5. 104   6. 105

Set 7 For use after page 44.

1. Count by twenty-fives to 300. Write each number.

2. Count by fifties to 400. Write each number.

3. What is the largest two-digit number?

4. What is the largest three-digit number?

Set 8   For use after page 48.

Follow the rule. Write five numbers in the pattern.

1. Start with 15. The rule is add 3.

2. Start with 85. The rule is subtract 5.

Set 9   For use after page 59.

1. Jose has 3 dimes and 8 pennies. He finds 2 dimes and 7 pennies in his shirt pocket. How much money does he have?

2. Helen has 4 dimes and 5 pennies. She finds 1 dime and 6 pennies at the bottom of her purse. How much money does she have?

Set 10   For use after page 67.

1. There are 262 children at Homestead School and 171 at Terrace School. How many children in all?

2. 342 children go on a field trip Wednesday. 282 go Thursday. How many go in all?

Set 11   For use after page 75.

1. Copy the triangle. Use the numbers 150, 200, 250, 300, 350, and 400. Put them in the circles so that each side of the triangle adds to 850.

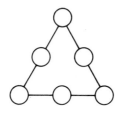

2. Copy the triangle. Use the numbers 25, 50, 75, 100, 125, and 150. Put them in the circles so that each side of the triangle adds to the same number.

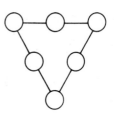

Set 12 For use after page 83.

**Add. Use = if the sums are equal or ≠ if the sums
are not equal.**

1. 1342 + 1213 ◯ 2030 + 525   **2.** 4539 + 1763 ◯ 5812 + 500

3. 3478 + 2521 ◯ 3624 + 2374   **4.** 7937 + 1570 ◯ 7535 + 1972

5. $8.91 + $5.49 ◯ $7.20 + $7.20   **6.** $5.37 + $4.83 ◯ $9.00 + $1.30

Set 13 For use after page 99.

Copy and complete these magic squares.

1.

2.

18	25	
31		
20		

3.

		22
	19	11
		24

Set 14 For use after page 107.

**The ⬚ in each problem stands for the same digit.
Find the digit.**

1.	2.	3.	4.	5.
5⬚2	2⬚⬚	5⬚2	9⬚9	⬚86
− 13⬚	− ⬚⬚2	− ⬚41	− ⬚8⬚	− 2⬚9
444	99	191	192	50⬚

Set 15 For use after page 111.

Subtract to find each missing number.

1. 189 + ⬚ = 424   **2.** 538 + ⬚ = 725   **3.** 94 + ⬚ = 863

4. 34 + ⬚ = 201   **5.** 47 + ⬚ = 410   **6.** 138 + ⬚ = 527

7. 123 + ⬚ = 403   **8.** 77 + ⬚ = 860   **9.** 136 + ⬚ = 214

Set 16   For use after page 115.

1. Tom has 6 dollars, 4 dimes, and 5 pennies. He pays $5.95 for a poster. How much money does he have left?

2. Beth has 7 dollars, 3 dimes, and 4 nickels. She pays $6.27 for a book. How much money does she have left?

Set 17   For use after page 125.

1. A movie starts at 7:30. It is 1 hour and 35 minutes long. At what time is it over?

2. A boat leaves Oak Grove at 10:15. It arrives at Denton at 11:00. How long is the trip?

Set 18   For use after page 129.

1. Lisa has 6 coins that are worth 19¢. What coins does she have?

2. Jorge has 5 coins that are worth 18¢. What coins does he have?

Set 19   For use after page 145.

Copy these number patterns. Fill in the missing numbers.

1. 10, 12, ▨, ▨, 18

2. 2, 5, ▨, ▨, 14

3. 11, 14, ▨, 20, ▨

4. 23, 25, ▨, 29, ▨

5. 11, 13, ▨, ▨, 19

6. 19, ▨, 25, 28, ▨

Set 20   For use after page 150.

1. There are 4 rows of 5 chairs and 4 rows of 6 chairs. How many chairs in all?

2. There are 4 rows of 4 chairs and 4 rows of 7 chairs. How many chairs in all?

3. There are 5 rows of 3 chairs and 5 rows of 4 chairs. How many chairs in all?

4. There are 5 rows of 2 chairs and 5 rows of 5 chairs. How many chairs in all?

Set 21 For use after page 156.

Multiply. Find ▣ to complete the pattern.

1. $2 \times 1, 3 \times 1, ▣ \times ▣$

2. $5 \times 10, 6 \times 10, ▣ \times ▣$

3. $1 \times 6, 1 \times 5, ▣ \times ▣$

4. $4 \times 10, 3 \times 10, ▣ \times ▣$

Set 22 For use after page 159.

Copy and complete. Remember, ( ) mean Do me first.

1. $(1 \times 5) + 4$

2. $7 \times (2 + 3)$

3. $(3 + 7) \times 0$

4. $(10 \times 1) + 8$

Set 23 For use after page 168.

1. Greg has 46 books. He loans 12 books to one friend and 5 books to another friend. How many books does he have left?

2. Kim is taking 5 classes. 3 classes require 4 books each. 2 classes require 3 books each. How many books in all?

3. Harold has a bookcase with 6 shelves. 4 shelves hold 10 books each. 2 shelves hold 9 books each. How many books in all?

4. Maria orders 25 books. They come in 3 boxes. 2 boxes contain 8 books each. How many books in the third box?

Set 24 For use after page 171.

Estimate each answer. Then solve the problem.

1. You buy a loaf of bread for $0.89 and a carton of milk for $0.59. You have $2.00. About how much change will you get?

2. You buy a baseball for $2.49 and a bat for $3.78. About how much money do you spend?

Set 25 For use after page 173.

Write a word problem for each number sentence.

1. $536 + 427 = 963$

2. $\$5.00 - (\$1.69 + \$2.75) = \$0.56$

Set 26 For use after page 183.

The names for shapes with five or more sides and angles follow a pattern. Make a large chart like this one. Then complete your chart.

1.

Number of Sides and Angles	Name	Shape
5	pentagon	⬠
6	hexagon	
7	hepta___	
8	octa___	⯃

Set 27 For use after page 193.

Make a graph like the one on page 193. Mark a point for each problem below. Number the points in order. Connect the points in this order: 1–2–3–4–5–6–1. What shape do you find?

1. 2 over, 1 up

2. 4 over, 1 up

3. 6 over, 3 up

4. 4 over, 5 up

5. 2 over, 5 up

6. 1 over, 3 up

Set 28 For use after page 205.

1. There are 11 players on a soccer team. 5 are forwards. Write a fraction to show what part of the team are forwards.

2. 4 children are playing tennis. 2 are girls. Write a fraction to show what part of the group are boys.

3. There are 5 players on a basketball team. 2 are guards. Write a fraction to show what part of the team are guards.

4. 4 people are playing catch. 3 are girls. Write a fraction to show what part of the group are not girls.

5. 3 girls and 5 boys are jogging. Write a fraction to show what part of the group are girls.

6. 6 boys and 4 girls are swimming. Write a fraction to show what part of the group are not boys.

Set 29   For use after page 217.
Copy and complete these magic squares.

1.

		2.4
		0.8
	1.2	3.4

2.

	3.5	2.9
	2.7	
2.5		

3.

0.4		
1.5	0.9	0.3

Set 30   For use after page 225.
Add and multiply. Use = for is equal to, > for is greater than, or < for is less than. Remember, ( ) mean Do me first.

1. $(4 + 5) \times 6 \bigcirc 24 + 30$

2. $(1 + 6) \times 6 \bigcirc 12 + 36$

3. $(6 \times 7) + 39 \bigcirc 23 + 58$

4. $28 + 19 \bigcirc (6 \times 3) + 31$

5. $(7 \times 4) + 15 \bigcirc 33 + 10$

6. $7 \times 9 \bigcirc (7 \times 6) + 21$

Set 31   For use after 231.
Copy and complete. Remember, ( ) mean Do me first.

1. $(4 + 3) \times (2 + 5)$ 2. $(4 + 4) \times (7 + 0)$ 3. $(5 + 4) \times (3 \times 3)$

4. $(2 \times 4) \times (6 + 2)$ 5. $(5 + 4) \times (6 + 1)$ 6. $(3 \times 3) \times (7 + 1)$

7. $(9 \times 1) \times (1 + 4)$ 8. $(4 \times 2) \times (3 + 2)$ 9. $(5 \times 0) \times (8 + 1)$

Set 32   For use after page 237.
The ⬚ in each problem stands for the same digit. Find the digit.

1.
```
  ⬚4
× ⬚
 48
```

2.
```
  2⬚
×  ⬚
 12⬚
```

3.
```
  5⬚
×  ⬚
 33⬚
```

4.
```
  ⬚9
×  ⬚
 117
```

5.
```
  1⬚
×  4
 ⬚4
```

6.
```
  31
×  ⬚
 27⬚
```

Set 33 For use after page 241.

1. Maria delivers 113 papers each day for 5 days. Then she delivers 111 papers each day for 6 days. How many papers does she deliver in all?

2. Tony buys 2 books for $3.49 and 3 books for $2.15. How much money does he spend?

Set 34 For use after page 257.

1. A store owner has 18 watermelons. She puts them in 3 equal piles. How many watermelons in each pile?

2. A produce clerk puts 4 tomatoes in each bag. How many bags does he need for 36 tomatoes?

Set 35 For use after page 264.

1. A factory produces 63 cars in 7 hours. How many cars does it produce each hour?

2. It takes 6 bolts to put on 1 car door. How many doors can be put on with 54 bolts?

Set 36 For use after page 269.

Divide. Add the quotients. Do they make a magic square?

1.

$8\overline{)32}$	$7\overline{)28}$	$7\overline{)49}$
$9\overline{)72}$	$8\overline{)40}$	$9\overline{)18}$
$9\overline{)27}$	$7\overline{)42}$	$8\overline{)48}$

2.

$9\overline{)45}$	$7\overline{)35}$	$8\overline{)64}$
$8\overline{)72}$	$9\overline{)54}$	$8\overline{)24}$
$9\overline{)36}$	$8\overline{)56}$	$9\overline{)63}$

Set 37 For use after page 275.

1. A store owner has 98 potatoes. She puts 8 potatoes in each bag. How many bags does she fill? How many potatoes are left over?

2. A baker puts 6 rolls in each package. He has 65 rolls. How many packages does he fill? How many rolls are left over?

Set 38 For use after page 283.

Make a bar graph to show the heights of these four children.

1.

Name	Height in Centimeters (cm)
Victor	160
Betty	120
Armand	100
Maria	140

Set 39 For use after page 286.

1. What is the perimeter of a flower bed that is 2 meters long and 4 meters wide?

2. What is the perimeter of a triangle with sides that are 5 centimeters, 4 centimeters, and 3 centimeters long?

Set 40 For use after page 292.

Use the thermometer on page 292 to answer these questions.

1. 26°C is how many degrees above the temperature at which water freezes?

2. 86°C is how many degrees below the temperature at which water boils?

Measurement Tables

Metric System

Length
10 millimeters (mm) = 1 centimeter (cm)
10 centimeters = 1 decimeter (dm)
$$\left.\begin{array}{l} 1000 \text{ millimeters} \\ 100 \text{ centimeters} \\ 10 \text{ decimeters} \end{array}\right\} = 1 \text{ meter (m)}$$
1000 meters = 1 kilometer (km)

Area
100 square millimeters (mm^2) =
   1 square centimeter (cm^2)
10,000 square centimeters =
   1 square meter (m^2)

Volume
1000 cubic millimeters (mm^3) =
   1 cubic centimeter (cm^3)
1,000,000 cubic centimeters =
   1 cubic meter (m^3)

Capacity
1000 milliliters (ml) = 1 liter (ℓ)
1000 liters = 1 kiloliter (kl)

Mass
1000 milligrams (mg) = 1 gram (g)
1000 grams = 1 kilogram (kg)
1000 kilograms = 1 metric ton (t)

Time

60 seconds (s) = 1 minute (min)
60 minutes = 1 hour (h)
24 hours = 1 day (d)
7 days = 1 week (wk)
28 to 31 days = 1 month (mo)
12 months = 1 year (yr)

Customary System

Length
12 inches (in.) = 1 foot (ft)
3 feet = 1 yard (yd)
1760 yards = 1 mile (mi)

Area
144 square inches (in.^{2}) =
   1 square foot (ft^2)
9 square feet = 1 square yard (yd^2)

Volume
1728 cubic inches (in.^{3}) =
   1 cubic foot (ft^3)
27 cubic feet = 1 cubic yard (yd^3)

Capacity
2 cups = 1 pint (pt)
2 pints = 1 quart (qt)
4 quarts = 1 gallon (gal)

Weight
16 ounces (oz) = 1 pound (lb)
2000 pounds = 1 ton (T)

Symbol List

+	plus
−	minus
×	times
⌐ or ÷	divided by
=	equals *or* is equal to
≠	is not equal to
>	is greater than
<	is less than
( )	do the operation inside parentheses first
. . .	pattern continues without end
8 r2	eight remainder two
20.7	twenty and seven-tenths (decimal point)
∟	right angle
°C	degree Celsius
°F	degree Fahrenheit
50¢	fifty cents
$1.25	one dollar and twenty-five cents
3:45	three forty-five (time)

Glossary

addend   A number that is added.
   Example $5 + 8 = 13$ The addends are 5 and 8.

addition (+)   An operation on two numbers to find how many in all or how much in all.
   Example $7 + 9 = 16$ 7 and 9 are **addends**. 16 is the **sum.**

angle   A shape formed by two lines that meet.

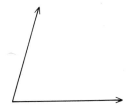

area   The number of units, usually square, needed to cover a surface.
   Example   The area of this rectangle is 6 square units.

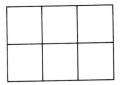

associative property of addition   The way in which addends are grouped does not change the sum.
   Example $(3 + 2) + 4 = 3 + (2 + 4)$

associative property of multiplication   The way in which factors are grouped does not change the product.
   Example $(5 \times 3) \times 2 = 5 \times (3 \times 2)$

bar graph   A graph with bars of different lengths to show and compare information.

capacity   The amount a container will hold when filled.

circle   A closed curve. All points are an equal distance from a center point.

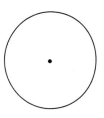

commutative property of addition   The order in which addends are added does not change the sum.
   Example $7 + 5 = 5 + 7$

commutative property of multiplication   The order in which factors are multiplied does not change the product.
   Example $3 \times 7 = 7 \times 3$

cone   A solid with one face that is a circle.

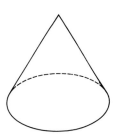

congruent   Having the same size and shape.

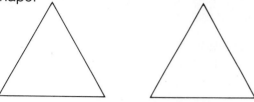

coordinate graph   A drawing of numbered lines that cross at right angles and are used to name the positions of points.

count   To name numbers in order, matching each number with an object, to find how many objects in all.

cube   A solid with six square faces.

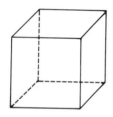

customary measurement system   A measurement system that uses inches, feet, yards, and miles as units of length; cups, pints, quarts, and gallons as units of capacity; ounces, pounds, and tons as units of weight; and degrees Fahrenheit as units of temperature.

cylinder   A solid with two faces that are circles.

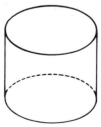

decimal   A number that uses place value and a decimal point to show tenths.
　　Example   5.7   Read *five and seven-tenths*.

degree Celsius (°C)   A standard unit for measuring temperature in the metric system.
　　Example   Water freezes at 0°C and boils at 100°C.

degree Fahrenheit (°F)   A standard unit for measuring temperature in the customary measurement system.
　　Example   Water freezes at 32°F and boils at 212°F.

denominator   The numeral below the bar in a fraction.
　　Example $\frac{2}{5}$ The denominator is 5.

difference   The answer to a subtraction problem.
　　Example $8 - 3 = 5$ The difference is 5.

digit   Any one of the ten symbols 0, 1, 2, 3, 4, 5, 6, 7, 8, or 9.

dividend   The number that is divided in a division problem.
　　Example $3\overline{)18}$ *or* $18 \div 3$ The dividend is 18.

division ($\overline{)}$ *or* ÷)   An operation on two numbers that tells the number of equal groups and the number left over, or the number in each group and the number left over.
　　Example $5\overline{)37}$ $^{7\,r2}$ 5 is the **divisor**, 37 is the **dividend**, 7 is the **quotient**, and 2 is the **remainder**.

divisor The number by which the dividend is divided.
Example $4\overline{)36}$ *or* $36 \div 4$ The divisor is 4.

edge Two faces of a solid meet in an edge.

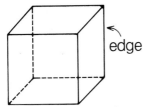
edge

equal fractions (equivalent fractions) Fractions that name the same number.
Example $\frac{1}{2}$ and $\frac{2}{4}$ are equal fractions.

equals *or* is equal to (=) Have the same value.
Example $5 + 7 = 12$ Read *five plus seven equals twelve* or *five plus seven is equal to twelve.*

equation A number sentence with an equals sign (=).
Examples $6 + 4 = 10$
$8 - 7 = 1$

estimate To guess a likely answer. One way to estimate an answer is to round the numbers before doing the problem.

even number A whole number with 0, 2, 4, 6, or 8 in the ones place.
Examples 6, 78, 112

face A flat surface of a solid.

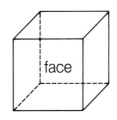
face

factor A number that is multiplied.
Example $6 \times 7 = 42$ The factors are 6 and 7.

fraction A number that names part of a whole or group.
Examples $\frac{1}{3}, \frac{3}{4}$

graph A drawing used to show and compare information.

identity property for addition If one of two addends is 0, the sum is the same as the other addend.
Example $57 + 0 = 57$

identity property for multiplication If one of two factors is 1, the product is the same as the other factor.
Example $17 \times 1 = 17$

length The measurement of an object from end to end.

line of symmetry If a shape can be folded along a line so that each half is the same size and shape, the fold line is a line of symmetry.

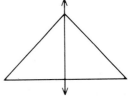

metric system A measurement system that uses centimeters, meters, and kilometers as units of length; milliliters and liters as units of capacity; grams and kilograms as units of mass; and degrees Celsius as units of temperature.

minus (−) A symbol that shows subtraction.
Example $11 - 3 = 8$ Read *eleven minus three equals eight.*

mixed number   The sum of a whole number and a fraction.
   Example $2\frac{1}{3} = 2 + \frac{1}{3}$

multiplication (×)   An operation on two numbers, called **factors**. If one factor is the number of groups, the other factor is the number in each group.
   Example $7 \times 8 = 56$ 7 and 8 are factors. 56 is the **product**.

numeral   A name or symbol for a number.
   Examples $\frac{1}{3}$, 2.3, 5, $15\frac{3}{4}$

numerator   The numeral above the bar in a fraction.
   Example $\frac{2}{5}$ The numerator is 2.

odd number   A whole number with 1, 3, 5, 7, or 9 in the ones place.
   Examples   9, 21, 243

parentheses ( )   Symbols of grouping. Parentheses tell which part or parts of a problem to do first.
   Example $(6 - 4) + 1$ Do $(6 - 4)$ first.

perimeter   The distance around a shape. The perimeter of a shape is the sum of the lengths of the sides.

place value   The value given to the place in which a digit appears in a numeral.
   Example   32   The place value of 3 is tens. The place value of 2 is ones.

plus (+)   A symbol that shows addition.
   Example $7 + 8 = 15$ Read *seven plus eight equals fifteen.*

product   The answer to a multiplication problem.
   Example $4 \times 12 = 48$ The product is 48.

pyramid   A solid. One face is a triangle, rectangle, or other shape with angles. The other faces are triangles.

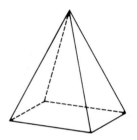

quotient   The answer to a division problem.
   Example $16 \div 8 = 2$ The quotient is 2.

rectangle   A shape with four sides and four right angles.

rectangular prism   A solid with six faces that are rectangles.

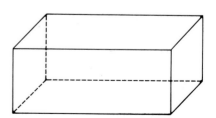

remainder The number left over in a division problem. The remainder must be less than the divisor.

Example   5$\overline{\smash{)}17}^{\,3\,r2}$ The remainder is 2.

right angle An angle with the same shape as the corner of a square.

rounding Writing a number to the nearest ten.

Example   34 rounded to the nearest ten is 30.

similar Having the same shape.

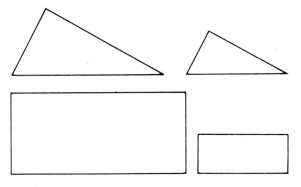

solve To find the answer to a problem.

sphere A solid.

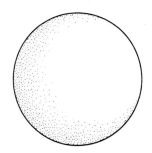

square A shape with four equal sides and four right angles.

subtraction (—) An operation on two numbers to find how many are left or how much greater one number is than the other.
   Example   12 − 7 = 5   5 is the **difference.**

sum The answer to an addition problem.
   Example   11 + 7 = 18   The sum is 18.

times (×) A symbol that shows multiplication.
   Example   4 × 5 = 20   Read *four times five equals twenty.*

trade In addition, subtraction, and multiplication, to make one group of ten out of ten ones or ten ones out of one group of ten.

   Example   14 = 1 ten + 4 ones

$$
\begin{array}{ccc}
\overset{1}{28} & \overset{4\,14}{\cancel{54}} & \overset{1}{37} \\
+\,36 & -\,27 & \times\;2 \\
\hline
64 & 27 & 74
\end{array}
$$

Also, to make one hundred from ten tens, one thousand from ten hundreds, and so on.

triangle A shape with three sides and three angles.

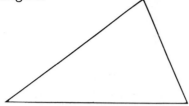

volume The number of cubic units needed to fill a solid.

Example The volume of this cube is 8 units.

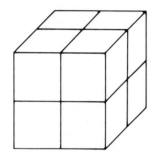

whole number Any one of the numbers 0, 1, 2, 3, 4, 5, and so on.

zero property for multiplication If 0 is a factor, the product is 0.

Example $17 \times 0 = 0$

Index

Facts
  addition, 3–5, 10–13, 16, 55
  division, 247–267
  multiplication, 139–144,
    146–150, 152–153,
    155–158, 223–230
  subtraction, 6–8, 10–13, 16
Fahrenheit, degrees, 299
Feet, 294
Fractions
  and decimals, 211–212
  denominators, 220
  equal, 209
  equal to one, 209
  equal to whole numbers, 209
  equal to zero, 209
  improper, 210
  and mixed numbers, 210
  numerators, 200
  ordering, 208
  for parts of groups, 202–207
  for parts of shapes,
    199–201, 204–205
  and problem solving, 207

Gallons, 295
Geometry
  angles, 182
  circles, 9, 180–181
  cones, 191–193
  congruent shapes, 186, 188
  cubes, 191–193
  cylinders, 191–193
  pyramids, 191–193
  rectangles, 179, 181
  rectangular solids, 191–193
  right angles, 183
  similar shapes, 187–188
  solid shapes, 189–193
  spheres, 191–193
  squares, 9, 179, 181
  symmetry, 184–185
  triangles, 9, 180–181
Grams, 289
Graphs
  bar, 283, 298
  coordinate, 193
Greater than, 33–34

Half hours, 123
Heptagons, 327
Hexagons, 327
Hours, 57, 123
Hundreds
  in addition, 56, 66, 76
  in multiplication, 238–240
  and place value, 38–41,
    43, 46
  reading and writing, 38, 41
  in subtraction, 104, 106, 113

Identity element
  for addition, 3–5
  for multiplication, 155
Improper fractions, 210
Inches, 293
Inverse operations
  addition and subtraction, 11
  multiplication and division,
    253, 263

Kilograms, 289
Kilometers, 284

Length
  customary units for,
    293–294
  measuring, 281, 293
  metric units for, 281–284
Less than, 34
Lines of symmetry, 184–185
Liquid measurement
  customary units for,
    295–296
  metric units for, 291
Liters, 291

Maps, 284
Measurement
  area, 287
  capacity, 291, 295–296
  computing with, 283–288,
    290–291, 295–298
  estimation, 282, 284, 289,

290, 292, 294, 297
  finding equal, 295–296
  length, 281–284, 293–294
  perimeter, 285–286
  and problem solving, 284,
    290–291, 295–296
  tables, 331
  temperature, 292, 299
  time, 123–126
  volume, 288
  weight, 289–290, 297–298
Meters, 282
Metric units, 281–291
  measurement tables, 331
Miles, 294
Milliliters, 291
Minutes, 123
Missing addends, 70, 97, 324
Missing factors, 143, 225, 262
Mixed numbers
  and decimals, 214
  and fractions, 210
Money
  addition with, 37, 58–59,
    65–66, 82–83, 115,
    127–129
  cent sign, 37
  dollar sign, 82–83
  estimation with, 37
  making change, 95, 103,
    114–115, 128
  multiplication with, 241
  and problem solving, 37,
    84–85, 116–117,
    170–171
  rounding, 37
  subtraction with, 93, 102,
    114–115
Multiplication
  and addition, 135–138,
    232–233
  and division, 253, 263
  factors, 137
  facts, 139–144, 146–150,
    152–153, 155–158,
    223–230
  missing factors, 143, 225,
    262, 328
  with money, 241